PRAISE FOR
SIXTY

"A compelling take on the joys and agonies of growing older. . . .
Brown peppers this memoir with crisp, self-deprecating asides,
and a wry point of view that holds up to the very end. Where
Brown really reels you in is with his sincerity. His insights, quips
and candid assessments of aging are to be enjoyed by any Boomer
nearing or having passed the big 6-0."—*LOS ANGELES TIMES*

"Mr. Brown is charming, thoughtful and edifying company.
There's loads to identify with in *Sixty*. More than that: There's
loads to flat-out adore. . . . Brown's reflections on friendship are
soulful and worth committing to heart. So are his meditations on
marriage and parenthood."—*THE NEW YORK TIMES*

"A rich new book . . . Brown can't help but turn some of the
absurdities he faces into humor . . . The laugh-out-loud passages
are tempered by a poignant theme Brown comes back to time
and time again: regret."—*FORBES*

"Brown asks all of the right questions in *Sixty*, an account
that is by turns witty and poignant. I laughed aloud."
—*THE WALL STREET JOURNAL*

"A spark of humor shines through even these
serious topics, which he handles gracefully. Well considered
and illuminating, *Sixty* allows readers to delve deeply into
the real meaning of maturity."—*BOOKLIST*

"Brown's humor is pointed inward as often as outward, and he neither glosses over nor languishes on the fact that he has fewer years ahead of him than behind."—*KIRKUS*

"Those turning 60 will appreciate and find resonance with Brown's honest grappling with his aging."—*PUBLISHERS WEEKLY*

"Finding out Ian Brown has turned sixty is like finding out my bad little brother has turned sixty: I'd expect him to have a disarming, slightly disreputable take on this least interesting of birthdays (long now in my rearview mirror). And with *Sixty*, I'm certainly not disappointed. Ever the witty, ever the mischievous, observant and likable, Ian Brown has written a book that other sixty-year-olds can keep on their breakfast table, to dip into with their Ovaltine. It's a splendid companion book to aging—a condition when ordinary companionship is, frankly, not always that agreeable."—**RICHARD FORD**

"Ian Brown is so wise and insightful and funny about the indignities of turning sixty that he makes those of us who haven't yet reached that harrowing birthday believe that maybe it won't be so bad. Surely, once we get there, we'll all be as wise and insightful and funny as Ian is. We won't, of course: This book, like its author, is one of a kind. A wonderful, inspiring, occasionally cringe-inducing chronicle of a very human year."—**PAUL TOUGH**, author of *Helping Children Succeed: What Works and Why*

"I've been reading Ian Brown since before I needed reading glasses. He's wise—poetic even—and willing to be unabashedly petty, which is what makes this book so funny and almost too true."
—**SARAH VOWELL**, *New York Times*–bestselling author of seven books, most recently *Lafayette in the Somewhat United States*

SIXTY

A DIARY

**My Year of Aging
Semi-Gracefully**

IAN BROWN

THE EXPERIMENT

NEW YORK

The Experiment, LLC | 220 East 23rd Street, Suite 301 | New York, NY 10010-4674
theexperimentpublishing.com

Many of the designations used by manufacturers and sellers to distinguish their products are claimed as trademarks. Where those designations appear in this book and The Experiment was aware of a trademark claim, the designations have been capitalized.

The Experiment's books are available at special discounts when purchased in bulk for premiums and sales promotions as well as for fund-raising or educational use. For details, contact us at info@theexperimentpublishing.com.

Library of Congress Cataloging-in-Publication Data

Names: Brown, Ian, 1954-
Title: Sixty : a diary of my sixty-first year : the beginning of the end, or
   the end of the beginning? / Ian Brown.
Description: New York : The Experiment, 2016. | "Originally published in
   Canada by Random House Canada in 2015"--Title page verso.
Identifiers: LCCN 2016012152| ISBN 9781615193509 (cloth) | ISBN 9781615193516
   (ebook)
Subjects: LCSH: Brown, Ian, 1954---Diaries. | Middle-aged
   persons--Canada--Diaries. | Middle-aged men--Canada--Diaries. | Authors,
   Canadian--Diaries. | Journalists--Canada--Diaries. | Aging--Psychological
   aspects. | Birthdays--Psychological aspects. | Aging--Social aspects. |
   Brown, Ian, 1954---Travel.
Classification: LCC CT310.B758 A3 2016 | DDC 305.244/1--dc23
LC record available at http://lccn.loc.gov/2016012152

ISBN 978-1-61519-396-7
Ebook ISBN 978-1-61519-351-6

Cover and text design and cover photograph by Sarah Smith
Author photograph by John Barber

Manufactured in the United States of America
Distributed by Workman Publishing Company, Inc.

First paperback printing August 2017
10 9 8 7 6 5 4 3 2 1

This book is dedicated to my brother,
Timothy Giles Brown, who is not as old as I am.

✤

But it is never over,
Nothing ends until we want it to.
Look, in shattered midnights,
On black ice, under silver trees,
We are still dancing, dancing.

—GWENDOLYN MacEWEN, "Late Song"

In 2004, when I turned fifty, I mentioned to a friend that I thought there was a book in the subject: that reaching what another pal optimistically called "the halfway point" entailed not just changes in the way I lived but changes in the way I looked at my life. I had spent fifty years looking forward, up the oncoming road, and suddenly I was just as interested in where I'd been. This did not feel like a victory. Then the busy details of family and professional life closed around me, and I put the notion—not just the book, but the very idea that I was in fact getting older—aside.

A few years later, in my late fifties, when I could no longer pretend I wasn't heading into the last turn, or for the back nine, or toward the clubhouse (someone should make a list of all the euphemisms we employ to denote the onset of aging)—after another cough that wouldn't go away, after the onset of the existential angst that seemed to set in after fifty-five, and especially after my parents died—I realized that I had forgotten the instances that made turning fifty feel unique. I resolved that I would not let the details slip away again, and decided to keep a diary of the year I turned sixty, from that birthday to the next.

After all, as Kafka observed, "one advantage in keeping a diary is that you become aware with reassuring clarity of the changes which you constantly suffer."

Alas, you also become aware of how hard it is to keep an honest, interesting, readable (to say nothing of publishable) diary. It's quite a lot of work, and it's hard to keep up, especially if you have a job, a life, and the discipline of a mayfly. The task also poses a recurring question, one I asked myself every day: what on earth would make someone think the life of a sixty-year-old middle-class journalist and husband and father in Toronto (of all places) was worth writing, much less reading, about? The answer was always the same: because I could find no satisfying record of anyone having done it before. I'm not referring to the countless newspaper columns and ranks of self-help books (some of them huge commercial successes) that celebrate seniorhood and try to reinvent aging as a new and ever-younger future. That kind of writing mostly made me want to run shrieking from the room. But original, truthful, sad but amused, authentic writing on the subject of getting older, is in quite short supply; it's a subject we don't care to think about when we're younger and can't bear to face when we're older. Gerontology (the sociology, psychology, and biology of aging) and geriatrics (the medical care of the aging) are booming fields of study, and there is a small but growing cadre of writers and scholars—mostly women, many of whom have spent their lives studying literature—now exploring the culture of aging and growing older. But those are still nascent movements. Up in the stacks of the Robarts Library at the University of Toronto, where entire floors are devoted to books about a single subject, I found but half an aisle of shelves (about twenty feet, and on only one side of the aisle at that) devoted to books about aging. The process of getting older, after all, as a young writer and academic named Amelia DeFalco first pointed out to me, is the process of becoming the Other—the unknown entity that we all fear, the ever-dying double that lives inside us, that we ignore for as long as we can, until we finally can't. Modern Western society still treats the aging and the aged the same way it has treated the disabled, women, and other thus-designated outliers: by pretending they don't exist. The irony of our insensitivity toward the elderly is that aging happens to every one of us; we're all getting older every single moment of our lives, from the moment we are born, though we spend most of our energy (commercial and otherwise) devising ways to pretend that it's not happening.

I admit that so far, I am the luckiest of sixty-year-olds. My health is steady, my mind is more or less intact, I can see and mostly hear, I am not in pain. I am not alone. I have hardly anything to complain about. And yet I, we, all of us, grow older anyway, and we feel it, even as we deny it. I thought it might be an interesting experiment to stare in the face of that denial, and keep track, at even the most mundane daily level, of the train coming straight at us.

Toronto, June 27, 2015

The most surprising change in the two-plus years that have passed since I decided to keep a diary between my sixtieth and sixty-first birthdays—the diary that resulted in a book, and now this new paperback edition of that diary—is the fact that I am now sixty-three. I know: What was I expecting? That I would write a book about having turned sixty, and that all forward aging would thereafter magically stop? But that is evidently what I *did* expect, because I am surprised to find myself this much older. Sixty was one thing; I was a novice at this "getting older" thing, an amateur, and could be forgiven for not understanding it fully. Sixty-three is well into the weeds of the experience.

Still, the human capacity for delusional thinking on the subject of getting older is bottomless, even among those who have written books on the subject. The other day I saw a man on the subway reading a crime novel. It was eight o'clock in the morning, and he was obviously on his way to work. He was probably in his mid-thirties. (I find it harder and harder to tell how old anyone is, so desperate am I not to have to compare my own age to theirs.) He was also balder than I am. That was the crucial detail. He was quite clearly a vigorous man nearly thirty years younger than me, and yet—and yet!—the thought actually passed through my head as I watched him: *Oh look at that poor balding fellow, how much closer he is to death than I am!*

The second most surprising development in the two and a half years since I finished keeping this diary is the number of people who approach me or who write letters and emails to say how much the book engaged them, or made them reconsider the prospect of getting older. Sometimes they tell me I am wrong to make a fuss about getting older. A month after the first edition of the diary appeared, for instance, I gave a reading in Calgary, followed by a talk about why I had written the book. I had answered a few questions when an older man—a white, prosperous-looking WASP of about seventy-five, with a distinctly non-thinning shock of silver hair—took the microphone and began reprimanding me for having spilled the beans about getting older, for having revealed what a harrowing ride it can be. "Why would you write a book about all these fears and worries?" the tough guy said. "It's unseemly. And there's nothing you can do about it."

Which is where we disagreed, of course. So I explained that I think aging is a subject we ought to talk about more, not less, if we can bring ourselves to talk about it honestly and authentically—without approaching getting older only as some kind of human failure, and something to settle into. I explained to the man with the silver hair that the diary of my sixty-first year was by no means all fears and worries; that I wrote about turning sixty because that age seemed like a threshold, physically and emotionally and intellectually, a slightly terrifying land, but one full of possibilities, as well. I explained to him that I started writing about being sixty because my hearing started to go, because I quite suddenly started (I still remember the first morning it happened) to think twice before dashing across a busy street in front of a bank of distant oncoming cars—but also because I suddenly cared a lot less about what other people thought of me. Yes, lots of changes made me feel my advancing age, but also other, newer experiences made me feel, if not younger, then at least freer, more engaged in the world than I had felt before. I even started to talk about how my sexual desire had changed—how it had become slightly less insistent, which was occasionally alarming, but also wider in scope, more catholic, so that whereas in the past I was attracted to slim brunettes like my wife, now I could have my head turned by someone in a propeller beanie on a skateboard, or by the light coming through a stand of trees. I was aware as I was responding that my questioner didn't seem to be quite as irritated as he had been at the outset of his question. I then explained that *not* writing about getting older felt like an abdication of the last quarter of my life, and that at least half the painters and writers I admired had turned out some of their best work after the age of fifty.

The man with the shock of white hair sat through it all. Then he nodded and said, "Thank you." I admit I was gratified. Of course, I understand his initial fear: Our collective fear of getting older, and our lifelong denial of the Other aging within us from the moment we are born, is a fear of being erased, of becoming nothing again.

Throughout history, human beings have reacted to that fear in one of three ways. There is the "Woe is me!" reaction, the lamenting of the leaking of life, beloved of poets and philosophers. There is the "To hell with death!" reaction, also beloved of poets and philosophers, and of the vast self-help industry. And then there is the third route most of us take, which is to bounce endlessly back and forth, day by day and hour by hour, between "woe is me" and "to hell with death." As I approached my sixties I was oscillating back and forth between these two extremes with such velocity that I felt compelled to keep track of the swings. Keeping a diary about the experience seemed then (and still does for now) like the best antidote to erasure.

The third and I suppose most gratifying consequence since I first published this book has to do with the enthusiasm I've discovered readers have for the diary form. Keeping a diary turned out to be quite a lot of work, a form of alchemy in which I attempted to turn the dross of the day into some more precious metal. Keeping a diary requires— to cite the motto of the alchemists themselves—patience (you have to wait for something to happen), courage (you have to be brave enough to write truthfully about that thing when it does happen), and continuous regimen—the discipline to keep recording small moments of time in your life until they inadvertently take on a shape you didn't see at the time of recording. More dauntingly, a diary is a record of what actually feels important, as opposed to what is supposed to feel important, or what others say is important, or what you think ought to feel important, given the sort of person you are supposed to be. That takes time, and thought, and practice. You keep pouring the totality of your life over the filter of your diary, and with any luck what you are left with is the residue of authentic experience.

I often felt that I was keeping track of tiny, ultra-personal, hyper-individualistic details that no one else would find relevant or even interesting, to say nothing of readable—all the times I took to the Internet to see who else was turning sixty the same year I was, all the hours I spent worrying about money and whether I had enough of it, the pleasure of swimming in the Atlantic Ocean, the reward of an outdoor shower afterwards, the bottom-less engagement of reading, the various ways people walk at the seaside, the thrill of my daughter's company, the way my relationship with my wife has never quite stopped moving, why it felt so dangerous, almost . . . transgressive . . . to break even the simplest routine. My diary felt too personal.

But to my persistent surprise, it is such small personal details that most readers respond to most enthusiastically.

"I thought I was the only one to feel such things," a woman of fifty-three, "preparing for what's to come," wrote to me not long ago. "I now feel like I belong to a bigger community, that I am not alone." Our most intimate and personal experiences—so particular, and private, and yet shared, and equalizing. That revelation—and it was a revelation to me—seems like a fine reward for the challenge of getting older—a gift, if you will. And I suspect it is only the first gift of getting older. I'm trying to be alert to others to come.

Toronto, June 10, 2017

SIXTY

I'm sixty today. My Facebook page (Facebook is celebrating its tenth anniversary) is full of kind wishes from Facebook friends, that is, from people I know, sometimes well, but also from people I don't know at all. I'm not sure how I feel about Facebook friends, but thank you all for the birthday wishes. I begin my sixty-first year underslept, with a brewing chest infection, and to be frank I am not looking forward to the day—standing as I am on the threshold of the no man's land beyond sixty. Sixty! I mean—if you'll pardon the expression—fuck me dead! How did I get to be this old? The answer is by not paying attention.

Downstairs, I discover that Johanna, my wife, has left a card on the kitchen table. It contains two photographs of me walking my daughter, Hayley, in her stroller in Los Angeles, when Hayley was an infant and I was . . . thirty-nine? Forty? And of course, we all know what that looks like: it looks thinner. Your hair is ill-advised, but you have so much more of it you don't really care. At forty, I looked like someone who thought he was twenty-one.

And just like that, standing there in the darkened kitchen at sixty, having been that sort of person—the kind who thought he was twenty-one when he was forty—strikes me as a terrible error. O you fool, I think, you did not realize upon what quiet foot The End approacheth. (My mental cadence takes on the rhythms of the Book of Common Prayer when I get anxious.) I mean, it's easy to forget, amid the pleasures and terrors and gentle draining sounds of everyday life, how it all goes by much too fast. Even if you pay attention all the time—and who, really, manages to do that?

And then, inevitably, the litany of my failures rushes into the vacuum left by all that speeding time—except that now, at sixty, those failures seem especially irreversible: not enough money, no retirement possibilities, no lush vacation home, no fast cars, no novels or plays or Broadway musicals or HBO series written, the rest of the usual roster of regrets. As well as all the moments I could have been more human, and less afraid. And in the place of those lost accomplishments, there's just the clock ticking on the wall, making its sound, which, as Tennessee Williams said, is loss, loss, loss.

This is the problem with turning sixty: it's so goddamn melodramatic.

———

In any event, that was my general frame of reference when I thumped downstairs at half past six on the morning of my birthday, the sixtieth anniversary of my squalling entry into this world to the very hour. I had one thought on my mind, beyond the aforementioned general despair, and that thought was: coffee. Where is the damn coffee? I can't believe I am out of coffee on the morning of my sixtieth birthday, when if ever a man needed a strong cup of coffee, it's now.

But I had no coffee. So I thought: "I'll have some maté." I did, somewhat eccentrically, have some maté in the house. I filled the kettle, stumbled over to the pantry cupboard—I don't know why, because that's not where I keep the coffee or the maté, but you know how it is after sixty, you start to remember things not specifically but by category (coffee= shelf=cupboard)—and furiously flung it open.

Then the thing happened. I had been planning to make a warm steak salad for dinner one day this week. Over the weekend, I had tried to buy some *fregula* at Fiesta Farms, the brilliant grocery store in our neighborhood. But Fiesta Farms was flat out of fregula, so I purchased instead a 454-gram Cellophane bag of *acini di pepe*, which is pasta that looks like tiny dried beads—even smaller than fregula or couscous. A pound of acini di pepe is a lot of pepes, brother.

And of course—because it goes without saying that this would happen to a man slumping on the threshold of sixty—in opening the wrong cupboard I inadvertently nudged the acini di pepe off the shelf. The packet hit the parquet, and burst, and 17 bezillion acinis, or pepes, or whatever the fuck those little bastards are called, shot across the ground floor of my house. I then spent twenty minutes trying to sweep them up out of the charming cracks and wrinkles and fascia of my slanted old floors, to not entirely successful avail. I now realize why acini di pepe is one of the less common pastas: it's a clean-up disaster waiting to happen. I spent the rest of the morning hobbling around the house, stepping on overlooked acini di pepe, which I now call *ouchie di papa*, because they hurt like hell. Not a great portent of the future, you have to admit.

But then my brother called, which always makes me feel lucky; and my wife gave me, as a present, some groovy (but wearable!) clothes, which produced a small surge of (mysterious) hope; and then I actually remembered to bring my cup of hard-won maté with me to the car, which is an absolute miracle. And then at work I ran into even more Facebook birthday greetings in my mailbox, from more people I knew well and people I didn't know at all. And it turned out that my shyness or snottiness about the nature of Facebook friends had become less resolute. At sixty, after all, you are suddenly looking into the beginning of the end, the final frontier where you will either find the thing your heart has always sought, which you have never been able to name, or you won't. And whether you find it or not—I suspect, or at least hope, that it doesn't really matter, as long as you look hard—that will be your life. I keep trying to peer into the distance, to see how the story ends, how it stacks up, how I did as a human being, but of course you can't know, no matter what the priests and professional soothers say. I suppose the only thing you can hope for is that it doesn't get too lonely too fast. And however well I knew or did not know my Facebook birthday-wishers, they kindly, if optimistically, reminded me that I was not yet all the way to the end. Not yet . . . not yet . . . not yet. Which is the other sound the clock makes. So thanks, even unto the depth of strangers.

FEBRUARY 6

A session on Twitter, at work. "We all want more followers. We all want to make connections," a young woman says. A brilliant former *Globe and Mail* employee named Steve Ladurantaye, now paid a relative fortune to work at Twitter Canada (at least compared with what he was earning at the *Globe*), is leading the workshop. But this is the thing: I sometimes don't want more followers, because I don't want to think about writing to please them. I want simply to write what I need to write. I know that sounds romantic and pointless, but I am convinced it is the only way to do any worthwhile work. The advantage of having this thought at sixty is that it doesn't matter: by this point, how people react to something you do is kind of out of your hands.

FEBRUARY 7

My father's birthday. He'd have been 101, had he not died two years ago. I don't think a day goes by—and I know people say this all the time, but I now know it's true—when I don't think of him, even if it's just a sharp memory of his face as I turn a corner in my car, rather than one of those wider gaps when I realize again, for the nine-thousandth time, as if I had never realized it before: *he's not here anymore*. I don't feel all that sad, I don't burst out crying, I'm not unhappy; but I miss him, I wish he were here, I wish I could call him up and say, "I might come round tonight. Are you free for a Scotch?"

I keep thinking about his brief decline. A year before he died, he was still going to work once or twice a week. He liked feeling useful. Of my siblings, I lived closest to him, in the same city, down the road from the retirement home he finally moved into after Ma died. Once he was freed from her fierce ownership of him, I finally got to know him a bit. I watched his transformation from self to spirit, saw the decline of his body—and he'd been a capable man who had put a lot of faith in his flesh—just as I began to feel the decline of mine. It was a kind of three-way lens: I watched the world watch me get older (and more irrelevant) while I watched him transform into what he considered pure irrel-evance. He wasn't irrelevant to me, of course: I loved our new relationship, the way we moved beyond obligation and expectation and failure into simple, unquestioning com-panionship. We traveled up and down the Atlantic coast with Tim, my brother; we went to England for a last tour. We got around, even if we needed a wheelchair to do it. By then his heart valve condition had been diagnosed; by then he had started crying at the dinner table or in the pub, and apologizing for his physical inadequacies. But his company was still pleasurable to me. I had always admired his physical skill and endurance, the fact that he was an athlete into his ninth decade. He believed in the physical, in hard work and sports and keeping moving, he figured it was his most valuable currency—that and being useful. At the end, of course, those were the two things sliding fastest. But by then I loved him just for being there. Now that he's gone, I miss his mere presence.

It was all very metaphysical: my visits to the old folks' home (where he was a man, and in the minority); our discussions of his children, my brother and sisters, who I would reassure him were fine; his reports on the copper market, an interest he carried over from the scrap metal business he'd been in; his especial thrill when my brother and sisters could come to town; the Scotches we shared, watching "the golf " and "the rugby" together, as equals.

I was watching something else as well, of course. I was observing his growing Otherness, his transformation into a non-physical (or at least physically less capable, noncompetitive) being. Because I remember that too: the accidents as we raced for the toilet; the strippings and the sluicings; hosing him down, as he held on to the taps for support; his terror of indignity, of being dependent on others, of being a bother; his steady apologizing for putting me through the Christ-like chore of washing the shit off his legs; my reassurances ("You did it for me, why should I not do it for you?"). Old age is the reverse of childhood, except that it's not the reverse of childhood at all, is it? As a child you are heading toward your more complete self, toward a bigger, better, broader, brighter self, a less dependent self, a self that exists independent of support; whereas as an old man you are headed in the opposite direction, toward oblivion (which is not the problem itself, after all, it's the getting to oblivion that is the problem, the slippery indignity of the stinking slide), toward a smaller and more shriveled and narrower and less brilliant self. And if you fight the slide, you are even more fucked, because then you are unhappy too.

I remember his body as though it is in front of me still: those purple bruises on his arms from every bit of contact, his fat-free flesh, the sagging, microscopically wrinkled quads, the horned feet, the crabbed fingers, the warped back, the primate stoop. The scent of him, half old man, half Eau Sauvage. The age marks like a thousand subcutaneous gravestones. And even so, there's a pretty good chance he had sex in that state, at the age of ninety-five. There's a chance he had a girlfriend after my mother died. Christ: imagine what carefree courage that exposure took. Or not: maybe the comfort of being naked with another human being never slides away.

––––––––

I am on the AirTrain, on my way from Newark to Manhattan, where I am to give a talk at the New York University journalism school. I have eagerly accepted the chance to go to New York on someone else's dime. It is the upside to becoming an elder, a mentor—whatever the hell that means.

On the train, a young woman smiles at me. I am chuffed. I am so chuffed I entertain a fantasy—purely a fantasy, I have no desire to see it through—of her wanting to have sex with me (ha ha ha ha ha ha ha) in the rhythmically rocking train bathroom, next to the sign that says N'ACTIONNEZ PAS QUAND LE TRAIN EST DANS LA STATION. (Do train bathrooms still have that sign? Well, not in the United States, you imbecile.) She's pretty, and wearing one of those artfully arranged slouch caps. It takes about five minutes for this thought to work its way into my brain stem: when you are sixty and a pretty young woman smiles at you, it's because you are old, and she is taking pity on you, not because she is contemplating asking you to accompany her into the rhythmically rocking bathroom of the AirTrain.

FEBRUARY 9

Johanna, who has flown down to spend the weekend with me, returns to New York, her old home, like someone slipping into a comfortable skin. After my talk we go to dinner with Rob Boynton, who invited me to speak at the school. He's writing a book about the Japanese who were kidnapped by North Korea; he speaks Korean; he's married to a Korean. He's probably at least ten years younger than me, though I feel I am physically just as youthful as he is, not as grey, not as heavy, in better shape. I spend an embarrassing amount of time every single day thinking about who is younger than me and who is older. I still imagine I am younger than all kinds of people who, on second glance, are certainly no older than me and quite often are ten years younger. I want to believe I am prey to this tendency because I am so young at heart—!—but I suspect it is because I am completely delusional. I still think I'm forty, because I sort of feel forty, or at least not that different from when I was forty (when I drank more than I do now, and smoked still, and occasionally smoked marijuana, and did coke now and then, and was a new father), before time and children made me serious.

Back when I was forty, I was about to be offered a job as the host of *Sunday Morning* on CBC Radio. Johanna and Hayley and I were about to return to Toronto, where Walker was born, where life changed completely. I think those days of first fatherhood in Los Angeles, with Johanna working at *GQ* and me trying to write a book, but still taking Hayley for early morning walks, and again in the afternoons, in her little pink jacket and her blue hat, and when I went to ski the Columbia Icefield, longing for her so much that I turned back in the middle of a blizzard and came home, were the happiest days of my life, of our lives.

But I knew nothing. I still had no sense that time works as a funnel: how the two decades from 0 to 20, say, take so long because they are your whole life; and the years from 20 to 40 still feel like a long time, because they are half your life; whereas the twenty years between 40 and 60 are only a third; and 60 to 80, if you even make it, is a mere quarter of a life span. Time speeds up as we go, as each year is experienced as a smaller fraction of the whole. There must be some mathematical principle that explains this feeling, similar to the way the water seems to rush out of the sink faster at the end than at the beginning, when in fact it is the same rate of draining.

I look back on my life before forty and deplore what I see; I hate myself for my lack of seriousness, my lack of productivity. The job as host of *Sunday Morning* was a good job (I'd turned down an even better one with National Public Radio in Washington, DC, because I thought the CBC job would give me more time to write), and my life was a "success," but I did not feel I was defining that success on my own terms. I knew nothing, understood nothing, had not grasped how one must start working and keep working, early on and every day, if one is to create something to show for one's life—as a writer, as a journalist, as a human being. I'm not talking about fame; I'm talking about something to show for one's existence on the planet, to pay off the gods of regret. Even a decent stamp collection would do it. In other words, what my father was unable to do, because he was too passive, too afraid, too worried about the future, which meant he never committed deeply to one thing, beyond the copper market and his wife. Although, why judge him? He lived his life as best he could.

I fear I have not. I know that fear is neither justified nor unjustified: it's just fear. But after sixty, you have less time to correct the mistakes. If you want to be Philip Roth, try to be Philip Roth early on: do the work, take the chance of failing, because it's not magically going to happen at seventy-five. If you tried, at least you won't regret not trying. I am never convinced I tried hard enough, because I never convinced myself that I had enough talent that it was worth trying, that I had the right, that I had the courage. I am a product of my class, and I am as I was treated growing up, having never nervelessly transcended that founding equation of my childhood: be seen and not heard. I repeated many of the conformities of my father (who was sent off to boarding school at four, or six, depending which version of his memory you believe), and am as a result wary of dedicating my life to a private, interior goal. We're decent guys. But what will decency get you, as opposed to discipline?

These are the circular doubts of someone who fears he put his faith in the wrong thing (i.e., youthfulness, a losing proposition all round). Or so it seems this morning, newly sixty.

My only consolation: maybe one day Hayley will read this; maybe dedication and drive has sunk in with her. Everyone tells the rest of the world the same thing as they get older: *pay attention while you can.* What did Johanna say the other day, as she was getting into bed? "Back when I was in my twenties and thirties, I always thought my fifties would be my heyday. When in fact I missed my heyday, which was my twenties and thirties." In any event, that would be satisfying, to know that we helped seed that hunger in Hayley, whether through what we did or what

we didn't do—that we showed her how rare and
life is. I don't care what her dream is; that's her
to tend. I do care that she grasps one, feels one, I
small or large or private or public: something that makes
her glad to have her time on earth. But maybe she already
has found it. I already admire the way she lives her life—
organized, compassionate, pointed at something she cares
about, taking advantage of opportunities, seeing what she
can see. I know she too has her moments of doubt, some
momentarily crippling, but I think I can see the pleasure
she takes in life as well, even in the way she makes a salad,
then forks into it with gusto. I know at least that I love
her with all I have. That, I am managing.

Ack, these dreary bouts of terror in the early morning.

FEBRUARY 10

Lunch with K., in the restaurant at the Bell Lightbox. She
arrives wearing eighteen layers of quilted this and stitched
that, a gigantic bedroll that then unspools for the meal.
She's, what, eight years older than me? I was in love with
her a long time ago, before I married; I've always been fond
of her. But as I get older, I am less afraid of her. I realize
now how bossy she was, how anxious, also how beautiful
in those days, with her blond hair, her perfect features,
her otter-like body. She is still slim, still stylish, her hands
are still appealing, but her face shows her age sometimes,
especially in the cheeks: care, weather, sun, a lot of time
in the mountains and outdoors. The conversation is the

usual effortless flow: there is nothing about her I find boring, down to her shopping and eating habits. We used to talk about my ancient obsession with her. Now it's simply amusing, even funny, great "material." Too bad I couldn't have seen it that way back then.

Still, there is always something slightly depressing about these lunches with old friends whom I don't see often. Each encounter is a new measure of time going by, as you notice some new wrinkle, a new pattern of spots on the hands, some new carefulness. For instance, K. has parked her car about half a mile away, because it was the only spot she could find where there wasn't a build-up of snow against the curb that she would have been hard pressed to climb over.

FEBRUARY 12

Here is something you should do: google who else is turning sixty as you are turning sixty. It's a little daunting, when they turn out to be hugely accomplished people. But the strange thing is that, after the initial wave of self-hatred, a wave of relief will settle in, as you think to yourself, as I thought to myself, "Hey, Oprah Winfrey and I are the same age." Admittedly, it stings a little that Oprah is richer than God Herself, while I . . . I am not. It's a bit of a slap to think of how hugely influential Oprah is, whereas I . . . am not. But then you will think, as I thought, "Okay, she may have all the money and power and glory in the world, she may be a magnificent person—but she's as old as I am anyway! Oprah is as close to the end as I am! Yeah, baby!" And that will be a solace, mark my craven words.

Who else hits sixty this year, in the middle of the baby boom bulge? Christie Brinkley. Very pretty, but hey—she's getting on, just like me. Matt Groening, who created *The Simpsons* and *Futurama* and won twelve Emmys. Talented, yes—but not getting any younger. Rene Russo, the former model and still extant actress (*Tin Cup*, the *Thomas Crown Affair* remake, three recent films). She offers the added bonus of being a knockout to this day. It is still possible. Patty Hearst, the heiress and Stockholm-syndromed member of the Symbionese Liberation Army, turns sixty in this, my year of turning sixty, and it's not hard to feel that perhaps you lived your life more fruitfully than she did hers, sympathies to her regardless. Recep Tayyip Erdoğan, the prime minister of Turkey, turns sixty this month, but he seems to be a sociopathic asshole. I would like to have accomplished as much as Ron Howard, who was Opie on *The Andy Griffith Show* and Richie Cunningham on *Happy Days* and directed or produced everything from *Parenthood* to *Cocoon*, but . . . we have the same amount of time left to accomplish things. No one can deny that fact. Ellen Barkin is now divorced from the Revlon millionaire, and she is my age. I find this bracing. Angela Merkel is my age and she is the chancellor of Germany. I have never wanted to be the chancellor of Germany. Michael Moore and Seinfeld are my age, and I admit that hurts more. François Hollande is the president of France at sixty, and still getting it, apparently quite regularly. This is reassuring. *The Tonight*

Show is sixty this year; that is a little depressing, because it means that I am as old as *The Tonight Show*. On the other hand, *The Tonight Show* was where Jack Paar cried on air. Lorraine Bracco and Scott Bakula (actor) and David Lee Roth (Van Halen) and Ang Lee (*The Ice Storm*, *The Hulk*) and Chris Noth (Mr. Big on *Sex in the City* and straying husband on *The Good Wife* to Julianna Margulies, who is forty-eight) and Joel Cohen (the moviemaker) and Chris Evert (the tennis player) and Ray Liotta (the actor, not looking as fair as Mr. Noth) and Annie Lennox (who is still astonishing, in any setting) are all sixty, and so am I. Comrades in age. I am surprised how cozy that makes me feel. Because Freddie Prinze (the actor from *Chico and the Man*, who committed suicide) and Vitas Gerulaitis (who died of asphyxiation thanks to a poorly installed pool heater) and Hugo Chávez (the colorful president of Venezuela) and Stevie Ray Vaughan (the musician) all would have been sixty this year, but they didn't make it, and so I do not envy them anything.

FEBRUARY 13

I have started reading *A Death in the Family*, the first of the six volumes (three published in English so far) of *My Struggle*, by a Norwegian writer named Karl Ove Knausgaard. He calls it a novel, but it's actually his diary: names and details of real people and real life, including his wife and kids and in-laws and cleaning routines, are unchanged. Admittedly, reading a six-volume autobiography of the moment-to-moment life of a forty-five-year-old Norwegian novelist named Karl Ove Knausgaard does not make me look like a youthful fellow. But at my age, with the time I have left, I'd rather read something that will stick in my head, if not for its content, then for the example its author sets, for proof that it is possible to take in the world on your own terms, and still speak to people. Knausgaard is the antidote to the communal, let's-all-experience-the-world-together promise of the Internet. It's a diary of everything that goes on in a head at once—of his inner and outer lives—a record of his consciousness of the world, complete with all the meandering memories that consciousness contains. It's a diary about time, and the things that make it stop.

A friend recommended volume one of *My Struggle* (*Min kamp*, in Norwegian) in January. "The whole book's about the inner life," he said. Two days later I saw a review in *The New Yorker* and thought I might have to read it. Despite the fact that—well, you know, I don't have unlimited amounts of time left, so why was I going to commit so much of it to the unproven diaries of some Norwegian wanker? Though on another level, why wouldn't I, since these days I am always looking for partners in the project of getting through to the end of life with verve, a kind of inner cabinet: "an aristocracy of the sensitive, the considerate and the plucky," as E.M. Forster famously put it in *Two Cheers for Democracy*. ("Its members are to be found in all nations and classes, and all through the ages, and there is a secret understanding between them when they meet.") The band of characters standing behind the Beatles on the cover of *Sgt. Pepper's Lonely Hearts Club Band* strikes me as such a group: the gaggle of influences and inspirations John and Paul and George and Ringo carried around in their heads, the friends upon whom they leaned for rhythm, for infusions of courage, when they needed it. As soon as I started reading *My Struggle*, I knew that Knausgaard would be joining my backup clan. The first sentence of the book is: *For the heart, life is simple: it beats for as long as it can.*

Knausgaard was nearly forty when he began the project. Writing fiction had suddenly made him feel nauseous, because he felt that the world was suddenly full of fictions, in books and on TV and in the movie houses. He found himself drawn instead to "the types of literature that did not deal with narrative, that were not about anything, but just consisted of a voice, the voice of your own personality, a life, a face, a gaze you could meet." A solitary voice, in other words, in a media environment the late David Foster Wallace once described as "Total Noise."

Knausgaard wrote six volumes in five years. Up to twenty pages of prose a day. I'm not sure what the appeal of this work is, beyond the way his eye picks out the details you want to know about. It's certainly not the plot. As volume one (*A Death in the Family*) opens, Knausgaard is a thirty-eight-year-old writer with three children by his second wife. Between descriptions of his daily routine, he recalls his life in intricate detail: the struggle of a smart, sad, overly sensitive but often drunk teenaged punk rocker coping with girls, school, self-hatred, a band (Blood Clot is its name), and especially his physically and verbally abusive father, who even mocks his lisp. A single set of memories— such as Knausgaard's step-by-step journey with his brother back to his father's house after the hated old man dies— can lope on for two hundred pages.

That quality of attention—to a moment and a detail, to the record of one's own existence—seems to be what I hunger for now, at sixty years of age. I need to stop time, and see what I remember and why, before I take a single further step. I need to remember what has truly moved me, however inconsequential the details seemed at the time. It's Knausgaard's talent for ascending invisibly from the granular to the grand view that keeps you pasted to the page. The book ends in a funeral home, to which Knausgaard has forced himself to return, alone, to see his father's body one last time. I remember that moment myself, with my own father and mother: the strange compulsion to see a parent's body, again and again, to keep returning to the open casket before it's too late, the fear that I had one last chance to put them into the right perspective, at the proper distance, one last chance to breathe that parental essence, one last chance not to be put off or afraid, one last chance to be intimate with the beings who brought me into this world. One last chance to be sweet and kind and yielding. My mother's body lay on a gurney in the emergency room in the suburban hospital where she had never come around after she had had a heart attack, where I raced after hearing the news, the first to get there and the one who told the others. She was not long dead, but so still. I held her hand and kissed her face (how soft it was! How clear!), and stroked her white, white hair, and what was in me went out of me, toward her, but she was not there anymore, for the first time. One last chance to prove that I loved her enough.

> Now I saw his lifeless state. And that there was no longer any difference between what once had been my father and the table he was lying on . . . And death, which I have always regarded as the greatest dimension of life, dark, compelling, was no more than a pipe that springs a leak, a branch that cracks in the wind, a jacket that slips off a clothes hanger and falls to the floor.

I can manage about forty pages before I have to lie down.

FEBRUARY 17

At Assiniboine Lodge, about 125 miles southwest of Canmore, for a week of all-terrain skiing with Al Kling and John Mitchell and John's wife, Maggie. Mitchell and Kling and I have done this, with or without others, nearly every year for thirty-five years—ever-older men doing daring things, to prove we're still daring, and therefore not older. We spent a night at the Mitchells' place in Canmore, caught up with each other, observing the progress of time upon the faces and bodies of each other, got up early, headed for the helicopter pad, and were dropped off at the lodge just before lunch.

We have been bashing up and down the mountains, skiing up, sweeping down. Until a few years ago it was the trudge up that reminded me I was getting older. The pattern of thought that occurs to an average skier making his or her way on back-country gear up the narrow forest trail to the Nublet, an outcropping below Mount Assiniboine, in Mount Assiniboine Provincial Park, about 112 miles west of Calgary by car and helicopter, or anywhere else in the middle of winter, can go roughly as follows:

Okay, okay, I'm not having a heart attack. I'm not. One hundred and twenty-eight beats a minute isn't a heart attack. It's a moderate workout. By the time the group gets back to the lodge, I will have burned . . . at least two thousand calories. Yes! I'll feel so good, I'll want to have sex incessantly. [Pause, gasping.] Too bad there's no one here for me to have sex with. My God, look at the size of that magpie: I've known smaller dogs. Whatever happens, it'll be worth it because once I get to the top, I get to ski down.

Now the descents are nagging at me too: I'm tentative, worried about falling, about what I might break. That's no way to ski. Still, this is easily the best skiing holiday I've ever had. Of course, I say that every time I go up into these mountains. Every time, I mean it.

FEBRUARY 18

We never ski the same slopes twice. Each morning's fresh snow comes up to our knees.

At the end of the afternoon, we skied back to the lodge and had a desultory sauna (we wear bathing suits in mixed company now) and a shower (which seems like a reward to me, every time I have one: I got that from my father) and snacks—cheeses from France and Quebec, charcuterie from Canmore, wine from Argentina and France and BC. I hurried to get to the lodge's living room: there's a chair I like to claim there, made from wolf fur and burled pine. (The race for available chairs in my father's retirement home made the Kentucky Derby seem like a slow walk.)

Our second night at the lodge, after the dishes had been cleared away, two guests—a professor of literature and her investor boyfriend—taught everyone, guests and staff alike, to dance the tango. The tango is all about tension and release—not unlike skiing up a slope you fear will never end and then rushing down, hoping it never does.

FEBRUARY 19

Today, we helicoptered out of Assiniboine; cleaned up in Canmore; and drove an hour west along the Trans-Canada to the fire road that leads into Lake O'Hara Lodge, just beyond Lake Louise. The only way in is to ski almost seven miles up the gentle slope of the fire road. We managed two and a half miles an hour. It's downhill on the way out, thank God.

There are twelve people staying in the lodge: an elderly couple in their seventies; a pair of dating thirty-nineish engineers from Houston, living for the time being in

Kitimat, BC, where they are conducting a feasibility report on Chevron's proposed liquid natural gas port; a fifty-something emergency room physician from Bragg Creek, Alberta, and her husband, a retiree who has taken up bison ranching; and their daughter and her boyfriend, a pair of surly professional protesters opposed to the Kitimat port. The young couple are the least accommodating people I have ever met. The young man keeps referring to everyone as assholes, making snide comments about people wealthy enough to be skiing here, even as he skis here; the daughter thinks of herself as a writer. Her mother told me, "If you could talk to the kid, she'd be very appreciative," but every time I try to make conversation, the girl farts, silently but pungently. I'm not kidding. She's on the paleo diet and must have different meals from the rest of us. I have rarely seen the presumptuousness of youth, the embodiment of the cliché "the world owes you a living," displayed so vividly. If aging is the process of becoming the Other, of shifting over into a state that everyone deplores and attempts to deny—which is pretty much what aging is, from what I can see—then I have found the source of the fear of such Otherness: young adults, whose freshness, or so-called freshness (the farter is never going to qualify), is based on being the opposite of old.

Lake O'Hara Lodge sits on the Continental Divide, and therefore experiences in the course of an hour every form of weather known to humankind: roasting sunshine, cold as dry as judgment, silent, steadily carpeting snowfalls, spooky ice fogs. The mountains that ring the lake always seem to have let you in just this once, as a special favor. The views are so spectacular, they're actually hard to fathom; John Singer Sargent painted here, as did Lawren Harris and J.E.H. MacDonald and Peter and Catherine Whyte, among others. The artistic history is part of what lures me back: painting was always one of my secret fantasy careers, what might have been. But it's too late now, at sixty. So I have settled into a routine instead: up at six to make some notes; coffee at seven in front of a second floor picture window; reading and writing until muffins at 8:15; full breakfast at 8:30. Pack a lunch from the array on offer. Skiing by ten, lunch and conversation in a sunny spot on the slopes, an afternoon of turns. Return to the lodge, thrilled and exhausted, at four. Nap—that seems to be a standard feature now (but it always was); reading, shower, drink; then dinner at seven. Everyone's happily in bed by ten. Wake up the next morning at six to find it is steadily, silently, endlessly snowing outside my window, the snow simply piling onto the earth in the windless dawn, silently seeding the ground for my day's pleasure.

I don't know if it's the exercise or the fresh air, but the conversation tends to be interesting. Last night, Alison, the co-owner of the lodge, told a story about scattering her grandmother's ashes in the woods a couple of miles south of North Bay, Ontario. When she returned a few years later with her grandfather's ashes, she discovered the highway had been expanded, and that Gran was resting peacefully under the new southbound lane to Toronto. I suspect all the men in the lodge have a bit of a platonic crush on Alison. I had one on her predecessor, Leslie Wake, as well. (I've been coming here, intermittently, for a long time.) There's something about women who can ski and knit. I still think of the way Leslie sat in the sauna, semi-naked and knitting, talking to me. I loved talking to her, yes (I had yet to meet my wife), and I also loved looking at her, in a non-lustful way, simply because she had a fascinating body and wasn't ashamed of it, and I, without any justification whatsoever, took that as both a gift and a compliment. (That's what I miss at sixty, in myself and everyone else: physical shamelessness.) I think she was pregnant, too. I was twenty-seven when I first met Leslie, who was—what, seven years older?—and just embarking on middle age. I was late to do that myself, and didn't have a child until I was thirty-nine. ("A long middle," as someone once said to me, not kindly.) Anyway, Leslie gave me the hat she'd been knitting as we talked. I still wear it.

FEBRUARY 21

On our last day, we follow Bruce, the owner of the lodge and our guide, up through the forest, climbing and puffing in the crisp sunshine for two and a half hours to reach the toe of Opabin Glacier. Then we ski down the moraine slopes that fall away from the ice. I yo-yo them, trekking up and swooshing down four times. Once you start, you never want to stop. I guess that is true of a lot of things.

After that, we ski the rest of the way back to the lodge, through glades and meadows and gullies and snow-padded rock fields, an hour and a half of soft, sublime descent. I miss snacks because I linger with my skiing friends on frozen Lake O'Hara in front of the lodge to watch the heartbreaking afternoon light crowd in over the mountains. It isn't just the scenery that keeps me there, of course, but the new thought that, at our advancing age, this might be the last time we see it together. Which makes me immeasurably sad. You can't just use this terrain, leave your tracks on it, and leave: it uses you, makes you earn it, makes you deserve it. The mountains near Lake O'Hara have been around, after all, for at least a couple of hundred million years; this was the rim of a great sea, later pushed up into synclines. We'll be around, if we're lucky, for eighty. Years. Is it the finite nature of our existence among the mountains that makes their beauty so achingly real and important? See us now, we hear them say, before it's too late. I like doing it on skis. That way, I get to feel how steep the slope is, up and down.

FEBRUARY 26

Johanna has begun to play the video game Candy Crush. She is obsessed. The last time this happened, she was addicted to Brain Age, which was some sort of memory strengthener, and would play late into the night, long after I had gone to sleep. Then she complains about not being able to sleep. She has started using what I call her "sleepy cloth," in one of those corny tenderisms husbands lavish on their wives. The sleepy cloth is an old scarf that she drapes across her eyes to keep the light out. She has begun to snore, ever so faintly, but still wakes me and asks me to turn over on my side when I do. I always reply in the same way when she does: "But I *am* on my side!" Then I am awake. She seems to develop these bouts of computer gaming before she takes on a new project, or at least whenever she doesn't have enough work, or work that satisfies her. I know all this about her. That seems like a decent accomplishment, at sixty.

I drove Walker back to his other home tonight. I do it every two weeks, after he comes for his visit from the assisted living group home where he has been a resident since he was eleven, after his condition (genetic) and his intellectual and physical disabilities got to be too much for us to manage. He's eighteen now, "transitioning," as the social workers say, from the children's care system into the even more inadequate adult care system. He still looks about twelve, and still has the mind of a one-and-a-half-year-old. He's the same, in other words: still can't talk, still can't reason, still can't live without twenty-four-hour care, still laughs, every time he laughs, as if he's never laughed so hard. I still wonder about the purpose of his life, if it has one. I suspect it does. When I was forty and he was born, throwing our lives into constant turmoil, I used to ask myself how I would manage him (change his diaper, stop him from hitting himself) when he was twenty and I was sixty. Now

I know. That was why we gradually moved him into a group home, at the suggestion of the care workers, at their urging. He comes home for two days every two weeks. He loves it, and we do too. But I dread taking him back again, every time. I dread the hour-long drive each way if I am tired, from having tried to put him to sleep at midnight the night before; I dread leaving him there. Olga, his nanny—we still have Olga, twenty-two years after she first came to look after Hayley—manages it better, but she spends more time with him, and is therefore less guilty. Olga's the same age I am, aging in her own way, but at the same pace. She talks more than she used to, whether or not I listen. She still likes to read the billboards out loud as we pass in the car, something she started with the kids and continues now with me, as if I were four years old. It seems to be a habit she picked up when she was first learning English.

Tonight I enacted the same ritual I perform every time I park Walker in the front hall of the white bungalow on the edge of the city where he lives when he's not with us, where the taxes are lower and a group home makes more financial sense: kiss him, say good-bye, high-five, kiss him again, three hugs, hold his hand, tell him I will be back soon, kiss him again, and leave, saying good-bye as I go, heading out to the car. I'm a parody of a man who can't say good-bye and I feel like I am abandoning him there every time. We can't handle him at home for more than a day or two, but I still feel as if I have let him down. Sometimes he's happy to be back but sometimes he's not. I keep hoping to find some time to raise some money to build a new kind of community for people like Walker—if only to have a place I wouldn't be ashamed to leave him, a community that could be measured by the forgiving standards of its inhabitants rather than against the normal world's so-called "standard of care." It's good care, but I wonder what kind of a life he has. Unfortunately, Walker can't tell me. I can't let the end come before I have finished that project. So I tell myself.

FEBRUARY 27

A drink and a hamburger at the Pilot with Q., an old pal from college. We meet up a couple of times a year. We're friends in the way you stay friends when you have endured emergent adulthood together, in close quarters: very little breaks that bond, even if you live very different lives, and even as time and age change you. He looks ten pounds lighter than he did the last time, which is ten pounds heavier than when he was at university, and is well turned out in a good shirt and grey trousers. He always dressed as an adult—blazers, ties, good sweaters—and thought like one too, which I counted on. Played football, was a deft writer, and genuinely funny: he listened to marching band music for an hour every Sunday evening, for the irony. He was eighteen at the time.

Today he is full of chagrin for other reasons; he has done something he wishes he hadn't done. I ask what the trouble is, but he won't say. He's not one to publicize his difficulties. I immediately try to make him feel better by lamenting my dire financial situation. The other day I saw my annual benefits statement, and it appears that working at the newspaper, and then moving to freelance, and then coming back fifteen years later to work there again has left me with a monthly pension of $800. I may have misread the form, but I am afraid to ask for clarification. I tell myself that when I retire I will be too lame to go anywhere anyway. But I have purchased a whole life insurance program to make up for it, which costs $1,800 a month, and is slowly driving me further into debt.

Hayley's birthday. She's in Edinburgh for her third year, a break from taking her degree at McGill. I sent her two hundred dollars and a box of chocolate meringues that I baked.

MARCH 3

Haircut. Howard has been cutting my hair for . . . Christ knows how long now. At least fifteen years. He was working for Civello when I first ran into him, then had his own place, and is now back at someone else's shop. He and his wife—a young lawyer, from money, mother of their two children—seem to be having some troubles. Howard has subsequently lost a lot of weight, has cut his hair in a young hip style, and is living in the basement. He's fifty.

The attendant washes my hair. I used to luxuriate and look up at the woman doing the washing. Now I am chaste, keep my eyes closed, and try not to think of her horror at bathing my balding scalp.

The haircut itself takes forty minutes and consists mostly of Howard trying to make the island of hair left on my foreskull look like something other than a random stand of corn that somehow got planted away from the main field. What the fuck am I going to do with it? "The day will come when we will have to shave it off," Howard said a year ago. While that day has yet to come, when it does, it will mark the day that I am officially, formally, unarguably, irretrievably, thanklessly, laughably bald. There is still fringe—yes! I am not yet as bald as my younger brother. Or as bald as my old man was at my age. Or as bald as my brother-in-law, or as bald as some guys at work who are *way* younger than me. No, I am not. I'm not as bald as Offman, for God's sake, and Offman is barely in his forties. This is my daily litany. For this is the thing: there is already a bald spot at the back of my head, a round, brown, hairless circle, a monky tonsure that denotes my oncoming celibacy and sexlessness, like one of those bare spots in the center of a Druidic circle of standing stones, the place where the sacrifices were made. What I would give for it not to be there. But it is. It's a spot I like not to think about, the Area 51 of my own head, the zone no one acknowledges. I forget that my bald spot is there, and then, when I find myself inflating the age of someone my own age, or thinking I am younger than a guy who is actually five or ten years my junior, the sudden memory of my bald spot smacks me down on the hard pavement of reality. I think, "Sure, that guy is at least ten years older than me, or at least he looks it, or—Oh, wait, I have a fucking bald patch, I am as old as that fucker and then some, plus he's taller than I am." That's what it's like in this balding man's brain, pretty much all the time. I remember the bald spot, and that reminds me how damn old I am. But at least Howard knows my secret, and he does his best to keep it one, and for that favor I am willing to give him ninety-five dollars quarterly. The rest of the time we mostly talk about Israel. He's a witty, well-read, extremely well-informed fellow. I hope he manages to weather his troubles.

MARCH 4

Hangover. They take more out of me now. But I still insist on having them. I have been in a near-coma for most of the day. There is the mid-morning nap, to recover from having been awake half the night thanks to the alcohol (got to bed at two, woke up at five); the early afternoon nap; the generalized horniness brought on by the fact that one's defenses are lowered (this is half the reason to have a hangover: your capacities are diminished, you can't be expected to follow the program, and as a result your mind seems to wander where it wants); the huge lacunae in one's operational functions (I left my reading glasses on three different displays in the supermarket). Underlying the physical longing is a slight paranoia about my upcoming twenty-two-hour flight to Australia (to give a speech, and the organization who hired me is paying for the flight); beneath that, another layer of anxiety pertaining to whether or not it is healthy for my heart rate to reach 164 beats a minute at the peak of exercise (if I'm not in pain, I presume it's okay); and, overlaying it all, the lovely off-kilter sense of time, which loses its authority in a hangover, so that every minute lost feels like two minutes gained. I sometimes think the only reason I drink is for the aftermath.

MARCH 10

The RBC Charles Taylor Prize luncheon at the King Eddy, my favorite hotel in the city: I like the association with Edward VII, and his wayward ways. I'm a former winner of the prize, hence my invitation. You would think this would make it more relaxing to stroll among the nominees and editors and publicists and envious fellow writers—especially the envious fellow writers—basking in former glory. But instead it just makes me wonder why I'm not a nominee again. The year I won this prize (three years ago now, Jesus wept), someone at this very luncheon walked up to me and said, "How does it feel to know you'll never write anything that good again, that your best work is behind you?" I should have replied, "It makes me feel like punching you in the face." Because, of course, that is precisely how it makes me feel to this day: what if I never again write anything worth it? What if I waste time and effort on bad work at an age when wasting time has such temporal consequence? Martin Amis regularly implies that a writer's career is pretty much over by fifty, but I notice that hasn't stopped him from trying. I suppose that is all there is to do. You keep trying.

Later in the afternoon (not sure if there is any correlation with drinking at lunch with a cohort of anxious writers and their publishers), I have a short but intense bout of jealousy, thinking about Johanna and what's-his-name, the guy who has been sniffing around her "work," or so he claims. She said she was off to dinner last night, some book club; I began to think how often her book club meets, and was convinced she was using it as cover. I had an entire fantasy in which I walked in on her, unannounced, and caught her in the act, then couldn't decide whether I would just walk out or demand one last accounting. Of course, this is insane: it turns out her book club was canceled and she sat at home all night watching TV. But at least I'm showing some signs of an inner life! Jealous at sixty: who knew it could be a point of pride?

However, tonight, a Monday, I am on my way to Australia. We arrive on Wednesday morning. I leave Sydney three days after that and arrive home Sunday. It's as if time and the calendar are in sync with the vagaries of my memory. I should count the number of times I forget things in a day, but of course I am afraid to do that. I have to give a keynote address to the Australasian Academy of Cerebral Palsy and Developmental Medicine—an entire convention of doctors and therapists who work with the physically disabled, some of whom have read my book about Walker and thought their fellow physicians should read the story of a father trying to figure out if his disabled son's life has any purpose. The conference is sponsored by the world's largest manufacturer of Botox, which is used mostly in cosmetic surgery but, when there is a little left over from smoothing out the wrinkles of the vain, can be used to relax spastic muscles.

My ticket says I am flying first class, but when I board, this is not the case: I am in some ever so microscopically bumped-up version of Economy. It should be called Economy-Huh. I am sitting in the middle of a family of six, the mother a steady worrier. I offer to switch seats with one of her children on the far aisle, and she gratefully accepts, and I even more gratefully move. I don't mind children on flights. I do mind children on me on flights, at least if they aren't my own.

I watch a passel of instantly forgettable movies. Why does a man who feels his life speeding by watch *The Shawshank Redemption*, or the *Bourne* movies, or *The Godfather*, or the *Die Hard* movies, for God's sake, for . . . what, the fortieth time? Why do I keep watching movies I don't have time left to watch? I want the comfort of the familiar, but then it disgusts me, as if I were some kind of whacking perv, and I turn to Knausgaard (I'm on to volume two, which is mostly about his divorce and remarriage and raising his kids). The Knausgaard makes a new path in my head, and I want that more, in the end, than I want the cozy time wasting of *Shawshank*. This makes me feel noble, I am embarrassed to admit.

Knausgaard seems to be able to write about anything, and he's so good I don't even envy him. He remembers not just details—the sound of doors slamming, the way his luggage falls down the carousel at the airport—but the emotional aura that surrounds each detail, the way one brand of cigarettes implies one thing, another brand another. The whole thing is a construction, but it doesn't feel like one; it feels like the consciousness of the moment, which he is getting down before it's too late. Action (a witheringly self-conscious birthday party for a child in his daughter's class) mutates into a meditation on aesthetics (on the triple consciousness of a late Rembrandt self-portrait: "in this picture he sees himself seeing whilst also being seen," which is also Knausgaard's way, and also the way of the sixty-year-old) and from there into his specialty: the moments in a life that suddenly step forward from the rest of it, and the subsequent feeling of inexhaustible awareness and watchfulness that great art inspires. He doesn't miss anything, or at least he leaves you with the sense that he hasn't missed anything. This jacked-up watchfulness then seems like the antidote to our pretense that time is not flying, that we are not dying every moment of every hour of every day of every one of our lives, from start to finish.

> *I got up, rubbed my hands on my thighs a few times, and walked down to the intersection. The passing cars left tails of swirling snow behind them. A huge articulated truck came down the hill with its chains clanking, it braked and just managed to shudder to a halt before the crosswalk as the lights changed to red. I always had a bad conscience whenever*

vehicles had to stop because of me, a kind of imbalance rose, I
felt as though I owed them something. The bigger the vehicle,
the worse the guilt. I tried to catch the driver's eye as I crossed
so that I could nod to restore the balance.

These are the moments that make a life, Knausgaard would have his readers believe. Given that a life is so fleeting, we should pay attention to every detail in it. But we never do. I think this is why I keep reading Knausgaard in such strange places: in the car in front of my house at the end of the day, or for an hour before breakfast. I read him whenever I can, because I can, because I don't want this opportunity to slip away with all the others. He makes me perk up, like my dog when another dog comes down her street. Time is elastic in *My Struggle*, but it is always racing by as I turn the pages, as if Knausgaard were playing a clever trick: he is stopping time, while I spend mine on him.

The specifics of a person's life are always arguing against the impersonality and generality of the larger world—a battle that feels analogous to the existential smack-down between seeing and hearing and feeling and smelling and touching and being, and therefore aching, on the one hand, and the total extinction that lies on the other side of the river, when you're dead. The question of what a life means and how it should be lived (not to mention how a writer should capture it) is at stake on every page of *My Struggle*, and it makes me cranky, but so is the answer to that question: just take note, it doesn't matter what you are

taking note of. You don't have to be having an a
a twenty-eight-year-old yoga instructor with l
and a body like a climbing rope, you simply h
the fantasy, and where it popped up, and what happened
next. You want to organize it later into a novel, fine. Do
that. You want to use it as a springboard into an essay on
the apologetics of girl-watching, do that. The key is to pay
attention to what is happening, not to what is supposed
to be happening. That might be as true of facing growing
older as it is of writing a book. That, I imagine, is also why
Knausgaard abandoned fiction for these volumes: fiction
was supposed to be literary, and literary didn't feel very real.

In my copy of the first book, close to an anecdote about
Knausgaard looking at some Constable paintings, are my
notes, in pencil, of the lunch I made and was eating as
I read: a sandwich of canned smoked tuna and mayonnaise and balsamic vinegar on toasted rosemary focaccia,
with a blood orange for dessert. The tuna was a stocking
stuffer from my wife the previous Christmas, a treat she
loyally buys me every year. I'd been reading and eating
and making notes in the kitchen when I heard a frantic
scrabbling at the back door. I jumped up to let the dog in.
She was happy to be back inside. There are notes about
that too, in the margins of my copy of *A Death in the Family*. Why am I making such notes? Because those things
happened in the course of the reading. Because they are as
real and as "important" as anything else within the frame
of the experience of reading the book. Because that is how

I read: I'm distractible. Most contemporary art, Knausgaard insists, suffers from two weaknesses: it considers naturalistic depictions of reality to be old-fashioned; and it doesn't care if it rouses any feelings in an onlooker. It celebrates intellect—ideas, and ideas about ideas, which are then pinged and pinned and shared and tweeted. But the moment Knausgaard focused on the Constable paintings in the book on his lap, he writes, "all my reasoning vanished in the surge of energy and beauty that arose in me. Yes, yes, yes, I heard. That's where it is. That's where I have to go. But what was it I had said yes to? Where was it I had to go?"

Those are the questions of an artist trying to make his art come alive. They're the same questions every sensate person asks him- or herself in the middle of the night: what, precisely, makes me feel unapologetically alert and alive? What will I remember as I die, if anything? Is it this? Is it the sandwich, made with such care? The dog at my side? Is it this book, or that one? Is it art or work or pleasure or people? Is it the faces of people I love? Is it whatever I manage to elevate into the realm of the memorable? In the days before the world went digital (and I say this not as a complaint, simply as an observation, because I live in the digital world as much as anyone), events and people and objects and sensations established their importance slowly. They earned their place in our memories. Today, on a smart phone—such an ironic name—everything is important at once, and so nothing is important. You remember little of what you urgently sought out. Then you wonder why your life feels so empty.

I'm finding that it's harder to read Knausgaard in Australia, though. Maybe it's the heat, which is baking, or the comfort of my suite—an entire floor of a house to myself, halfway up a quiet hill, overlooking a pond and a golf course—or the parrots, or the conference attendees, the predominantly female doctors and occupational therapists who treat cerebral palsy, who waft and glide back and forth past my windows. Maybe it's the barkless eucalyptus trees, their thin, silvery leaves flashing in the air like schools of airborne herring. In any event, it is only on the bus back to Sydney, on my way home again, that I once again feel the need to read Knausgaard.

The Pier One hotel, where I am sleeping over until my plane leaves first thing tomorrow morning, is the kind of place that makes you feel special when you check in and not so special when you come down the next morning and have to pay twenty-five Australian dollars for fruit and yogurt. My room is the epitome of contemporary cool: white, narrow, uncluttered, hanging breathlessly over Sydney's famous harbor. There is a miniature glass dome over the hand soap in the bathroom, as if it were a tiny pastry. And the alarm clock is one of those silver, electronic cubes whose alarm is impossible to set—I can barely see the icons, and God knows what they mean—but which lets you play your iPod, because you have to have your music, right? Your music is like oxygen: there is no way you can go somewhere without access to the plasma of your personally curated taste to insulate you from the reality around you. In any event, the hotel makes me feel lonely, so I plunge into Karl Ove again. I certainly prefer it to hotel room porn.

MARCH 14

In *A Man in Love*, book two of *My Struggle*, Knausgaard recounts, over the course of 573 pages, his struggle with domesticity. He's become a classic dad and husband of almost forty: he hates himself for being conventional, but he's afraid to live any other way. (Does this sound familiar?) His disillusionment with "the prefabricated nature of the days in this world I was reacting to, the rails of routine we followed," his frustration with "the sameness that was spreading through the world and making everything smaller," is the predicament of successful modern Western culture. Hegel said this would happen. We've replaced an all-knowing God, the authority that made the world mysterious, with the authority of ourselves—know-it-all pipsqueaks by comparison, who actually know nothing. Everything is accessible to us, but very little of it reaches into us.

Is that bad-tempered enough? After all, I'm sixty.

Here's the strange thing: it's only by coming home, to my little house and my little garden, to the front door with the screen frame that needs to be painted, to my pleasantly familiar wife and my fond dog and my dilapidated kitchen and the jumbled fridge, to the objects and beings I know well enough to describe intimately, that I regain a small if resentful sense of belonging. Is that age, and a concession? Or is that just the old human gratitude?

MARCH 18

Cathrin's birthday: I take her to lunch at Canoe, on top of the Toronto-Dominion Centre, with a view, all around, of the city I decided to live in.

Cathrin's a year younger than I am, but seems younger still: I like her ready laugh, her good story sense, and the fact that she's never intimidated by her age. She's fearless, and at fifty-nine, fearlessness is increasingly rare. I've had an amateur crush on her since I met her and her husband . . . twenty-five years ago. Jesus. They were having kids just as we were, so we became fast friends; she and Johanna are close, even screen-writing partners. She was one of my favorite editors: when I lived in Los Angeles, and she was running a magazine in Toronto, we had long afternoon conversations on the phone, discussing everything, as only a writer and a great editor can. She separated from her husband about six years ago (he's still a close friend as well, I refuse to choose between them, as so many people think they have to). Though they are still in the process of divorcing, she is now dating a new man seven years younger than she is. He has a fancy job and flies all over the world. "I only feel lonely at two times," she says, over a lobster sandwich. "When I go to bed, or when I wake up in the middle of the night. And when I walk into a party alone." I understand the loneliness of the middle of the night. But I prefer to be anonymous and alone at parties; that way, I can stay anonymous and alone. That hasn't changed with age.

I tell myself that if my own marriage ended, I would not marry again. But there's no predicting. Afraid of dying, of what's coming down the road, I feel I ought to hedge my bets and behave, but there are no set rules, no matter what the self-help books say, and posterity doesn't give a shit how you live. Everyone over sixty feels the public prejudice against them, feels vaguely compelled to be sedate and proper, but everyone wants to smash the prejudice as well.

I love the view from Canoe (though I am slightly embarrassed by the brilliant service, and by the fact that I am spending too much money eating here): the intricacies of the city, in grid form. Makes me feel like God, or like the bridge painter in Tom Stoppard's *Albert's Bridge*, who spends all his time painting a bridge that spans a valley below him. When he finishes, it's time to start over again. Eventually he can't stand it any longer and trades places with someone from the valley. But soon he's back, seeking the cool loneliness of isolation and the view from above.

Reading that play was when I knew Stoppard was a genius. He was thirty-two when he wrote it. He was twenty-two when he became a playwright, having already been a journalist and drama critic. And here I am, at sixty, contemplating writing a play for the first time. I should be ashamed to put such words on the page—shouldn't I? This is failure, a lack of nerve—isn't it? That's the real crime against the self. But then I think of that poem of Yeats's, "The Choice," the fundamental decision to pursue "perfection of the life, or of the work." Choose the latter, Yeats says, and you "refuse/A heavenly mansion, raging in the dark." And for what? Hard work, no money, and insistent regret: "the day's vanity, the night's remorse."

MARCH 20

A visual field test at Mount Sinai Hospital, ordered by Dr. Robert Wagman, my ophthalmologist, who a couple of years ago found a small dent in my optic nerve. Because my father had a touch of glaucoma, Wagman tracks me and makes me put drops of Xalacom in my eyes at night. To my surprise, I am religious about it, despite the fact that the drops sting, and that I often forget to turn the overhead lights off before I throw my head back to receive the drops, thus blinding myself; despite the fact that the drops come in a tiny, plastic, pain-in-the-ass bottle with a bright yellow cap that needs replenishing every three weeks. It is not cheap, either, and would be fifty bucks a bottle if I didn't have a health plan, which I have, thank Christ. The active ingredient— a synthetic prostaglandin analogue—lasts about three weeks outside a refrigerator, hence the tiny bottle.

Glaucoma, or at least the potential for the "open-angle" kind, which is what I could face, is caused by high intraocular pressure (basically, high blood pressure of the eyeball). The prostaglandin reduces it by improving uveoscleral outflow of liquid aqueous humor through the trabecular meshwork in my eyes, and thence Schlemm's canal. (The eyeball is like a secret British club, full of rooms named for exotic and now-forgotten explorers. It's like having a small museum in one's head.) The prostaglandin has side effects: spontaneous abortion, the possibility of a wheeze, and so on. About 45 million people suffered from glaucoma, worldwide, in 2010, and the number is expected to rise to 59 million by 2020; it's the second most common cause of blindness, after cataracts. You pretty much know you're a candidate by the time you're sixty, if you don't have sudden-onset closed-angle glaucoma, which is another order of darkness entirely. My kind of glaucoma affects one in two hundred people under the age of fifty, and one in ten over eighty. The point is, you have to take the medicine to have a chance of not developing it, so I do. Despite the fact that every time the cold drop lands on the surface of my eye, I have to push a small bolt of fear back down into my chest, the fear of going blind from glaucoma, which for me, in its entirety, is the fear of not being able to read. I don't know how I would handle that. Would I hire a reader? Do they exist? Audio books? It all sounds clumsy, unhelpful. It sounds less than private.

I know these are minute concerns, but they occur to me perhaps half a dozen times a week. These are the physical pings that undermine my emotional confidence.

The field test is nervous-making, too. You cover one eye and stick your face into a rig that lets you survey a cavernous white space inside the machine. Looking straight ahead, you have to press a button whenever you think you see a light flash somewhere in the dome of white emptiness around your head.

"What if I just think I see a light, but I'm not sure?" I ask the attendant.

"Even when you just think you've seen one, press the button!" she says.

The whole ordeal lasts half an hour, with the waiting. As is my habit, I assume I am twenty years younger than everyone else in the clinic. I use the hand sanitizer on the way in and on the way out again.

Did I mention that since my return from Australia I too have picked up the habit of playing Candy Crush, the computer game to which my wife and 93 million other human beings are currently addicted, in between bouts of reading *My Struggle*? I can't imagine it is doing anything for my brainpower. I took it up in the first place thinking it would be like mental calisthenics for my aging, everslackening brain. (I read the other day that one in eight North Americans over sixty ends up with some dementia, and that over eighty-five the number is one in two. I can't look at those numbers without mild despair.) Reading Knausgaard makes me afraid that I have not seized the opportunities of my life, which in turn makes me anxious; playing Candy Crush, lining up shapes and colors and making the tiny screen burst with connections and cheers, makes me feel better again, at least for a few seconds, until the ensuing wave of self-disgust forces me back to Knausgaard, hoping to cleanse myself.

Sometimes all it takes is a passage. *Boyhood Island*, book three, is Knausgaard's seamless memory of growing up on a freshly minted suburban housing estate in Norway after 1975. He captures the boundless specificity of childhood, when everything is new to us: the gravel and asphalt of freshly laid driveways ("Oh, that alone, the driveways of childhood! And the 70s cars parked in them"); the distinctive smell of a friend's house; the way children anthropomorphize everything ("It was strange how all large trees had their own personalities . . ."); the "immense antiquity" of houses and cars; the thrill of a new pair of running shoes. Childhood is its own world, but so is aging, from what I can see. The difference is that, for an infant, the bigger world, the completing world, the world that you want to become part of, is outside you; but when you are aging, the completing world, the world where you will find peace, is inside you, in part because the outside world doesn't much want you anymore.

When you get there, the question is what you do with your aging. Do you treat it simply as evidence of your decay and failure? That's the common reaction. But maybe it is an opening as well, a small tunnel to a different window of perception. Dealing with the really old (as opposed to those merely starting the trip, as I am) is like dealing with an entirely different consciousness.

I was trying to explain this to someone the other day, and likened it to the losses and gains I encounter dealing with my son, Walker, who can't talk or reason or keep his attention on anything for longer than a few moments. His company is always a challenge, often a pleasant one, but I cannot cure or fix him, or alleviate his bewilderment, or solve his loneliness, or even, except by force, stop him from whacking himself in the head (which he sometimes seems to enjoy as much as he hates it). In his company, the rules of engagement are completely turned off, and I am as disabled and as ineffective as he is. In terms of our ability to engage with one another, we are equals—equally hopeless. All I can really be is company, more or less imaginatively, depending on how on-the-ball, how daring, how flexible I am. It involves a kind of passivity, rolling with whatever happens, using the present moment. When those moments work—and they don't have to, because you can try again and again—they are instantly memorable, original, real, true. They actually make me feel ageless.

This is often the case in the company of the very old as well. They make you wait, and you have no choice but to use the time to look around, not just at their lives but at your own, and at your lives together. This is one of the central premises of every memoir and novel and play and poem of old age ever written. It's a leveler, age—not just of the aged, but of everyone in the company of the aged. You have to notice its details and treat them as new, the way Knausgaard remembers everything being new when he was a kid:

> All you had to do was stick your head out the door and something absolutely fantastic happened. Just walking up . . . and waiting for the bus was an event, even though it had been repeated almost every day for many years. Why? . . . Oh, because of the wet snow. Because of the wet down jackets. Because of the many good-looking girls. Because of the bus rattling along with chains on its tires. Because of the condensation on the windows when we went inside . . .

It crushes me to admit that I tend to notice such details less as I grow older. The fade starts early, at puberty, when we begin to believe the outer world is what matters most, when we start to think we've seen it all before. The details are still there, of course; we just pretend they aren't worth noting anymore, because we require more instantly affirming thrills, whether it's Candy Crush or the steady suspense of *Breaking Bad* or the come-on of a new email message arriving in our inbox. We begin to stop noticing details when we begin to notice that time is always running out.

Even Knausgaard admits to this devaluation of detail. By the time he turned forty, he writes, "I hardly read books any more. If there was a newspaper around I would prefer to read that. And the threshold just kept rising. It was idiotic because this life gave you nothing, it only made time pass." He and his wife mean to watch serious art films, but when evening comes and the kids are in bed, they gravitate to fluff like the rest of us. "We wanted to be entertained. And it had to be with as little effort and inconvenience as possible." The laziness of the unlived life is its worst feature.

The redeeming trait of old age—or of aging into old age, as the gerontologists put it—is that finally, you can begin to look at the unlived life and appreciate that it is still life. If you take the trouble to write down the details, paying attention to the truth, and not the official version, you get a second chance to live it. That is the real discipline of getting older: to force myself to pay attention to details, as if they matter still.

MARCH 21 (FIRST DAY OF SPRING)

I am on hold at Ward Funeral Home as I type, listening to their pre-taped "on hold" message, which touts, in unsensational but still modulated and velvety tones, the Ward family's four generations of experience in the business of bereavement. I am waiting for Chris, my representative at Ward's, to find my father's remains, which I can pick up only with my brother, as he is the one listed on a form as the person to whom the funeral home will release things. Thank God my brother is still alive, then! He's coming to town in a few weeks and we'll be able to make that trek together, out to the Brampton suburbs where our parents lived, a place we fled as quickly as we could. His visit is something to look forward to: I need my brother's company, his friendship. He was my ally against my parents, growing up, and he is my ally still. And we're better friends now than we were as kids. He told me he was gay pretty early on, and I told him of my own travails with girlfriends and work. I don't know what I would do if he were not here to help me through the world. I write this almost casually, but the thought of not being able ever to see him makes my heart race.

In any event, when Chris comes back on the line, having found what's left of my dad, he tells me I must apply to the provincial government of Ontario for the certified long-form copy of the death certificate of Peter Henry Brown, the one the doctor signed, because, "officially speaking, doing it by the rules," that is the form we need to transport cremated remains (as they're called; I prefer the shorter and more efficient *cremains*) on a plane to England. Which is what we are going to do, in May, so that I and my brother and our sisters and other relatives can scatter my good-natured father into the North Sea, where he can at long last join my impatient mother. He has been sitting in a canister at the Ward Funeral Home since his cremation almost exactly two years ago.

According to Chris, bless his and my soul (the spirit of the Ward Funeral Home on-hold message seems to have inhabited my on-page voice), this certified governmental death form is exceptionally difficult to obtain. "They are very reluctant to let those out of their grasp," Chris has just said, unwittingly employing a metaphor of rigor mortis. He recommends, in addition to trying to go the official route, that we take a copy of the standard death certificate (which I believe my brother, the signee, has) and the certification of cremated remains (which Chris will tape to the engraved wooden box currently housing what there is of PHB) in our carry-on luggage. This is what he advises all his customers to do, he says, and notes that, in thirty years, he has never had anyone turned back at the border as long as the cremains are in an X-rayable container, which wood is. Even so, I need a copy of the death certificate.

But the challenge of obtaining a form so that I can obtain my father so that I can throw him into the sea has put me in mind, again, of my own death. I can't get away from the nagging feeling that somewhere along the path of my life, I misplaced twenty years. I am not sure when or where. It may have been the years I somehow forgot to pay close attention to, from twenty to forty, before I had kids (and when I was too ignorant and ill-read and self-conscious and [mostly] afraid to pay close attention to what was around me and daringly make something of it). Or it may have been the twenty years between thirty and fifty, when I believed I could make up later for all the time that was spinning by in the constant now of life with young children. More recently, I thought the missing years were the indulgent ones from forty to sixty, but I am not sure anymore. Certainly ten of those years can be excused: the decade of Walker's childhood was not good for much of anything except enduring. But that still leaves the last ten years, and the ten between twenty and thirty (what on earth was I doing then? worrying? trembling with fear?), and the ten between thirty and forty (same questions), which means I may have wasted as many as thirty years. I could have written fifteen books, say. I could have made some money. I could have loved more, especially. I could have been less guarded. I could have worried less about failure, which always made me reluctant to take a risk. (Like father, like son. I find the idea of being a cog in a genetic wheel discouraging.)

I still hope to catch it all up, but if I am really lucky and can keep writing for twenty more years—and that will be a stretch, because it gets harder, not easier—I can gain only a fraction of what I misplaced, a third at most, I figure. And who knows what quality it will be, as my faculties droop, along with everything else? What will I be able to remember? For instance, I have almost forgotten what a young woman's body looks and feels like. I ought to have taken better notes. Too late now.

Too late now. That's the problem.

It's as if I have lost my keys. I know they are in the house, but I simply cannot find them, so they are gone. They are within my orbit, but they are not graspable. They are the keys of time.

So what do I do? Take the last great risks? Write the shit out of what is left? Live the shit out of what is left? Try everything in the time I have? It's hard to choose what to concentrate on, given how little time there is, and how much I have to make up. A life lived the way I lived it, always thinking I'd get another chance, is an indecisive life; a life of indecision prepares one poorly for making the existential decisions one is forced to make later on. Which of the various projects that are still viable and tri-able should I choose? A novel, given the low historical odds of post-sixty novels being worth more than a whiff of accidentally released intestinal gas? (But of course, that's not true. The history of good post-sixty novels is long and rich.) A diary of turning sixty, called *Sixty*, lighting the path for a few in an oncoming generation? Start a whole new life altogether?

I don't want to go down the way the old girl did, in a flaming column of regret and bitterness, or as the old man did, in a hobble of inertia. I mean no disrespect to my parents. I loved them both, and I now view much of what they did as an honest accomplishment. But I don't want to be passive anymore. So I am going to try, I hope. Famous last words. Like the actor (I've forgotten which one) who said, "I've never felt better in my life!" and dropped dead. I'll save some money, quit my job, and write my life out, aim-ing to complete a project a year until I drop. It may not be pretty. I hope my brother will still be my best friend. He may want to disavow me for stretches of time. But I would rather manage not to regret at least the last bit of my life than regret it all, given how much I regret already. (Not Hayley, by the way—never Hayley, not for a second; not even Walker; and not my marriage; and not my brother and sisters and friends, though I wish I had been warmer.) Regret, at least *lifelong regret*, is the real enemy.

All right, enough of this endless recrimination. I should write my brother a letter. He's two and a half years younger, just hitting the steady anxiety attack of the late fifties. He's also in the market for a Manhattan apartment, and is considering one that overlooks the interior courtyard of the building. I should caution him against that. No view, no light, no outward aspect. No horizon. No vista. It's the real estate equivalent of being ninety.

Then lunch. Although really, I should hold off. I made a vegan Reuben for dinner last night, substituting smoked-salt roasted beets for the pastrami. If a gas company had built a pipeline to my ass, its stock price would have skyrocketed, based on undeclared reserves. Such are the indignities of life after sixty. One of these days I will have to start being careful about what I eat. The last time I visited the doctor for a general checkup, the nurse found my blood pressure a little high and cautioned me against salt. How is one supposed to taste anything without salt?

MARCH 27

The day of Sandra Martin's departure from the *Globe*. I go to half a dozen farewells a year now, partly because the newspaper business is in deep retraction, but mostly because this is the beginning of my cohort's time to say good-bye. Very few seem to regret leaving. Sandra's had a long and glorious and gossipy career at the newspaper, having written for most sections and most editors. She's a very good writer, and sexy, game, intelligent, vain, unrepressed. She likes attention and admits it. She's also a grandmother to small children, and is besotted with them. It makes for an unusual combination, the flirting followed by a fanning of photographs. But this is the thing about being older: the recombinations are always surprising. At least she has not been reduced by her age to a fraction of herself.

I return to Barbie Casselman, a nutritionist, in my ongoing hopeless attempt to get back to 180 pounds. I am 208, as much as I weighed when I first went to her. Which is bad. But also not bad, in another way, because it means I am no heavier all these years later, and that was a hell of a long time ago—a decade, no, fifteen years. She tells me that I can eat eggs if I am not a cholesterol producer. I never even contemplated the possibility that I might be one. But what if I am? In any event, it was a depressing encounter, and no way to begin the day. A day, incidentally, that is grey and wet and cold, drizzling, not unlike my life.

Last night, because Johanna and her women friends were having dinner at our house, I went out. I read Knausgaard until seven, then headed to the Oxley to have dinner. This was on my bike. It was chilly, but I wore a synthetic down vest and a sports jacket and gloves (and orange socks), so while it was brisk, it was not unbearable. (I'm strangely proud of the orange socks.) Dinner was a beet salad, fish pie, Diet Coke, for forty bucks, more than I can afford, and then I went to a movie (*The Lunchbox*, excellent, though to my shame I wanted a happier ending—I wanted the older man to get the pretty girl, and find happiness, literary happiness, the happiness that can be had from writing to one another). I ate a bag of popcorn and a package of almond M&M's. Unbelievable. And drank a bottle of water. A combo, and how. As I stepped out of the theater and was unlocking my bike in the freezing chill— the world feels colder since I turned sixty—I found two emails and a phone call from home, jealously asking where I was. Jealousy seems to go both ways, even after all these years.

But I cannot go through this seventh decade like this, physically. My goals are no drinking, take up meditating, write every day, exercise. Maybe read in place of TV. The goals of a fantasist.

APRIL 5

Woke up in a full-on panic at 5 AM, terrified, my throat constricted and my heart racing, over: no money, the cost of my savings/insurance policy, my deadline on Karl Ove Knausgaard (I've decided to write about him and his books for the paper), the state of my relationships and my life, my lack of discipline, the fact that I haven't looked at an essay of Hayley's, as requested, the state of my eyes/ears/ health, the documentary films I have to screen for my gig on TVO, the local public television station where I have been hosting a show for more than twenty years, the applications to Banff I have to read, the possible mold in the house, the need for a kitchen reno. At last the wolf is at the door, and I can't feed him. I spent most of my first six decades on earth imagining these panic attacks would soon be a thing of the past. They are, if anything, more common, more insoluble.

I jump out of bed and come downstairs and start typing.

My life is such a failure next to my brother's comfortable, financially responsible example. And my blood pressure must be going through the roof. What about the soy sauce in the meal I ate last night? It was salt-reduced, but still.

What did Casselman say to me? "Don't run, not at 208 pounds."

"Why not?" I said. "I've done it before."

"Really?" she said. "It's so hard on your joints."

Really.

APRIL 6

Just had a call from Tecca. Al, her husband, training on his bike this morning, as he has many mornings for twenty years, passed out going around a corner downtown. He came to five minutes later in the back of an ambulance. He's sixty. He's broken a few ribs, and his left eye won't open or close properly: if he forces it, he sees double. But there's no evidence of stroke or heart attack. The incident seems to be another one of the mysteries of the seventh decade, the Decade of Living Precariously.

Meanwhile, he'll be in the hospital for a week. It's an alarming development: physically, Al is the strongest person I know, and has the endurance of an ox.

When I go to visit him in the hospital, he doesn't seem diminished in any way: full speech, full memory, and only the lazy eyelid. A huge relief. He tells me the doctors are flummoxed, and keep referring to the injury as a "stroke-like" event. But it's not a stroke. Al's late father had a habit of fainting, and they think Al may have inherited the tendency too. Still, I find it profoundly alarming, though I admit this only to myself: Al has been my traveling companion for a long time, a fellow adventurer, the guy who first took me into the mountains and up onto glaciers. I've entrusted him with my life many times, and vice versa. I don't want to leave him behind—but this is the asshole part: I don't want to be kept behind, either. It's like a race: we don't want to win it alone, but we don't want to come in second.

I plan to call him this afternoon—right after I get back from a bike ride, because the sun is out, and the clawing urge to prove to myself that I am still alive, that at least *I* am not in the hospital, is undeniable. I always wondered how my father endured the culling that marked the last twenty years of his life, the incessant dropping off of his friends and co-workers, and now I know: with the shameful, secret pride of the last one standing.

How is it that every day knows how to remind me that I am another day older? I just typed *April 8, 1914*. I am convinced it's early-onset dementia, brought on by a string of prepubertal concussions, but mistyping the date is nothing, a mere ripple of forgetfulness across the ever more watery surface of my brain. This morning, confronting my sagging dog of a face in the mirror, I reached for a tube of hair gel, in an effort to tame the few disobedient sprouts I have left. I squirted a blob into my hands, appreciating as always the satisfying poop of the gel ejecting, rubbed my palms together—and proceeded to apply it to my face and neck, sure it was sunblock.

Now that I am sixty, I have to wear industrial-strength sunblock with a minimum SPF of 4000, protection so strong rescue teams could have worn it after the meltdown at Fukushima. Age spots now show up on my body with such speed and frequency I feel like a special effect—the man who is turning sepia before his photograph can. The other week at work, I walked into the bathroom, entered a toilet stall to perform my duty, and began to unbutton my shirt.

APRIL 10

My life has become a steady series of meetings with specialists—and I'm only sixty. This is just the preamble to real old age. I'm still part of the herd: you make it through this culling and you might last for a while.

This morning I am seeing Dr. Malicki, the respirologist I first went to two years ago, for recurring bronchitis and not being able to catch my breath. I was still a smoker. Malicki is an Egyptian Muslim; we sometimes discuss the Arab Spring, the unrest in Cairo, though I get the impression he doesn't care for politics. At any rate, the first time I saw him, he made me blow into a series of gizmos, then told me I had stage 3 bronchitis (there are four stages in all, just as there are four stages of cancer, and the fourth is not good news at all) and that my lung capacity was down by 30 percent, handed me a prescription, and told me to come back in a month.

I immediately stopped smoking, which led to more exercise. By the time I returned, I was up to capacity again. Recently, I have been cross-country skiing. When I blow today, my lung capacity is off the chart, and Malicki says I can stop seeing him. This makes my day. I smoked, on and off, for thirty-odd years. What was I thinking? Hayley once said, "Don't you want to play with me for a long time?" I quit that day for seven years.

But now, at least, I've made one tiny repair to the aging mechanism, in the face of my potential glaucoma, and its treatments, my advancing baldness, my failing hearing, and the memory lapses, my flare-ups of rosacea, knee pain, arms that fall asleep at night, what seems to be a higher resting heart rate than I used to have (although my doctor denies this), age spots, and an alarming bout of my plantar

fasciitis, a consequence of fallen arches. Oh, and the hemorrhoid. But that will have to wait until tomorrow.

APRIL 14

So, that hemorrhoid. At my last checkup, I'd gone in
fearing rectal cancer or some prostate aberration. "Well,
Ian," my GP, Dr. Abe Hirsz, said, in his nothing-fazes-me,
what's-on-sale-at-the-deli-today voice, while poking into
the arroyo of my ass crack, "you certainly have a hemorrhoid." This hemorrhoid—George, I am calling it—George
is now almost as big a part of my life as masturbation was
when I was a teenager, and just about as Roman; it's a
rich, lustrous, steamy affair, full of itching and compulsive
scratching, a *Satyricon* of the perineal world. Christ knows
what's going on down there, but it feels like the clover-
leafed interchange of two multi-lane highways.

The treatment, of course, is the ointment Abe recommended. The act of applying this ointment ought to have
been painted by Bruegel, given his eye for the hopeless and
the absurd. I am the afflicted burgher in the vast painting,
hiding in the corner of a little room while all about me in
my vast house a party rages—but there I am, locked in
desperate privacy, invisible to all (or so I hope: in fact, two
teenagers are leaning over the wall of my hideout, peering
in and laughing at the fatso as I stoop and crab blindly,
trying to separate this from that and find that right place
to . . .). Honestly, there is no greater indignity known
to man. It's as if someone rented out my nethers while I

wasn't paying attention, and now I have a tenant. George. Abe tells me he's never really going to go away, he'll just eventually settle in and become more comfortable. This seems like the perfect metaphor for the fade of age.

Indignity is so much a part of my life now that I barely notice. Really. Of course, indignity has been a part of my life all along, but now, at sixty, my body has become an objective correlative for all my imagined psychological shortcomings. If I were writing a self-help book, I would tell people to get their psychological shit together by the time they turn sixty—but who can do that?

Today, after giving a talk at work about writing about the Arctic—a talk I was asked to give, that I was embarrassed to give since the story took me so long to write, why would I want to draw attention to it, but which I desperately wanted to give as well, so bottomless is my vanity—after that display, I was dragged over the editing coals for my essay on Karl Ove Knausgaard, which the editors have decided should be 2,500 words, not the 3,500 words they assigned. It's as if they believe that eight weeks of reading and thinking and writing can be resized, stretched, or shrunk at will. I haven't written an essay at all: I'm simply the Gap, and anything you find on my shelves can be exchanged by the customer. So Knausgaard is delayed a week while I wrestle its length. Instead, they are running a profile of Narendra Modi, the nationalist Indian prime minister. By someone else.

Back in January, when I had that annual checkup that revealed George, I was supposed to get the standard blood tests done too. I have been putting them off, but this morning I finally got around to the task. I went to the local lab to have my blood work done, to get my PSA score (the prostate, looking for sudden jumps), to get an ECG for my heart. Ever since my father's death from congestive heart failure (a leaky atrial valve, as it turned out) at the age of ninety-eight, I'm keen to have a full workup from a cardiologist. ("If they'd operated when he was seventy," my father's specialist told us six months before the old man passed away, "he would have gotten twenty-five more years"—then he stopped himself. After all, my father was ninety-eight.)

I arrived at 7:45 AM to beat the crowd, and found I was twelfth in a line all roughly my age or older. Forty-five minutes passed before they called me. The nurse drew my blood and told me to take off my shirt, rolled up my pants at the ankle, and attached the leads for the ECG. She did the test. "Do you feel better now?" she asked me afterward, laughing. Does she think I'm a hypochondriac? Or is that the kind of joke one makes with the crowds who come through the lab, all these people with some secret in them, some physical miscue?

APRIL 16

At a story meeting at the *Globe and Mail*, the downtown daily newspaper where I work, where I still go into the office every day, a reporter in her thirties raises what she believes to be an up-and-coming issue: do old people deserve medical care—such as transplants—as much as young people? After all, they are not going to live as long. Everyone thinks this is an excellent idea for a story.

APRIL 17

The sprinkler guy came this morning to check out my underground watering system, the single greatest boon to gardening ever invented. The pear tree is in blossom, as is the Japanese cherry; the bulbs are on their way. I still miss the mulberry tree I cut down twelve years ago because of the mess the berries made on the limestone of the patio. I made the decision on a weekend Hayley and Johanna were away, in a fit of insanity, three years after we moved into the house. They didn't want me to cut it down, and most of the time neither did I. Mulberry trees are famous: the Tudors planted them, and the berries figure in the myth of Pyramus and Thisbe, the myth that eventually gave the world Romeo and Juliet.

But I had personal reasons for keeping the tree as well. I still remember looking up from the patio and seeing Hayley and her friend Daisy leaning out of the sunroom on the second floor, picking and eating mulberries from the tree. I remember thinking, "This is why you have to keep the tree, because it gave you that moment of beauty. That moment was worth the whole thing."

I even devised a few schemes for spotlessly harvesting the mulberries into a turban of muslin, but it's hard to quartermaster a hundred yards of muslin, and in any event it never came to pass. And then some difficulty occurred—our son was sick, we were arguing, our whole life was messy—and I wanted this mess, at least, gone. I ran into an arborist who said he could take it out quickly, that he'd haul the mess away, and to my surprise one day I asked him to do it. Margaret Atwood once wrote that gardening is not a rational pursuit, and she is right. Today, the pear is taller than the mulberry, and blossoms every spring. I didn't ruin the back garden, and my wife and daughter seem to have forgiven me. But I regret cutting down the mulberry tree every day.

I rode my bike to work today. I still insist on this, in all but the worst of winter. It feels like the least I can do. I may have been wearing my helmet, even. I was waiting at the light at King and Spadina when a woman in her fifties walked up and smiled at me. She was blond, fit, but wearing sunglasses: I am not sure I could have been expected to recognize her. She took mercy on me, said, "Hello, Ian, Samantha——." Samantha, G.'s wife. G., who was a senior when I was a freshman in high school, later a breeder of horses. Twenty, maybe thirty years had passed since I'd seen her last. I remember thinking, when I first met her, "G. is a lucky man." One of those moronic thoughts. In any event, this morning she was wearing a maroon jacket—I think it was maroon—with a racetrack logo on it. She was about my age, and looked younger, though I automatically thought of myself as younger, because I was younger than her husband. Then she put her hand, tanned and slender, on mine where it rested on the handlebars. I thought, "Maybe she is younger than me, her hands look young, you can always tell from the hands."

Then I started to scan my reaction to her. Was I still attracted? Was it hard to talk to her, did I care what she thought? She looked fit, as noted, perhaps a bit more lined around the eyes. I wasn't interested in knowing if she found me attractive, that wasn't the point; though of course, who would mind that? I wanted to know what time had done, to me, to her, to us. I was not interested in satisfying my physical desire, even if I had felt any: I was simply interested in ascertaining and understanding my own reaction, in examining what it is I wanted, an entirely private affair—though these days many people do not consider such thoughts to be proper for men, especially men over the age of sixty. You're not supposed to have any desire beyond the age of sixty. You are supposed to be an insensate stone. Or, at best, cuddly, grandfatherly and cute.

A few years ago, I wrote a controversial column about the problem of the male gaze, about looking at women on the street (discreetly, I hasten to add, not shouting out comments), and whether men should feel guilty about looking. Half the women who responded to the article accused me of sexism; but how can simply noticing someone on the street be sexist? I presumed nothing, wanted nothing, reached for nothing.

It took months before I understood my crimes: One, the piece was told exclusively from a male point of view. Two, I was too old. I am not supposed to be having anything but fatherly or even grandfatherly impulses. I am happy to have all those impulses, but I have the others as well, and while I am not about to act on them, I think I have a right to understand them, even in this repressive, censoring age. I have no desire to subjugate women; I have only a desire to liberate myself, at no expense to anyone else. But the thought of getting older is so terrifying to everyone, we would rather the elderly simply disappeared, and stopped having impulses at all.

All this passed through my brain as I chatted with Samantha. Then she patted my hand on my handlebars once more and said, "Good for you! The mad cyclist going to work!" It was one of those things you say to an older person who is doing something zesty for their age, like riding a bike to work. I felt like pulling my cock out and saying, "I still have one, you know." It was possibly the most ageist thing anyone had said to me since I had turned sixty. And it came from someone my age.

APRIL 27

Al's mother died this morning—at ninety-eight. Like my father. It's an immense accomplishment to live that long, a thing of courage. Maybe too long: Al figures she stopped eating on purpose, to get it over with, just as my father did. I have replied to his email announcement of her death but have not yet phoned. I am dreading the call, as always. Calling friends whose parents have died has become a kind of subroutine, like cleaning out the fridge. A.'s father; B.'s father; now A.'s mother; C.'s father; D.'s mother. That's in the space of six months. I never know how to describe the gap a death inevitably leaves in someone's life, and so I hesitate to call.

I am hungover from drinking a bottle and a half of red at dinner. Johanna's away, so I grilled a paltry chicken breast and opened a bottle of *tempranillo*. Then I found half a joint in a cup—God knows how long it has been there—and, throwing all caution to the wind, smoked that and aimed for Drew's twenty-eighth birthday party. Drew was one of the younger participants in the Banff literary journalism workshop last summer; he's a brilliant writer and editor. But he is twenty-eight, goddamn him. I imagine him as one of the writers of the generation of, say, Sheila Heti or Zadie Smith, because they're very modern and a generation younger than me—when in fact they're forty and more. I still think of writers like Heti and Smith as twenty-four because I don't want to admit that another generation has inserted itself into adulthood, which puts my own generation one stair closer to the exit. This incessant age competition carries on in my head incessantly, and it's exhausting.

I arrived at Drew's party at 10 PM; there were three people there, one of whom was his sister. There were six people there when I left an hour and a half later. They're like Hayley's friends: they don't go out until midnight or later. They also don't really start conversations, though they are very good at talking once you get them started. Is this a generational response, or is it to me specifically? I always feel compelled to ask them questions: where did you go to school (this woman is still going to school!), what are you studying, what do you hope to do, where did you grow up, what did your parents do—nothing difficult, just trickles to get a conversation flowing. They look at me as if I am a thing from Mars. Maybe they don't want to talk to me. They're not talking to anyone else, though. Maybe they don't like talking? Maybe there's no point in talking to a relic like me? Maybe they're just young? Maybe I'm just high and paranoid/self-conscious?

In any event, I'm trying too hard, and over-asking, and making jokes, and being too jolly, and laughing too hard, even shouting in exclamation, whereupon I start apologizing for shouting. If I was twenty-five, I wouldn't give a shit; if this young woman doesn't know how to carry on a conversation, that's her problem. At sixty, I'm convinced I'm the problem. I am like a turd in the living room that everyone would like to disappear. And so I leave, wishing everyone well, full of heartiness, but the moment I am out the door I shake my head and laugh at myself.

It's undeniable: I am beginning to cut an eccentric older figure. The other day someone told me that Johanna entertains her female friends with imitations of the sounds I make while reading the newspaper and eating my breakfast.

It's a very funny bit; she's done it for me. Half the time I make the noises to make her laugh, but I worry, all on my own, that I am becoming the joke I am trying to tell. God knows what I will be like if I make it to eighty.

A small party at H.'s, to see her new "retirement" residence. Her only child, a daughter, is out of college and living in another city, and now that H. is on her own, she has moved into a luxury condominium building in midtown Toronto, next to the sports club with the whitest clientele in Toronto and overlooking a cemetery. This is the sort of thing people my age talk about all the time now—where we are going to live when we retire, and how we will afford it—at least when we are not discussing medical procedures. (I promised myself after I met my mother-in-law—she was fifty-five or so at the time—that I would never talk about operations and strokes and hernias the way her friends did, incessantly. No. I would talk about literature and ideas. Now I talk about operations and strokes and hernias. Hemorrhoids, even. I used to talk about sex, but no one wants to anymore.) In general, the older I get—this has been happening for a few years now—the less I talk at a dinner party. It's harder to hang on to a rigid opinion, and easier to listen from the margins.

The current dream plan popular among my crowd is to buy a larger residence among a group of friends, a small building or a multi-unit dwelling, and turn it into apartments, with a common dining room and medical help included. The question is, whom do you want to spend the rest of your born days with? The same people? New people? No one?

H.'s apartment is on the ground floor, and huge; she bought two apartments and knocked them into one. I figure she must have paid . . . well, more than a million and a half. Anyway, she gave me a tour of the building's swimming pool—she's super-keen on the pool—the gym, then her place, including its various bedrooms. I delude myself into thinking she might consider sleeping with me if I made a move (not that I would, but the fantasy runs on in some corner of my brain); we shared a slight past long ago, and she has always been unconventional that way. I admire the fact that she still is.

"It's cheap, relatively speaking," she says, speaking of the units in the building. "And there are lots of them. The funeral home pulls up and takes the bodies away, and new people move in." The odds of my being able to afford a place like this are so minuscule it's shocking, even if I win the lottery. (I now buy tickets to something called the Heart and Stroke Lottery, whose proceeds go to research on heart attacks and strokes, which of course at my age could mean a double win. Ghoulish, yes. But I still buy them.) "They have a party room, because your own place is too small to have a party," she says, then adds, "No one ever uses it." This apparently saddens both of us.

I stay a long time at the party. The time slips away. Then I stop in at a bar for a drink on the way home, alone. These little adventures occur so rarely nowadays they're like exotic half-hour holidays. By the time I open our front door, Johanna is furious: it's nearly two, and she has been worried. I am a selfish prick. Everyone has these spats, I presume, though pointlessly: at this stage it should be clear that neither of us is about to change. We have a fight, in any event, and I go to sleep on the couch. That hasn't happened in years. I wake up in the morning feeling as if my veins are filled with sand, as if my tires are filled with water. I cannot move. I didn't think I had that much to drink. But this is sixty.

MAY 2

Yesterday, walking the dog—along Bernard to St. George, to the eyeglass store, to see how much graduated trifocals cost, then over to Josephson's on Bloor (where they are a third again as much), and then back again, in a light rain on an overcast day—I suddenly become afraid. I am standing at the corner of Spadina and Bloor, with Ginny, waiting for the light to change, watching, on the other side of the street, a guy in a modern slim-line jacket so tight that he looks like an overstuffed cannoli. It is so tight I can see his political inclinations. I don't understand why people buy ultra-fashionable clothes: they'll be unfashionable in a year or two, and then they will wish they had bought some kind of classic cut.

Eventually, I cross against the light out of frustration, but as I do, I notice how fast the cars come up Spadina, how tearing loud their tires are on the road. And then I have a thought I have never had before, in sixty years of living: "Maybe I had better step back behind the telephone pole, behind it and then back three more feet, in case one of these cars careens out of control and hits me and the dog."

As I describe that strange, fearful moment, I realize that wasn't the first time I have had the thought: it happened the other day as well, riding my bike to the dietitian's (without a helmet! no coward I!) along Temperance Street, where half a dozen construction sites compete to eat up half the lanes of the road in either direction. I suddenly looked up and thought, "This is the kind of place where the freak accidents you read about in the paper happen, where a steel plate falls off a crane hook and crushes that unsuspecting passer-by." The random apprehension of danger has become a new companion in my life. I biked quickly to the end of the street. The truth of the matter is that the odds of bad things happening are higher everywhere for me at sixty. Twice now I have signed up for a doubles squash round robin and then canceled, because I don't want to injure myself before I go away to England in a couple of weeks.

This is new—planning inactivity so I don't ruin an upcoming holiday by being too active. "Take it easy," my

Korean physiotherapist says. (Yes, I have a physiotherapist, a reliable specialist who can quickly cure my sudden ailments, and not just here, but another one in Banff as well, when I head out west to chair the literary journalism program at the Banff Centre for the month of July.) It's hard to take it easy. It feels like a concession to death. When I am making my way along King Street these days to buy a takeout lunch at Fresh and Wild (something with kale in it, or something green and nutty to go with a few unfattening shrimp, for never less than seventeen dollars, because that might stave off a premature death), I notice how deliberate my pace has become, how measured, as if I am trying to pace out the time left. God knows I don't want to accidentally lose any of it. It's like a reversion to childhood, to the obsessive-compulsiveness of trying not to step on a crack. It feels that nervous, and that infantile. And I am that powerless to stop it.

This is new to the seventh decade: I can sail along secure that I will not put a foot wrong on the trail, and at exactly the same time be worried that I might put a foot wrong. I have a feeling this is the first sign of the doubleness of getting older, of becoming two beings in one—the aging decliner and the on-sailing stalwart; the settling body and the still-soaring mind—that defines what aging is, in many cases. (I would prefer that to a sailing body but a disappearing mind, or so I tell myself.) Suddenly there's a ghost in the works, the ghost of the old man in me. What I can't figure out is why I am so afraid of it that I try to ensure an orderly progress to the end. When did I turn into a metronome? When did this happen? Was it the report of higher blood pressure? Was it the first time I really thought I couldn't catch my breath after running? Was it the suddenly serious after-effects of a third beer? Was it that erection that for the first time didn't work the way an erection is supposed to work? I'm not talking about a lack of hydraulic enthusiasm due to insufficient tenderness or persistent texting, or because of work and anxiety, or because one would, in the end, prefer to read tonight—and that goes for either party. Everyone must have experienced that strange wan afternoon of the soul at least once or twice by the time you're sixty. No, I am talking about the first time you have a dead battery. That's a shocker. I was fifty-seven the first time it happened to me. Johanna thought I didn't love her anymore. I said, "It's a mechanical issue, I think. The engine's turning over, but the alternator won't catch."

But what changed to erode my confidence at the foundational level? What stole my nerve? I never used to worry about consequences because there so seldom were any, until I turned fifty or so. Now, as they say, anything can happen.

Last night, I went to the movie *Marinoni: The Fire in the Frame*, about Giuseppe Marinoni, the Montreal bicycle maker who recently broke the record, in his age group, for distance covered in a velodrome in one hour. Eddy Merckx, the famous Tour de France king, held the old record. Marinoni himself was at the cinema, in the audience. He's seventy-five and still rides a hundred kilometers, or about sixty-two miles, most days. He is thoroughly with it, still working, still riding that century a day, still collecting mushrooms in the woods, as he used to do as a boy: up the mountain, pick the mushrooms, back down again. In the movie, if he seemed slightly distanced from events around him, it was only because he was more single-minded in his attention to what he was doing, as is the habit of the elderly.

The movie made me want a Marinoni bike, but more importantly, it made me want to rise every day and ride a hundred kilometers. He said he wanted to keep working, keep making bikes, until a week before his death. "One week of holiday," he said. That's all. Not the worst idea I'd ever heard.

Instead, we are urged to retire, to take the buyout, to aim for contented retirement by the age of fifty-five, and to feel like failures if we don't get there. Most people don't get there, statistically.

MAY 9

Hakim Optical wants $364.65, before tax, for a pair of trifocals, complete with diamond coating. The distortion at the edges of the lenses, however, is like a funhouse mirror at a carnival. The Nikon lens, which is lighter and offers, the lady behind the counter says, "less distortion"—I would have thought distortion was what we were trying to avoid in an optician's store—is $493. But Hakim will give me a two-pair special for $502. Josephson's wants $800 for the Nikon lens.

Wagman told me to get the trifocals. "You don't care about looking young or, what's the word—hip—do you?" he said as he slam-dunked me through the usual checkup. He was wearing slacks and an open-collared shirt and had been haranguing me, in a pleasant way, about the paper's coverage of Israel. "Because if you don't care, get the straight trifocals. Do not under any circumstances get the graduated. You want distance on top, reading on the bottom, and plain glass in between, with the lines visible."

But the guy at Spectacles on Bloor, a German, says he can't make straight trifocals any more, that I have to get the graduated. Five hundred dollars for a single pair, ready in time to go to England, to scatter my old man on the sea.

MAY 11

I pick up my new graduated lenses. The distance part works, and the reading part is okay, if a little narrow: I have to be holding my book in my crotch to read.

But the mid-zone is impossible. The plain, unscripted part of the lens is a small circle—I'm talking about the size of a pea—somewhere on the nose-side of center-lens. "Move your eyes to find the spot, not your head," the optometrist insisted. I look like a lunatic, my eyes rolling and rolling in search of focus. Add one more indignity to the list.

MAY 19

Leaving for London for a two-week vacation with Johanna. We start at the famous Chelsea Flower Show in London, at the instigation of Al, who is a landscape designer, but I am more interested in English gardeners than I am in plants: my mother was English, and a furious gardener to the end of her life—she experienced the heart attack that killed her while looking out at her garden. Her garden was the calm spot near the center of her raging soul.

The visit to the show will be followed by some walking in the Cotswolds with Johanna and our good friends— Al and Tecca, and John and Maggie Mitchell. Everybody but Johanna has turned sixty in the past few years. Then Johanna and I will head to Suffolk to meet Hayley and scatter my dad's ashes in the North Sea, in the company of my brother and sisters and many, many Suffolk relatives. Whereupon Hayley, Johanna, and I will hike through the Yorkshire dales on our way to get Hayley's gear in Edinburgh and bring her back home. It's a busy two weeks, and will be an uncharacteristically lavish holiday. I don't actually know how I am going to pay for it.

MAY 20

If I were a gardener, a serious gardener, someone who lived for gardening, I would never again worry about having wasted my life. The gardener has a built-in engagement with failure, because Nature always beats you down, but then you never expect to succeed, and are always slightly pleased when you occasionally do.

The Chelsea Flower Show takes place on the grounds of the Royal Hospital Chelsea, the famous veterans' home in fanciest Chelsea, and is dedicated to English gardening. Some twenty thousand people are wandering through today. Many of them are over fifty, and all of them obsessed with their gardens. It gets them outside, it gets them moving around, but mostly, if English gardeners are any evidence, it gets them inside themselves, thinking, feeling. It gives them something to emote about, given that emoting about your fellow human beings is largely frowned upon here.

I followed a well-heeled group of sponsors around the exhibits this morning: tailored spring suits and ties for the men, floral spring skirts and bum-freezer jackets for the women, plus purse and flats—expensive flats with shields and heraldry—and the classic English complexion everywhere to be seen. That's before they hit seventy. At seventy they turn into the Pepperpots John Cleese made famous, except that they don't argue about whether Jean-Paul believes in personal freedom. They cheer for the garden designer of the year with the same enthusiasm we reserve for the winning goal in an Olympic hockey game. The central theme of this show is the anniversary of the start of the First World War, but there are others: the use of water, recycling, sustainability. After an hour of wandering around, I met Baroness Fookes, a large, seventyish woman in a turquoise suit and black broad-brimmed spring hat that looked like a giant, overturned serving dish. She was walking the grounds with Mother Catarina Boyer, a wise-cracking American nun with a Chicago accent who lives in a nunnery called Our Lady of the Rock on Shaw Island near Vancouver. I felt like I'd wandered into a Wes Anderson movie.

Baroness Fookes is chair of the House of Commons' all-party Garden and Horticulture Group. Of course she is. "I have a particular interest in the Great Pavilion, in plants," she warbled. Of course she does. Robin Williams Sr., no relation, redesigned her personal garden; she'd asked him to center it around a pergola and various "features." I nodded, yes, fascinating, do go on. "And I actually said, 'Gosh!' because he has translated my wishes into a cohesive whole." The English are so eccentric, and so tolerant of eccentrics, that you never feel out of place: everyone is tolerated, if not exactly accepted, even if you are the hideous fucking age of sixty.

At the same time, in the same country where the cultivation of the garden has been raised to historically unparalleled heights, an investigation is currently underway in Rotherham, a town in northern England, where for the past twenty years a gang of Pakistani-born Muslims has been raping, buying, selling, pimping, and otherwise sexually abusing as many as four thousand young, lower-class women—the lowest of the low in Britain, single white uneducated girls with no jobs. They've been getting away with it lo these many years because the police and the authorities have been turning a blind eye. It's the Jimmy Savile story all over again: no one gives a shit about these women, and the society seems to condone those who don't. It's a monstrous story, and a monstrous contrast to this gorgeous green day I'm having, surrounded by man-made beauty. The same British culture has permitted both this zenith and that nadir of civilization.

I saw a garden for the blind and another for the deaf. I saw enormous poodles and Great Danes made entirely from rosebuds and rosehips (£30,000); fully insulated armadillo-like sheds, complete with a bed and composting toilet, for the bottom of the estate or for the backyard or "for the shooting fraternity," as a salesman told me. "The solar toilet sounds disgusting, but it basically boils away the waste, and in two weeks you have feed for the roses," he explained. He'd sold six hundred sheds. They were made of Siberian larch, which doesn't crack.

I saw begonias the size of dessert plates, from Blackmore and Langdon, plant growers by appointment to HRH The Prince of Wales, orchids, bulbs, *Acer palmatum*, entire ranges of lupines, you name it. I ran into a woman named Angel Collins, a landscape gardener who was ordering plants for delivery June 9. "And I'm also choosing the flowers that I particularly like." She was here because she had to see the plants in person, so to speak: "You'd never be able to tell from the catalog what color they are. You wouldn't know that the Nonia is quite upright. Whereas Deli is quite dumpy." The problem, she said, was that "the more you look, the more beautiful they look." She gazed at the vast exhibition hall, filled to bursting with examples of the flowers that people in England want to put in their gardens. "I mean, Ashby's quite beautiful. Looks like a pansy."

She does big gardens. Her current client owns a six-acre estate with five different gardens on it, including an ancient medicinal abbey garden. "Dream job." Apparently it's going to take her two years. "Is that enough?" I asked, by now flirting. "No. Not really. Not enough," she said. She was in her fifties, I guessed, and wearing a brocade dress with black and gold embroidered white flats. She was sexy, though I couldn't really tell you why. Maybe because she was willing to speak to me? Maybe because she was nattily, proudly, cleverly, wittily, consciously attired? Because she had a nice figure, trim but not daunting, from all that stepping about in the beds and the pastures? Because she was intelligent? Because she was passionate about this thing she did with her hands and her brain? All of the above.

"Are you particularly interested in pelargoniums?" a woman asked me after I'd left Angel, as she noticed me writing down a few names. "Because a lot of people call these geraniums. But that's wrong. A geranium is a hardy, heirloom perennial. Pelargonium is a tender wood shrub." She felt the distinction keenly.

I kept writing down not the Latin names but the common names breeders had given to their plants, more evidence of people taking pleasure in what they did. In the peonies alone I encountered Coral Sunset, Many Happy Returns, Cheddar Gold, Kansas, and Risky Business. The hostas were more obviously sexual: Hanky Panky and Strip Tease. ("That was because it had a strip of white in it," a salesman said, confirming my hunch that there is a tradition of naming hostas after raunchy pursuits. "Most of them are bred in America," he added.) Occupied people, focused and obsessed people, many of them my age, spent hours on end investigating lupines and clematis and topiary *Sarracenia*, so they were not bored, they were not lost, they were not sitting around wondering what their lives had amounted to. I daresay they all had such moments, but the garden is the boss: what your ground and soil will let you grow is what dictates your day. But you can't be too responsible, because you are not in control of what Nature delivers. There is a modesty and a humility and a sense of resignation and an acceptance of failure built into gardening that gives it dignity and grace. It's a bit like fly-fishing. Oh, and like aging. Like aging might be.

I think—this seems obvious now—the notes I have been making about plants are really notes about my mother. I am still trying to figure out the layout of her soul. She was a mad gardener, and I grew up as a garden slave, weeding the perimeters of what seemed like her vast suburban tracts, forced to work outside instead of reading ("Get some fresh air! That will do you more good than a book," followed by some flung projectile) for hours and hours at a time, for no money. Later, when I started gardening myself, she was no fan of my efforts. "You don't seem to have the talent for gardening, the way your brother does," she once said to me, peering askance at my tiny city plot. She was right. Gardening might have been her feminism, given that she was too young for the first wave and too old, and family-laden, for the second wave. There's an entire generation like her, intelligent, clever, thwarted, furious women denied jobs and power who perfected the household arts instead. Gardening was her route into her own world, where no one could tell her what to do. The last time I saw her alive was over lunch on her pretty patio, teeming with flowers, four days before she died. I was trying to make her laugh. She was so famously severe, it took some doing: her laugh was a process of gradual but quickening expansion, rather like a kettle coming to a boil, but if you knew what you were doing you could get her there. I was telling a story about a series of books my mother bought for us as children, to make us better behaved. They were called Uncle Arthur's Bedtime Stories, and they were hideous: strict, mean tales published by a fanatical Bible society. They had one purpose: to make the child reader feel eternally guilty.

The story I remember best was about a boy named Bobby, who loved baseball. Bobby loved baseball so much he played baseball every day after school. Bobby wanted to be a baseball player, and every day Bobby played baseball.

But one morning as Bobby left for school, his baseball mitt on his hand, his mother, a small, thin woman—all the women in the Uncle Arthur stories were small and thin and tired—said, "Bobby, I wonder if just today, this one day, you could not play baseball, and come home after school to help me. Because I'm all alone." All the women in the Uncle Arthur stories were alone: some strange plague seemed to have wiped out all the husbands. "Just this one day, no baseball," Bobby's mum said.

And of course Bobby, like any good kid, said, "Yes, Mum, I certainly will." And then, like most kids, he promptly forgot, and went to play baseball anyway. And when he came home late he found his mother—dead! On the floor of the kitchen.

I'm not kidding. That was the story. I found it upstairs in my mother's bedroom, and I brought it down to the table, and read it to her in her garden, and she collapsed with laughter. Then Tim said, "We've found the original code! The mother lode of Cicily Brown's Handbook of How to Make Children Do What You Want Them to Do!"

It was a great day. It happened in her garden. By week's end, she had died looking at that garden. And here I was at Chelsea, searching.

At half-past two, Victoria Wakefield stepped into my life and introduced me to the three flowers of the year: the winner, a double *Hydrangea macrophylla*, Miss Saori, in pink; a black and pale lavender iris, Domino Noir, number two; and in third place, *Gerbera garvinea*, Sweet Glow, in orange. Mrs. Wakefield and the Royal Horticultural Society Plant Committee Panel (which sounded like a formidable thing) had chosen them the day before from seven finalists, culled from forty-three entries. Mrs. Wakefield was straight out of a Beryl Bainbridge novel, a thin strand of kind dignity topped with a puff of white hair that she would have paid more attention to were it not for her beloved plants.

Mrs. Wakefield lives at Bramdean House, in Hampstead, where she has spent years conducting official trials for *Nerine bowdenii*, a multi-stemmed bulb-grown perennial that looks fresh and pink, but which flowers at the end of August or September, bringing color to the fading garden. Which of course we all long to do. "Well, I'm not doing it myself," Mrs. Wakefield said, of the actual digging involved in her garden endeavors. "You get a proper man to do it." Indeed. I asked for the plant's common name. "There isn't one really," she said. Indeed.

She suggested I visit Kiftsgate: to Mrs. Wakefield, Kiftsgate is the most beautiful garden in England, the product of three generations of women gardeners. I don't know why, but she made my day, Victoria Wakefield did. She gave me hope that my life as an older person did not have to be a long desert of loneliness and pain and rejection, that trying was all I could reasonably do, provided I had a cause, a passion, a focus. That was all I needed, something to become obsessed about.

I cruised the show for the remainder of the day, torn between exhaustion and curiosity, amazed over and over again by the things people find to love. There were life-sized and strangely realistic driftwood sculptures of horses

(£22,000) and gold swans (£7,000). "We generally sell every-thing," the driftwood horse salesman assured me, or maybe himself, toward closing time. There were waterproof rubber gardening clogs covered with images of flowers and vegeta-bles, and an entire display of gardening garb at the Welligogs booth, including the stylish leather knee-high country boot so popular with Chelsea hipsters, which made me think I should procure the North American franchise for a photo-appliqued clog dealership: they'd go over well in Canada and the United States. (I will never do this.) The people selling the gardening clothes were all young and striking, and therefore somewhat unlike most of the attendees.

I met a man who claimed to have invented and was selling wool compost, an "ericaceous wool-based compost with a pH of 4.5–5.0," and thus a part of what he called "the peat-free movement," which is gardening's under-taking to slow climate change. I encountered a crocheted gorilla named BOJO, after Boris Johnson, the Lord Mayor of London (who had written a book about Winston Chur-chill that I later bought, which informed me that Churchill didn't become prime minister until he was sixty-three). The gorilla had been made by a hippieish-looking woman in glasses who was sitting near it, crocheting.

The entire show was the English mind on display. "You've got to let your inner butterfly out sometimes," a sixtyish man in a navy-blue and green striped jacket and red pants said to me as I made my way toward the exit through the artisanal gardens, and before I passed the guy in the

Le Corbusier glasses who was wearing a striped green and pink and brown suit with knee-length trousers, and before I made the acquaintance of Michael Funnell, one of the Chelsea pensioners who lived at the Royal Hospital. He was wearing a red uniform. "This is my fourth Chelsea Flower Show," he said, "but I live here." He'd joined the army at twenty-four and had been a paratrooper in Palestine. "The job was to keep Jews away from Arabs, and vice versa," he said. "There's always trouble there." He was eighty-six. "I've been free of every encumbrance, like wife and children, for years." His wife had died in 2010, in September, and he had moved into the veterans' home right away, though he said he had kept his house until he knew he liked it here. "We come down just to add a bit of color," he said, indicating his red uniform. People seemed to like to talk to the pensioners, and the pensioners seemed to like to talk back. His role was ornamental. I am beginning to understand what that must be like.

There was such an array of things to know about: pond gloves, and Dubarry gardening boots, and chemicals for duckweed control. It was all strangely erotic, but not sexual, in the way of the English, and this was unexpectedly freeing. As if someone had forgiven me. Perhaps it was my mother, looking down and finally approving. It surprises me how much I hope she has, even now, when I am sixty.

"It's cyclical," one gardener said, trying to explain why she liked it. "You can always have another go. Never surrender! Although a lot of people get very controlling about

it. And then the weather comes along and screws it up."
The trick, she said, was to know your land, your soil, your
weather, your circumstances. "If you ignore what you've
got, then you will fail." She paused. I suddenly realized she
was about twenty-five, a garden designer in training, and
that I had spent the day thinking of the garden as a sym-
bol of the end of life, as an acceptance of my own aging.
It was such a stupid, self-involved, narcissistic take on it,
as if gardening (how dull and ancient) was a reflection of
who I was (dull and ancient, content to putter about amid
the pots and bushes). Yet we all do this: we all slot everyone
we meet according to age and rank and background. We
expect them to be a certain way because of who we think
they are. I do it to young people at work, and they do it to
me. The difference is that as you begin the walk (short or
long?) toward the end of your life, you notice how often we
do it, and you wish we did not. The girl was still talking.
"My experience of gardening is that it is a huge thing that
we can share. That you're not alone. Common ground.
Literally, common ground."

As I made my way out of the gates of the garden show
into posh Chelsea again, I passed a woman in her sixties
going in. She was wearing cream pants, a citrus-green her-
ringbone jacket with a large orange and red flowered bag,
an appropriate layer of jewels, and white ballet flats, as well
as a black and white polka-dot scarf. She looked dashing. I
keep reading about the depressing shift women encounter
as they reach their fifties and sixties: how a world that has

excluded them, and valued them only for their beauty, or as wombs and servants, suddenly ignores them even more resolutely as their bodies mutate and change. At my age, superannuated and desexed by the presumptions of the culture around me, I can finally begin to understand that rejection in a first-hand, physical way. We should become allies. But the brave woman in the cream pants wasn't accepting the verdict of the younger world. She was putting the full joy of spring on display, and with no self-consciousness, no apology. "Good for you," I thought. "Good for you."

Johanna and I headed to Al and Tecca's flat in Chelsea afterward for a drink, and then made our way back to our hotel in Bloomsbury—nearly an hour in transit, to my chagrin. I was tired. I can't just put my head down and keep going like a bull, the way I used to. On the other hand, you never notice anything with your head down. On the Tube, slumped into a seat against Johanna, I had no choice but to simply absorb the world around me, to let it in, wash through and over me—to be passive. I was simply happy to be there with her. Whereupon the Tube made itself into something for me: a tunnel of living Henry Moore sculptures and Walker Evans photographs and twisted Francis Bacon paintings. Back at the room, I fell asleep in my clothes, and awoke at 2 AM in a tizzy, confused but at least not panicking.

MAY 21

A day of kayaking on the Thames with Mitch and Al. It's Al's idea, Al's treat. We paddle downstream to Traitors'

Gate, the tunnel entrance from the Thames, now blocked off, to the Tower of London. We stop for lunch on the bank of the Thames under the Tower, and ride the incoming tide back to Chelsea. The last urban river I kayaked with Al was the Hudson, the time we circumnavigated Manhattan. That was before I was married, when Johanna lived in New York. It took us eight hours to go about thirty-five miles. We've skied or hiked or boated or motorcycled or walked together for more than thirty years.

It was a gentle outing, interesting, original if somewhat mild even by sixtyish standards. At fifty, on glaciers, we had a rougher measure of success: "At least no one's died yet." We wouldn't make that joke today. It's too close, too much a possibility.

I keep worrying about Al, this condition they are investigating, this unknown "stroke-like" event that occasionally shuts one of his eyes but that isn't a stroke and that his doctors do not understand. I keep wondering, darkly, Who will be the first to go? What will it be like with one of us gone? Will we keep having the adventures? Of course, I assume it won't be me.

The Lutherans, Johanna's people, have an old tradition at the burial of their dead: they circle the grave and link arms as the body is lowered—to prevent anyone else from slipping in. But it's when you are not watching that they slide by you. I think of all the time I have spent in Al's company: on glaciers, on mountains, on rivers, in gardens, walking Manhattan, walking dogs, drinking, smoking, cavorting, playing squash, chatting, driving, skiing, camping, in the north and south and east and west, discussing everything for literally weeks on end. He made me braver, showed me a world I had never seen in the mountains. If he wasn't there to take the next trip, I would be crushed and would think of all the matters I had never found the time to speak to him about, the things I never found time to say about his generosity and his bravery, and his self-lessness, and how smart he is. Stuff I've never said, because while we are alive we think we still have time. Why do I only understand now, at this late stage, that we never have enough time to say everything we ought to say? That we should stuff the words in at every opportunity, through every crack? I should have grasped it a lot earlier, felt it more acutely; some people do, but none of us do all the time, and very few of us do it anywhere enough. How have we managed as a species to progress this far without shattering the illusion that time stretches out before us? It doesn't. It runs past.

We shower at the flat, the flat the Mitchells and Klings have rented in Chelsea, and eat dinner in an Italian meat shop I spotted on the way into Chelsea this morning. The steak is thirty-five pounds a kilo, if I remember correctly. Every pound I spend feels as though it's coming out of my future: every treat today is one more can of cat food for the two of us later.

A hired driver takes us to the Cotswolds. Christ knows how much this is running us, but John and Maggie Mitchell, our friends from Edmonton, have arranged the Cotswolds tour, and they have more money than we do. I am so aware of the crushing cost of everything we're doing, it's almost hard for me to enjoy myself. Admittedly, my heel—that plantar fasciitis—is acting up, an affliction I can't always remember the name of, which is not a good sign. The fact that I can't remember its name doesn't make it hurt any less.

It never ceases to amaze me how difficult it is to talk about money. We have had our troubles of late: it's a difficult time in journalism, everybody's losing money and pulling back. Johanna has taken a cut in her fee as a columnist at the *Globe*; I still have a salary, but my work as a host at the local public television station is dwindling, and the CBC never hires me anymore. (Maybe I've been banished; maybe they feel twelve years as the host of *Talking Books* was enough. Seems like a reasonable assumption to me.) So my pre-tax income has bumped down by at least 35 percent in the past decade. I still make a decent living, but it's not as if anything more lucrative is in sight ahead of me. I am beginning to see that John Stackhouse, the editor-in-chief of the *Globe and Mail* who has just lost that job, was right: the era of getting paid to be a writer, on a salary with benefits, was a historical blip that may be over. As a writer it was one of the more discouraging things I have ever heard anyone utter.

At any rate, as we are driven to the Cotswolds, I mention, calmly, to Johanna that I have spoken to our mortgage broker, and that she is going to come over to the house when we get back, and that she has suggested we take advantage of low interest rates to borrow some (more) money and fix up the house and the basement (which Johanna wants to rent out, but without fixing it up), which in turn leads to a tense conversation about retirement and retirement savings and what we have and (mostly) what we don't have. Talking about money makes us both nervous, even at our age, when you would think we'd be over it. But no one is ever over it, ever. I even understand her logic: if we're short on money for a remunerative basement reno, surely we are short on it for a kitchen reno. But I am optimistic that a better kitchen will pay for itself when we sell the house. In the meantime, I spend a lot of time in the kitchen, and like to cook; I have done so for ten years in a room that discourages me. Does that have to continue?

This is the daily debate in a life pushing beyond sixty, in someone who is coming to realize that his or her life could end at a moment's notice: how do you want to spend the life you are living at this very moment? In a less beautiful room or a more beautiful one? But Johanna is eight years younger than me: maybe the question is less pressing for her.

We have our skirmishes. She takes issue with my absent-mindedness (a lifelong trait). I take issue with her tone. She in turn says I am reading tone into her tone, that there was no implication there. It's a thirty-year-old liturgy, and still a weekly ritual. We're old mates, so she has the luxury of dismissing me. And she is eight years younger. She is younger, therefore (it is automatically assumed, by me as well) more with it. Never mind that it's true, and always has been: I'm still offended by my own presumptions! But it stings me more now than it used to. It bothers her that I can't always hear her properly, which makes her sigh and raise her voice in quite reasonable impatience, asking if I have my hearing aids in, which in turn makes me think that she thinks that I am some sort of doddering fuckwit who has forgotten to insert his earhorns when in fact I have been downstairs writing and reading for two hours while she sleeps, and simply haven't put them in because they're in the bedroom and I don't want to wake her up. I, of course, would give anything not to be going deaf, and can't stop it. I fear I am no longer worth repeating things for. The prospect chills me.

I mean this as no complaint. Every couple has dips and lulls and estrangements. We like each other. My wife is never unalert to the passing parade, and I am never bored in her company. Our sex life isn't the antic honeymoon luxury cruise it once was—and I refuse to write about it in detail, even here, because that is for no one but us—but no one's is. We're about average. But in its place our companionship gets greener and wider, more forgiving. We seem to think we have some duty to stay together—not for the children, but for the idea of being together. Because we can make each other laugh, reliably, and because we have a past together, which we don't want to throw away. It will mean very little when we're dead, but while we're alive it helps us believe that we accomplished something; it gives us (and everyone else) the illusion of some permanence. And of course the prospect of starting over is daunting, I suspect, for both of us—financially disastrous, for starters, but also frightening. Perhaps less for her, given that she's younger. What would happen? Could we survive on our own, as friends and not as companions? Would it be worth it, not to be spoken sharply to, not to have someone imply that you are behaving foolishly, not to have someone forget to compliment the way you are dressed before going out to dinner, not to have someone forget to hold your arm from the front door to the taxi? Would being single be a boon?

We've been married for twenty-six years as of this fall and together for thirty-one, and yet I am sure we both still entertain the occasional thought of . . . what? Starting over again with someone else? I'm not even sure that's the impulse; the impulse may just be to avoid the same sameness for the time that is left.

Don't get me wrong: there's a lot to be said for sameness, familiarity, comfort, not having to find a new apartment, etc. My friend Z. recently got married again for the third time. Each divorce has been more toxic, and more expensive. His exes show up at dinner parties across the city, telling bitter, funny stories. He would say—at least, he would if he had the emotional vocabulary to say it—

that sixty is the time to take the greatest emotional risks, if only to stay spiritually alive. The question is, which is the greater risk: staying together or leaving each other? The risk of emotional sameness or the risk of a solitary dwindling? This is what I have come to realize, at my advanced age, my children: It doesn't matter which risk you choose. It matters what you do with it.

Before we headed off on this jaunt to Britain, I visited my insurance agent. I have something like half a million dollars' coverage, which seems like a hell of a lot, especially when I have to pay a premium that leaves me broke every month, and thus deeper and deeper into a line of credit, and closer and closer to fatal heart disease, to judge from the actual electrical buzz I experience in my balls and chest every time I look at my bank overdraft.

So I raised the possibility with my agent of cutting my premium by more than two-thirds and my coverage to $150,000. I mean, look: I am going to be dead. That amount would still pay the immediate debts and the funeral costs and give Johanna a year of income. This too is love, baby. She'll own the house and have my pension, such as it is, and my retirement savings. I need to cut back, because my income is not increasing, as noted: I've had two increases at the *Globe* in six years, each one 3 percent, which comes down to 1 percent a year for six years, not compounded, and not equivalent to inflation.

My insurance agent is happy to help out, but she also thinks I need to find new sources of income, at sixty. "Are you familiar with the kids on YouTube?" she says, ten minutes into the meeting. I am coming off a hideous, knock-me-down cold, the first I've had in years (another bad sign!), and want to decapitate her on the spot. Her name is Jodi, with an *i*. She's a perfectly fine person, a friend, and she has been a good adviser. But this . . . telling me to look to YouTube for a living . . . decapitation did come to mind. But of course I did not decapitate her, because I am an older person now, and I should listen to the young hipsters who think they know everything. So instead I say, "Which ones?" and she rattles off a pair of kids who make a science show, "which is really good, and teaching kids about science." She claims they're making between half a million and a million a year on YouTube. The implication is clear: if I wasn't such a stiff old fuck-up, I could be making half a mill on YouTube. Which is so unlikely someone should write a pop song about it. "There're very few of those people," I point out, but she then claims to have met ten of them. (It turns out her boyfriend did a job for Google, and as a result they were both introduced to the top ten under-25s on YouTube.)

"Who else?" I demand. By now I have my notebook and pen out, and am writing shit down.

"Well, I don't want to violate their privacy."

"Don't be ridiculous. I'm not going to tell anyone."

"Those two guys in Montreal, the bacon guys? Who cook bacon all the time on YouTube? They make me ill, but they make over a million a year."

She means Harley Morenstein and Sterling Toth, who are twenty-five and twenty-seven, and created the weekly online bow-down to gluttony called *Epic Meal Time*. They have millions of subscribers and about 34 million views—easily topping a million views an episode. One of their Thanksgiving creations was a turkey, a duck, a chicken, a Cornish hen, and a quail stuffed into a twenty-pound piglet. They cemented it with mashed bacon and pork sausage and the like, to the point where it created a feast of just over 79,000 calories. Their hope is to monetize their concept so that they do not have to return to graphic design and supply teaching. I admire them; really, I do. They must be having a blast, and they are obviously energetic guys with a knack for popular fare. I am just surprised that my insurance agent was pushing me to emulate them. I can't really see a YouTube channel called *An Old Guy Who Loves Bacon*. Perhaps I could do *An Old Guy Who Doesn't Like Anything and Is Old Before His Time*.

But my agent isn't done with me. Soon she is talking about how the future is changing so much and so fast, and how she is reading Peter Diamandis's books, *Abundance* and *Bold*, about the world's five greatest problems and how we are going to solve them with "solar panels the size of a fingernail that can heat an entire village."

And of course I resist all this. I resist books like *Abundance* and *Bold* on principle because a) I loathe intellectual certainty, and they traffic in it, and b) they're successful, and c) such books generally read poorly (though *Bold* isn't bad), because they aren't written elegantly, with an eye to the quality of the prose, and that's what matters to me. I realize this is old-fashioned and defensive and asinine, and likely counterproductive and self-destructive too; this is the view of an aging man. But I can't respect the ideas of anyone who won't make at least an effort to say something in a way that brings the reader some pleasure or awe. But then again, it is the height of idleness to decry the present. Whatever else you say about it, the present is unavoidably real and here in front of our eyes. I think Martin Amis said as much in one of his books, I can't remember which one. And if there are people living in the present who believe they can predict the future, all the better for them.

I prefer to describe the present: it feels more human to me; it is something I can see with my own eyes, hear with my own ears. It is what I have more of. It has the distinct texture of the here and now, and it resists simplistic analysis. It requires holding contradictory ideas in the brain at the same time without having a nervous breakdown, and I think that's good for my sixty-year-old brain. The present beats the future. But of course I would say that, wouldn't I?

But on the way home from the insurance agent's, I have an idea. I'll finish this effing diary and then I'll create my own YouTube channel. I'll call my show *Ow, What Happened?* And on it I will describe, while applying the hemorrhoid ointment to my nethers and chowing down on Metamucil, what it feels like to be sixty in a world that doesn't want to admit that one day it is going to be sixty too.

MAY 23

I am sitting in one of the many living rooms/parlors/games rooms of Buckland Manor, trying to get some writing done. It is six-fifteen in the morning, the last hour of the day I have on my own before the programmed activities start.

Spent yesterday morning at Sissinghurst, the country residence and garden of Vita Sackville-West and Harold Nicolson. (A plaque describes them as "Writers and Gardeners." Classic understatement.) They were a radical couple, both of them taking male and female lovers yet remaining married, and having children, despite Vita's vow with one of her lovers, Violet Trefusis, that they would not sleep with their husbands. (Vita broke it off after learning Violet had, in fact, shagged her mate.) Virginia Woolf wrote *Orlando* after her affair with Vita. Vita seems to have been a bit of a heartbreaker, even of Harold's class-hardened heart. His diaries—of his war service no less than his personal life—are some of the most engaging ever written.

I wander around the gardens for three hours, imagining what it would be like to live here: to have a study in the long house; to have a study, as Vita did, in the Sissinghurst tower. Harold, being a classics man, kept planning the garden, restricting its colors, shaping its beds. Vita had no plan and wanted none, operating on instinct and forever trying to stuff a bit more drama into its already overstuffed parterres. Harold later admitted that she had won that lifelong battle, and that it was a just victory in that his vision was too restrained. They kept loving each other through all these comings and goings. In one of the side gardens, at the top of an allée of beeches, I come across a couple: he sketching, she reading. In their late sixties, I'd guess. Eccentrics, together. It seems to be a good way to go.

In the afternoon we head over to Great Dixter. It is planned chaos to Sissinghurst's barely contained order. The house has been around since the Middle Ages, a concept that simply will not take root in my brain. Our vacation plan, concocted largely by Maggie Mitchell in conjunction with a knowledgeable local guide, seems to be to take a well-known walk every morning—the Heart of England Way, the Monarch Way, all parts of the Cotswold paths between Bath and where we are, almost 125 miles east—and visit gardens and country houses in the afternoons.

The walking is fantastic: the map is not always reliable, and we spend a lot of time lost, then finding ourselves, and discussing the route. Tecca, Johanna, Maggie, Mitchell, Kling, me: it's a bossy group, so there are a lot of opinions. The scenery has been here forever, and gains from the effect.

Buckland Manor, where we arrived two days ago in time to set out across the fields for a gigantic ploughman's lunch in a nearby town, was formerly a monastery, at least until the dissolution of the monasteries by Henry VIII in 1536, whereupon it became the property of a Lord Mayor of London. It's a fantastic, and fantastically expensive, hotel: the room rate is twice what I thought it was. I feel I have to use every room in the place to get my money's worth, along with the croquet lawn, the gardens (especially beautiful at dawn and dusk), the dog, the maids and waiters, the breakfast room (like eating in a Jane Austen novel), even the fleet of Aston Martins and Bentleys that are available to rent. We do not rent them because we still have available to us the car the Mitchells hired to drive us to and from our various walking paths and end points.

I like to get up early and go down and write in the most remote and ignored of the three vast sitting rooms. Life as a monk could not have been all that bad—until the end, of course.

MAY 24 *(WRITTEN IN THE EVENING)*

More walking today, on various paths. This is my idea of a good time—walking for miles with great friends through fields of fresh green, along ancient paths that we more or less have to ourselves, across this (mostly) still-unchanged landscape. Everything is in bloom: lilac blossoms the size of footballs, hundreds to a tree, roses (singles, doubles, quadruples), irises, hawthorns (the flowers are so white, the hawthorn-crested hilltops look snow-covered). We walk and talk, moving up, moving back, changing chatting partners, sometimes going it alone (which seems to be my preferred mode, which I feel guilty about: what about all those things I planned to say to my friends?). It started to rain ever so slightly, but not really perceptibly. It was like walking around in a vast humidifying facial mist.

Our afternoon destination today was Stanway House, which was also an abbey for the first eight centuries of its life, whereupon it shifted ownership to the Tracy family, who have held it for another five hundred. This is what I love about England: its history is bigger than any one individual, however big those individuals were (Henry VIII was massive). The house was being used to film scenes for the TV version of Hilary Mantel's Booker winner *Wolf Hall*. The current owner, the thirteenth Earl of Wemyss, was not at home. We wormed our way into the good books of a woman who seemed to live there, and she showed us around: photos of the earl as a boy, carrying the train of the Queen Mum; the earl riding camels in Egypt; sketches of his grandparents in charcoal by John Singer Sargent; the original exerciser chair (by Chippendale); Flemish tapestries; William Morris wallpaper hung by Morris himself. Johanna pointed out that the earl's family tree—which occupies most of one wall—begins in 640, and includes Charlemagne (768), Ethelred the Unready, and William the Conqueror. The first de Tracey may have been one of Thomas Becket's murderers.

Later, we headed over to Snowshill Manor, which was built in 821 and later given to Catherine Parr by Henry VIII. Parr was the Queen of England for four years, and was Henry's sixth and final wife, and outlived him, and was Elizabeth I's regent, and was the first English queen to publish a book under her own name (*Prayers or Meditations*, I think it was called). The house was bought in 1919 by an eccentric—make that extremely eccentric—architect with a West Indies sugar fortune, Charles Wade, who restored it, mostly to house his collection of anything handmade that caught his eye: twenty-two thousand items, none of them labeled. Cloth shoes, miniature spinning wheels, looms, dozens of suits of samurai armor, slings, thousands of costumes, wooden boxes, toy soldiers, drawings on playing cards, dominoes made from dinner bones carved by French prisoners. Chuck Wade, as he quickly became known to us, was also a confirmed bachelor, until he turned sixty-four, whereupon he married a local woman to take care of him. He continued to sleep in a wooden box, though, and so did she, behind a locked door.

We began to make up limericks about Chuck Wade and his snozzle (*Snowshill* was once pronounced like that). It was amazing how much this childish pastime occupied my brain, as I tried to get the scan and the rhymes right, while also finding a good place to park a triple entendre on the word *snozzle*. (*Chuck Wade's wasker was a whopper/Ugly, large, a real flopper/He collected others, in his hall/Red ones, French ones, big and small/Until his snozzle came a cropper/And he had to marry a pauper*.) Then it was back to the manor, by car, a nap, drinks, dinner. I was happy to see my bed.

Our last day in the Cotswolds. We visit Kiftsgate Court Gardens, which had been recommended to me by Victoria Wakefield, the *Nerine* grower at the Chelsea Flower Show, followed by Hidcote, which is just down the road—two vast gardens, the most impressive we've seen. Kiftsgate was created by three generations of "lady gardeners": Heather Muir in the 1920s, her daughter Diany Binny in the 1950s, and Diany's daughter, Anne Chambers, for the past thirty years. Ms. Chambers and her husband are in residence during our tour, showing a couple—including the first non-white man I've seen in days (gardening is not what I would call a widely integrated activity, at least in National Trust gardens)—around the ornamental pool, the rhododendron-drenched rambling hillsides, the lower patios (with pool, and a view that would lead to the town but for a forest that, Chambers says, "Mummy planted to block the view of it"). I fall into conversation in a wooded part of the garden, under an actual cedar of Lebanon, the real thing, with a woman who tells me of having finished her own garden recently. (This might be my favorite part of turning sixty: sixty-year-olds will talk to anyone. They're grateful for conversation. You don't even need to say hello, just start yakking.) "It's only an acre," the woman says. She has been at it for twenty years. "My friends ask me what I will do now," she says, laughing. "There's always maintenance." Her challenge was sandy soil, which—she tells me, a keen but ignorant gardener—is like a death sentence.

In fact, she has been writing a memoir to document the experience.

Then it's on to Hidcote. Our pace is not exactly leisurely; I could spend days in any one of these gardens. Though perhaps not this one: there are hundreds more people here. The National Trust has been running Hidcote since 1947. They're even showing a movie under the stars soon—*Grease*, that classic movie about hybridization. But then, Hidcote has always been a bit of a hybrid. It was owned by Lawrence Johnston, an American veteran of the Boer War. He spent three decades importing plants from other parts of the world. What has amazed me about gardeners is their gravity: they may talk about color and form, but what they are always trading in at bottom is the prospect of death, facing the reality that a garden done well outlives you, hence the overseeing majesty of five-hundred-year-old pines and cedars of Lebanon.

There are so many different, parallel gardens at Hidcote—the white garden, the iris garden, the topiary zone, the bulb slope, the sedum corner, sectors devoted to roses, to climbing roses, to water plants, you name it—that it's bewildering, almost overwhelming. At one point I come to the end of an alley and look out over what seems to be the perfect thirteenth-, fourteenth-, fifteenth-, sixteenth-, seventeenth-, or eighteenth-century Constable countryside: green, rolling hills, the odd stone wall, a few sheep. This is the pastoral view someone in England has always wanted to preserve. A vision of stillness, of nothing changing. There is no death in this picture, or if there is, it is simply continuation: what was, is, and will be. It is the antidote to the sadness of aging.

That has to make the onrushing end a little easier to take, doesn't it—knowing that you tried to keep important things important? That you shored up the world's chance to admire beauty and husbandry and care and knowledge? That your life meant something, even if it was just consistent, conscientious, care-bound weeding? My wife later tells me that Vita Sackville-West called Hidcote "a jungle of beauty; a jungle controlled by a single mind," but I'm not talking about anything so megalomaniacal.

I thought about this all evening, and well into the night, lying in my expensive bed in my rented manor for the last time. Tomorrow we are heading to Suffolk, by car, me driving on the left-hand side of the road, to scatter my father's ashes (there was no trouble with the death certificate at security at the airport: I carried the old man in my suitcase, and the woman at the scanner was quite solicitous) in the North Sea with my mother's family, the only family he ever wanted to call his own (because his own was so cold and proper and uncommunicative), the only plot he ever tended (beyond slaving in my mother's extensive and time-consuming flower garden, and carefully tending his own ten-by-five-foot vegetable garden, over which he waged great war with an army of rabbits).

Lying in bed, I couldn't overcome the fear that I have wasted my life, wrecked it, spoiled it. For instance: I have been reading *Wolf Hall*. As I read, I try to figure out how Hilary Mantel does it, this seamless inhabitation of Cromwell, and it reminds me that for years now I have been convinced that the summer of 1759—the siege of Quebec, when France lost Canada to Britain—would make a great sexy novel. But now there isn't time left to figure out how to do that.

As a writer, I never specialized. I paid too much attention to individual blossoms and not enough to the garden itself. A blossom is a great rush, but it's a passing thing, like writing an article. A garden is a bigger project: it will always defeat you, it will always be a picture of your strengths and weaknesses—good on the bower of shrubs, not so great on borders or overall cohesion. I wouldn't have minded breaking the rules—I am not sure overall cohesion is possible, or even admirable—but I wish I had taken on the challenge of an entire garden, instead of just a few flower boxes or a stand of poppies.

If you feel you have to do something perfectly, you will never attempt it. If you know you will fail but figure what the hell, you might just try. Of all the object lessons I should like to pass on to my daughter, this is the important one. She'll be waiting for us in Suffolk when we arrive.

MAY 26

Everyone is meeting at my uncle Pat's seaside cottage in Thorpeness: my brother, Tim, and his partner, Frank; my sisters, Maude and Daisy; the vast ranks of my mother's family still in Suffolk—her sister Audrey (her other sisters, Judy and Tossie, are not here) and brother-in-law John, some of their children, various cousins and wives and children and dogs.

I rose in the morning, hobbling on my plantar fasciitis–afflicted foot, embarrassed by my rosacea-strewn face (another outbreak, and me with no hydrocortisone), paid a shuddering hotel bill of £1,300 (after a breakfast of fruit and kippers, which I was trying to pretend was healthy after reading a Giles Coren column in the *Times* in which he suggests that North Americans still labor under the impression that animal fat is the enemy, rather than carbohydrates; my answer has been to eat everything), and drove, haltingly and on the wrong side of the road and often in the wrong gear, across Britain to the seaside my father loved so innocently and unreservedly from the time he was a boy.

I keep thinking about my father in my suitcase. The dust of the old man. I was on a motorcycle in Argentina when he finally died. I'd cared for him for those last years along with my brother and sisters. I was the point man at home base in Toronto, visited him regularly, and then when it came to that long-planned trip, when I'd offered to stay at home, he'd said, "Go, I'll see you in two weeks." I came back; he didn't. I missed his death by days. It didn't matter, because I was there for years caring for him until he died. But it mattered not to have seen him at his last, not to have been there to help him through the gate. I wonder who will be there when I go, whose face will be the last I see, if I am lucky enough to have that kind of death. The other night I imagined it might be Johanna or Hayley, their kind smiles in full view. I guessed they might cry, and then I would say, "Don't cry. You don't need to be sad. Because this is the best company I have ever had." I think about this stuff now.

We arrived at Thorpeness (slight fight in the car prompted by the GPS voice's stubborn refusal to take us the way we both wanted to go: eventually we reverted to a map) just in time to find the Canadian flag flying on the deck, and the UK flag beside it. The first person I saw was Hayley, arrived from Edinburgh after a semester there: that was lovely, maybe the best moment of a serious day. Then we kissed and greeted everyone else; and forty minutes later, at the prompting of various busybodies, set off three flares (which required four members of the coast guard to be present, almost like an honor guard), two of which exploded prematurely; and then made some speeches. My sister Maude consistently dissolved into tears; I simply told the assembled that to my father, with his cold upbringing (English middle class, boarding school at four, sent out to work at sixteen, to war at twenty-five; he was a virgin until he was thirty-eight, by his own admission, though I did not say that), the family gathered here was the only one he had, and the one he loved most. Then we made our way down to the water.

Timmy (my brother) and Maudie and Daisy (my sisters) and Johanna and Hayley and two of Isobel Betts's kids (Isobel is my goddaughter, and I was glad they were there so we could pass something along, whatever it was, maybe just the future memory of having been there, so they might take an interest in who my old man was) were in the waterside gaggle. The others gathered quietly on the beach behind us all the way back up to the house.

My father blew into the water more easily, more obediently than our mother had, less in our faces; that was like him. He drifted to the northeast. I was worried the tone of it all was too light and peremptory, too sunny, but he would not have wanted to stand on ceremony, as much as he would have been thrilled to be honored by so many people (which I'd said in the speech). I cannot think that he is gone; he is more alive to me now than he ever was, as a companion, as a reminder, as a warning.

The whole thing happened very fast, in any event: one minute we were on the beach, the next he was in the sea, and after that we set to eating. "No point prolonging the misery," someone said. But it wasn't misery. He'd been with me still, even as dust. Then he was not. I told myself to pay attention to the living, as he would have wanted.

MAY 27

A visit to see my uncles and aunts in Suffolk. Pat and Judy, my mother's brother and sister-in-law, have put us up, kindly, in their beach house at Thorpeness; they have to be in their eighties now. Then to tea with Auntie Audrey and her husband, John. Audrey was the aunt who became a second mother to me when I couldn't live with my own, after I had headed off to boarding school; the one who helped me re-establish contact with my English family after my mother declared she would never speak to anyone again after my grandfather remarried (too soon, she thought). John took me in, became a pal. He is ailing; this is the first time I've seen him since my mother's funeral, and he is in tears.

When I was sixteen, we drove to the Lake District together, went on a hike or two. He was a quiet guy, and a good listener. He must have been forty-four then, still owned a pub. My own mother was fifty-six. They were all younger than I am now. Time is sliding all around me. I promise myself I will come back and see him before he dies. Same with Audrey, same with Pat. But it is harder to say good-bye to John than it was to scatter my father's ashes.

MAY 28

Or so I thought. This morning, before we headed north to Yorkshire and Edinburgh, having cleaned the beach house and locked the doors, I took a last glance at the pebbled strand where we'd left my dad. This is the strange thing: I couldn't leave. I stood there for an hour. Hayley and Johanna sat in the car, out of the wind, waiting. I kept staring at the spot where he had been handed onto the water, kept looking out at the small waves—it was early, the beach was empty—kept looking up at the grey sky, thinking: "Is he there? Is that wave him? Or is it that one?"

I tried to take pictures, but nothing would do. Nothing was memorable enough to replace him. We look alike, but we are not the same person: he was too cautious, too conservative, too afraid to take a risk, too afraid of change, too afraid to offend my mother, didn't think he could stand alone, thought he was nothing without her. In other words, we are often exactly alike. I got to know him in the four years after her death; we became pals. We weren't the same person, but of course we were. He had his marbles until the end, felt the pain of his physical slide too keenly, couldn't stop being ashamed of his growing fragility, used to call me at 5 AM, out of his mind for not having been able to sleep. He became a bit crazy then. He worked until he was ninety-seven, still calling the copper market correctly. Died within a year of stopping. If I last as long as my parents did (I haven't been as well behaved, so that's a significant "if"), I may have another thirty-five productive years. Let's say twenty-five, conservatively, if luck is with me. Let's hope for it. That's the same as being twenty-five and getting to fifty. That's enough time to become the thing I want to be, whatever that is, time for another career, another self, another life, time to get it out of me, onto the page, into the air, into the heart. I wish it was not so hard not to be afraid.

Eventually, I made my way back to the car. Johanna seemed to understand why it had taken a while. She asked if I was okay. From the back seat, Hayley gave me a kiss. I felt a bit better after that. I was passing him on.

Had a chat with Hayley about books and writing and publishing (she has a summer internship as an editorial assistant, to see if she likes it). I told her to pay attention to her instincts, to what she likes and finds bottomlessly interesting, because that matters. I have no idea if this is good advice: so much for the wisdom of sixty. She doesn't seem to expect me to have answers, which is a relief.

But even as we talk, I am plagued by the fear of having no money to retire on: it looks as though I will be working until I drop. I realize the disgusting self-indulgent irony of this: here I am traipsing around the Cotswolds, heading on to Italy, taking ski trips in British Columbia (albeit on someone else's dime, at least for two-thirds of it), and I have the gall to worry about money. But I can't seem to avoid it. I don't have the money to spend, but I don't want to say no to what life is left. So I keep spending, and thus must keep working. As I watched my father carry on as a scrap merchant into his nineties, always keen to know what was happening in the world that would affect the price of copper, working until I drop seems acceptable: I like writing, why would I want to stop? I'd rather go out writing, like the Montreal bicycle maker who only wanted a week of holiday before his death.

But in the past year or two, I've clumsily realized that my ability to write or not write, think or not think, drool or not drool, is largely out of my hands. I am a hostage to the fortune of my health. I should have planned to be financially free by the age of sixty, and then any gravy I earned beyond that would be just that, gravy. I am better off than most people, given that the newspaper tells me two-thirds of Canadians have no retirement savings whatsoever, but actual financial independence? A retirement without work? Impossible now. I am sure this is my fault, but there you go: I moved around, thinking it would be good for me as a writer, and all that movement punished my disloyalty by interrupting my pensions. If we sell the house, we can survive, provided no one is maimed or chronically ill, but it's not going to be lavish.

But then I think: why does it have to be lavish? In a few years, I'll be grateful if my anus is still in one piece.

So it won't be a cottage by the sea, but it might be a condo in Leaside. Whereupon, some days, I think: you can still write in Leaside. And on others I think: where can I buy a bottle of arsenic?

Worst of all, I am plagued by thoughts of not writing everything I would like to write before it's too late. Regret: this is the real killer. And why, Ian Brown, do you have regrets?

IB: Because, like I already said, I didn't write what I wanted to write.
IB: Why not?
IB: I was afraid it would be no good.
IB: Why were you worried about that?
IB: Well, isn't it obvious?
IB: Lots of people produce stuff that isn't any good. Didn't stop them. Does it change the way you think of them?

IB: No. Even if I wouldn't read it, I admire their effort, mostly.

IB: You'll never produce anything good or even bad if you don't try. Why are you so worried about failure?

IB: Do we have to talk about this?

IB: Yes.

IB: Because success is the measure of one's worth. I was taught that.

IB: But you don't believe it. You never believed it. You became a writer because you didn't believe it. And you've had a lifetime to disprove it, a lifetime to try other approaches. Perhaps you ought to have tried a few.

IB: What can I say? I was afraid that trying and failing would be more painful than the failure of never trying at all.

And so on. The other day, sitting in a restaurant with Hayley and Johanna having a cup of tea, I forgot myself and panicked and threw my head into my hands and moaned, "Oh, I have so much to do." And Johanna said, "What's the matter, did you forget an obligation?" And I said, "No, I meant in my life," and that is true. It all feels rather urgent. Then Hayley said, "I don't know why you haven't written fiction." I pressed her, but all she would add was that she was loving *Barney's Version*, and thought I could easily have written as good a book. I am in tears thinking of it, because as hypothetical as it is, it is still the best compliment I've ever had.

Have been away in Halifax, up and down the Eastern shore, writing about lobster fishermen. Driving through the country I came upon a house festooned with local Nova Scotia folk art carvings—masks, Jesuses, talismans, totems. I stopped the car and tried to buy two devils nailed to the wall near the door: one was Satan, upside down, with GOING DOWN written on his chest; the other an upright, surprised devil, bearing the words I AM NOT WELCOME HERE. But the artist wouldn't sell them: "If I sell them," he said, "I'd have to make two more"—to protect his house, in other words. I want one for my house.

I miss Johanna. I think this is an accomplishment. We've been married twenty-six years as of September, and I still relish her company, wit, style, warmth, fashion sense, empathy, seriousness, adaptiveness, organizational abilities, looks, tenderness to our children, sense of adventure, tenderness to me. She can be bossy, and judgmental, and she leaves the kitchen a pigsty more than I do, but at this yearning stage (sixty), these are forgivable faults. I especially cherish (I think that is not too strong a word) her eccentric sense of humor, which matches mine. She talks to the dog as if the dog were an old high school girlfriend. I like that, too. The world is often a horrible place, and at sixty it is no longer possible to dismiss its pain, in all its emanations. Johanna is a good person to face that darkness beside. For all my persistent and growing crankiness, I keep coming back to that.

JUNE 28

At least, I think it's June 28. I have been in Siena, in a villa, free and courtesy of Joanne Green, my generous mother-in-law, and I have to say the rest of the world doesn't really affect you here. The house is vast, and privacy is actually possible, despite the presence of nine people (Hayley and Johanna included). The countryside is green and gold, and the weather has been perfect, complete with a massive thunderstorm last night in which a bolt of lightning knocked out the power. We'd had *bistecca fiorentina* for supper, done in salt and pepper with olive oil. We'd walked through the nearby woods, and along the road, and picked up a dog, from another *podere* down the way. The dog stuck with us all day. We eventually called the number on his collar, and got his owner, a journalist, who came by and picked him up. The dog's actual name was Pollock, after Jackson Pollock, because the dog was crazy and he had a sister named Peggy, after Peggy Guggenheim, who I believe was Pollock's lover in her beautiful palazzo in Venice. But we started calling the Italian dog Rovere, and Rovieri, and also Cane, which means "dog" in Italian. It was nice to have a dog around. I miss our dog, Ginny (she's staying with Gab, an unattached fortyish friend of Johanna's who buys her treats and calls her Gidget and sometimes pretends to people they pass on the street that Ginny/Gidget belongs to her; needless to say, she is very fond of Ginny and threatens to steal her heart away from us). I have become even fonder of her (the dog, but I like Gab too) as I have grown older. I feel her loneliness, her need for companionship, as I feel my own. Getting older is a process of getting lonelier and lonelier until, at the end, you are completely solitary, and then you are officially dead.

It's 6 AM, and I am sitting in the upstairs kitchen of the villa, trying to write. Most of all I am trying to figure out if what I am writing has any value at all, and why I am doing it. Does it have to feel like terribly hard work for it to mean anything? Is the only meaningful human activity, in fact, struggle?

We had an interesting conversation driving through Yorkshire with Hayley. Hayley maintained you could bully someone even in your mind, after hearing a story from her mother about the only girl who ever bested Johanna academically at school, XY, the Little Shit™—a name coined by Johanna's mother. Johanna told the story of how she and her friends Judy and Patty and Maureen had defaced a picture of the girl in their yearbooks, writing under a photo of her with her arm around someone, "XY with her only friend."

Hayley objected to this behavior, saying that she thought it was just as much bullying to denigrate someone in private as it was to do it to their face—that the effect of either was to poison the world against someone, and that the victim often felt it, despite the lack of a public forum. Johanna's reaction was that public denigration is public denigration, but that trying to prevent people from writing their true feelings in private in a notebook amounted to policing someone's thoughts.

"Yes," Hayley said, "precisely."

It's a manifesto that's popular with progressives these days, though Johanna stood fast. But I could see Hayley moderating her ideas as we spoke; I could see her taking everyone's ideas into consideration, and trying to get to a position with which she could feel comfortable. That's what young brains do.

I was like that once, but I am more resistant now, more stubborn, less willing to change my opinion, because . . . because why? Because my identity is wrapped up in these positions. Surely they are who I am? I need them to be, because my body is becoming unreliable; God forbid that my mental self should waste away as well. And so the cranky old man is born. Every time I find him forming inside me, I want to drive a stake through his chest. But that, from what I can tell, is the challenge of the next—oh, what?—thirty years? Staying open. I suspect it will be the hardest thing I have ever done.

Apart from that, I have two precise aspects of turning sixty to report; one concerns the persistence of envy as a motivating force. It's a few weeks now since Liz Renzetti's launch party for her novel *Based on a True Story*. It was a good party, not that I noticed, because I was a turning worm of envy the entire time I was there. To me, almost everyone at the party seemed to be an asshole, and that's a clear sign. I have long been a fan of Liz's excellent writing and her company, but it's her apparent confidence I admire most. (I'm sure she has racking stretches of doubt, but they never leak into her prose.) Liz took a chance most journalists can't—to make something up, to tell a story of her own creating—and so owned the time it took to tell it. Branding a stretch of experience as your own is the reward for the daring it requires to say, "For once I am going to ignore the curling, disdainful lip of the world," which frowns on anyone stepping out of line, whether it be a middle-aged first-time female novelist or Sir Francis Chichester sailing around the world, on his own, at . . . what was it? Sixty-five? I loved Chichester's story.

And yet here I am in Tuscany, as the morning comes up on the land, filling a page with my thoughts, thinking: Am I writing in the wrong room? Is there a better view to be taking in while I do this? Would some other place in this vast house yield more inspiration? Am I writing about the wrong thing? At the age of sixty, one would think these doubts would wane. But apparently not.

I am beginning to understand them a little more, however. They're a way of avoiding the real difficulty of writing anything (beyond the hard discipline of reporting and composing and revising), which is to find something you care about to the point of agony, because those are the things worth writing about.

Before we left for Italy—this is the second revelation I need to record for this diary—I bought a new pair of pants. Very light grey, for the summer. I wore them with a blue shirt and the jacket of my seersucker suit, and grey Cole Haan suede shoes with bright yellow soles. I thought I looked like the cat's ass, until someone said, at some event I went to—a public lecture about whether the city needed a creative director—actually, it was Deborah Kirshner who walked up and said, "What are you wearing?" Deborah was a gifted violinist until she was in a car crash, and now she's a gifted writer. She seemed to imply there was something circus-like in my presentation, and of course that was all it took for me to suddenly see myself as some old fart in his bright, I'm-still-young-at-heart! duds, or, alternatively, as some cancerously obstinate old shit in his go-to-hell clothes. In an instant, I was transformed from flying cockatiel to caged parrot. It was all I could do to wait until I was home to get the clothes off my body. Especially as, reading that afternoon in the chair near my desk, I had nodded off with a fluorescent yellow Magic Marker in my hand, which then fell into my crotch and left a yellow spot the size of a fifty-cent piece. It looked as if I had leaked a little pee. Very becoming and youthful.

The thing is, where clothes and aging are concerned, *you never want to appear to be trying to look younger than you are.*

Dapper is okay; stylish is fine; well dressed is excellent, even if you're wearing a T-shirt and a pair of Levi 501s. Classic is ideal. Even counterintuitively attired—jacket and tie at a picnic, bow tie at Woodstock—is permissible. But trying too hard? Forget it. And trying too hard to look younger than you are (which is actually impossible: as Baryshnikov once said to me, the body never lies) is, at least for a man, this man, the great mistake, the sin of self-imposed indignity.

Johanna has tried to get me to wear hipper clothes for years, and I could have experimented more, but they always seemed somehow inauthentic. (She goes classic now, and buys quality, and hits the mark more often than I do.) And while I worry about what I wear ever so slightly less than I used to (vanity is a very persistent flaw), I tend to either grey flannels or jeans, high or low, never in between, because it makes the decisions easier, and I don't want to waste time on a decision when my time is running out! But the dilemma of what to wear is increasingly irrelevant anyway, because, especially nowadays, no one is looking. This is the most certain thing I know, and the fact I am most unwilling to admit, as liberating as it is.

Anyway, I've decided I like the light pants regardless. They fit well in the crotch, proud but not blatant. There's a motto.

I get one email at a time here in the Sienese countryside, once every hour, if that. We're way, way out in the country: the nearest corner store is a twenty-minute drive away. Nice place, though—a four-hundred-year-old pigsty and cattle barn (seriously), fixed up over the course of a decade. But the Internet is so fragile that every time someone turns on a cellphone, the whole system goes out.

I spent a good hour fantasizing that Johanna and I could stay here for the rest of our lives, provided we could get into town every once in a while, to Rome or London. The countryside is hyper-intense: the greens are ultra-green, the heat is broiler quality, the light is twenty-four-karat golden, the dust is super-dusty. Did I mention the bees in the tree next to the patio? Even the bees embody the idea of beeness, and are storm-trooper defensive and ultra-buzzy. It's as if someone has boiled the idea of the Tuscan countryside down to an essence, and then injected it into our brains: herbs and cherries and fields and flowers everywhere, and unbelievably quiet, except for the bees. My mother-in-law, Joanne, has committed us to a busy agenda, some of which quite reasonably involves paying attention to Bob, her boyfriend. Johanna and her sister Anne are gifted and faithful in this regard. Bob is ninety-four, and a bit grumpy, brought on (I suspect, and understandably) by his growing physical incapacity. On our tour of the villa when we arrived, we were walking down a driveway between two of the buildings, a very mild slope, but slope enough for him. Bob and I were in the rear, about six feet behind Joanne and Hayley, when Joanne suddenly stopped to make sure she didn't take a header, which in turn created a reverse conga line of backups and stoppages, and almost caused stooped and bent Bob to fall on *his* face. I offered him my arm, but he shook it off. "I'm all right until people suddenly stop and cause a traffic jam," he said fiercely, glaring ahead at Joanne. She didn't hear him. I could see him regret the words as they flew out of his mouth. My father hated his own age-related moments of pique. I'm up to about a dozen a year myself, all prompted by having to wait for service. "Don't you realize I'm dying?" I want to shout at the obliviously texting twatwipe behind the bar. "Every second takes me closer to the end!"

What I like most about the farm is the hot stillness and its long-unchanged views across the fields—that is, unchanged for the past five hundred years or so. The farmhouse we're staying in seems to date to the 1400s, which makes it even older than Bob. You encounter the odd car when you walk, but you can't hear them—and there are no trains, no trucks roaring along highways, no downshifting motorcycles. The odd dog barking. Old people: there are lots of old ones out here in the country, shuffling slowly to nowhere. Oh, and some hens clucking, a few moments ago, and a rooster earlier this morning, though he couldn't seem to make up his mind about when or how long to crow. (I know how he feels.) That's it, sound-wise. In other words, here there are no expectations, beyond being in the world—and that, it turns out, is a good place to be, at sixty.

JULY 3

The villa has seven bedrooms. Johanna and I are on the very top floor, with a view of the fields over the saltwater pool, in which you can do laps.

We're twenty minutes from anything, by car—and I do mean anything, including the sound of a car. All I have heard for the past three hours is someone splashing in the pool, the distant conversation of my family, and, at one point, a faint patch of music. Today is a non-traveling day. An excellent idea, and Bob's. He finds the wheelchair demeaning, and resists it. Maybe a trip to explore the hill towns of Tuscany was an unwise choice for a man in his early nineties?

I am the only one who is licensed to drive the nine-person van, so I spent yesterday from one to nine chauffeuring Johanna, Anne and Mark, Hayley, Zach and Noah (the sons of Johanna's brother, who isn't here), Joanne and Bob from here to Brolio (ancestral home of the noble Ricasolis, who aligned themselves with the German pope—mistake!—before the Florentine papists beat the living shit out them, whereupon they reinvented themselves as winemakers, and modernized wine production in Italy) via Siena and back again. I figure I have about four input channels at best these days, but for that trip I needed ten: all the bosses, snapping out driving instructions and commentary, plus the road itself (Italy), the stick shift (Fiat), the Italian signage (incomprehensible), the GPS lady (speaking English but programmed by Italians, therefore just a little late with the information I needed to turn right and left and go through the roundabout). Not to mention the scenery, which I gather is very nice. Plus I had begun the day with four Italian espressos, which really get things moving now that I am sixty but utterly incapacitate the attention span, so you spend the day running around in circles desperate to take a shit.

I have to say the food is quite good, and I have been eating incessantly when I am not drinking espresso. Have I mentioned Italian country plumbing? It resembles Italian GPS and Italian Internet service . . . *spotty* is one word that comes to mind. In fact, the plumbing works exactly like the wifi: nothing for the longest time, and then a flood of input and output, then nothing for a long time. Christ knows how this country has lasted as long as it has, infrastructure-wise.

And trying to claim the van at the Hertz counter when we arrived in Florence? Jesus Madonna! An hour's wait, and then they did not have the automatic transmission van we had reserved six months in advance. Six people behind the counter, two of them actually working, and one of those not exactly efficient. (I would confess to suffering an impatient senior moment, except that the Hertz crew would have tested the patience of Pope Francis himself.) I noticed a closet full of GPS units, which struck me as unusual, and then I tried the one we got. Eventually they handed over the keys to the only nine-person van they had, a stick-shift Fiat. "Eet ees the beegest van een Eetaly," the Hertz woman told me, and she was not kidding. Christ Himself knows how we will pass through about 50 percent of the streets in Tuscany.

But beautiful? My God. And calm? Also my God. I can't actually remember the last time I stayed in a place where you could not hear the hum of motorized life . . . maybe at my brother's in Rockport. I never realized what a hallucinatory and freeing effect silence has, perhaps because I have often worked in newsrooms, where you have to train yourself to ignore the screaming and shouting and character assassination going on all around you. I should bring my brother here.

I am astonished at how . . . freed from the usual self-hatred I've been. It is as if I no longer feel sixty, and a failure. But then, I don't speak Italian, so I am allowed to be hopeless and incompetent. All I have to do is write things down for a few hours in the early morning, before the day begins. This turns out to be enough.

Last night was the last in Italy for Hayley and me and Zach and Noah. Johanna and her sister and her sister's husband are staying on with Joanne and Bob for another week. (I would have stayed, but as of Sunday I have to go to Banff for the rest of the month.)

So we made our way to Siena for the trial running of the Palio horse race, with about forty thousand other people, from what I could see. Hayley and I stood at the rail that marks the racecourse around the edge of the central piazza, watching the horses dash and prance and wander by. Hayley is a great favorite of Italian men, who stare at her and smile and flirt and talk to her as she passes. She looks but otherwise ignores them. But everybody looks at everybody else here, men at women, women at men, men at men, women at women, etc. A woman from Montalcino in a red print dress explained the potential ins and outs of the race to Hayley and me, and how one *contrada* in Siena might hire a jockey from another neighborhood, who might then be paid off by his home contrada to throw the race. This celebration of corruption goes back a long way. Tonight, in the pre-race rehearsals, for instance, the Montalcinese are allowed to go first in the race because they supported the Sienese in a battle against Florence centuries ago. It felt memorable just to be there, with so much to hear and see.

Italian women are so lusciously brown it's shocking. But I wonder: if I weren't married, would I, at sixty, do anything about it? Unlike many Italian men, who have no shame where women are concerned—they stare and comment and grope like Gollums—I was always too diffident to be much of a ladies' man. Now I'm too old, and too jealous of my privacy. But it still feels like a loss. I know what fiftyish women mean when they say they have become invisible, but I do not know what fiftyish women mean when they say they prefer invisibility.

After the race, we ate at a good restaurant, a local place with large slow-food gastronomical ambitions. Outside, on the sidewalk, there was a party of eight, all Italians from what I could hear, in which I noticed a man, maybe in his late sixties, possibly older. He was slightly balding, but wearing his salt-and-pepper hair longer and swept back, and with a mustache (white), linen blazer, blue shirt, smoking a cigar. He was charming everyone, including me, twenty paces away. He was, as Johanna said, "obviously the most interesting guy in the world." I wanted to talk to him, learn his secret: how did he stay so vital? Then I saw: he did it by listening. He spent a lot of time saying nothing, thinking and watching. It seems to be the ideal post-sixty default setting.

JULY 8

Was in Italy Friday morning, Toronto later the same day, Alberta the next. Am now in Banff. My schedule seems crazily unmoored, without gravity (literally), as if I'm futilely attempting to stay busy as I get older in order to prove that I am still essential to the rest of the world. I left my cellphone at the villa in Italy. That has to be age-related: I've never done such a thing before. Unpacking and repacking weren't such a problem, however, because KLM also lost my luggage, the same clothes I need in Banff. No one's accusing KLM of being a sexagenarian! Apparently, the suitcase is somewhere between Amsterdam and Toronto. Hayley got a little upset with me at the airport, when I rather too openly expressed my disdain for KLM's complete lack of knowledge of, and curiosity about, where my bag might be. She kept apologizing to the clerk, who then apologized to me, whereupon I said (again), "Apologizing isn't really going to accomplish anything, is it?" But Hayley had a good point: it was not the clerk's fault that KLM lost our bags. But anyone of any age would go insane talking to these boobs, who treat me like a blip to be managed.

Oh, and my plantar fasciitis, which is still bothering me, has now been joined by a horrible rash that has spread out in lines across my chest and up my neck. I look like Spiderman's costume. It's some kind of allergy to the sun, it seems. Fantastic! I'm now allergic to light.

To add to my rash and my lameness and an incipient cold, I also have a raging pain in my ear and jaw. Fifteen years ago I would have shrugged it off. At sixty, any rogue symptom at all makes me want to hire a lawyer. It's either an abscess or an ear infection . . . but where could I get such a thing? On the plane from Italy, of course. I can picture the (unprintable adjective) guy who sneezed on me in line at the airport. Since I entered the aging zone, I'm like an early-warning ballistic missile sensor, always scanning for an incoming germ missile . . . Bastards! At this rate of paranoiac attitudinal aging, I'll be voting like an old conservative for Stephen Harper in a year. That really will be the end of my gracefulness.

I feel like a dried pepper, old and flaky and hung in a corner. Seriously, it's depressing. I've already lost my Tuscan serenity, and climbed on the old see-saw: since there isn't much time left to accomplish anything, I might as well not even try to accomplish anything. Anyway. There you have it. Obviously dying.

But laugh away. As the creators of memento mori used to engrave inside their tiny silver coffin pendants: today it's me, tomorrow it will be you. It's always someone. In the waiting room at Pearson, on my way to Calgary, I run into T., an acquaintance from university. I haven't seen him in . . . three years? And I barely knew him at that. But within a minute of saying hello, I know he's five weeks out of prostate surgery. "They got it all"—these are standard chats for me nowadays—"but it was a more invasive kind of cancer than they thought. But apart from a slightly leaky bladder, I'm fine," he said, not lowering his voice for the benefit of anyone nearby. "When I turned fifty, a friend of mine gave me a case of Depends as a joke. After the surgery, I said, 'I'm not laughing now.'" Pause. "I never thought I'd be wearing Depends." Another pause. "But hey: I'm still here. The collapse that occurs at sixty has advantages."

"Such as?"

Perhaps he meant candor. He had been an optimistic realist even in college.

"Well, grandchildren. When the first one came along, I felt a bit old. But that changed as soon as she got home." They're not his kids, but he is allowed to love them, the best of both worlds. "A chance to do it better."

"What else?" I said. "You said there were several advantages."

"Well, just perspective, I guess. Having survived this thing."

This *is* the thing, you see: I am on my way to being an old man. But at sixty, I am still the youngest of old men. I still don't know which way to dodge.

JULY 11

My brother's birthday. Called him this afternoon, and that made me more optimistic. He understands exactly where I'm coming from. I worried after the death of my father that my brother and sisters and I would fly apart, but it has not happened; we see each other less, but more regularly. We observe the holidays, visit when possible, given that they are scattered across North America. My first allies.

The plantar fasciitis has become almost crippling: walking is now hobbling, and the pain wakes me up. "Does the pain wake you up?" is a question doctors ask me now. If something wakes you up at night, it's worth paying attention to, apparently. If only I had known, I would have reported my existential angst to the doctor in my twenties, when waking up terrified, not of the night but of the shape of the day to come, became a regular feature of my life.

Because I can't walk, I can't hike. Rebecca, a physiotherapist in Banff, tells me that I can ride a bike, but I can't walk up Tunnel Mountain, my usual daily constitutional. And under no circumstances am I to run.

So I have taken up reading about my decaying body, boning up on the physiology of aging. This is not for the faint of heart, not least of all because there is no agreed-upon standard for what is "old." If you listen to the monologues of Jimmy Kimmel, anyone over fifty suffers from a kind of generalized foolishness. I like Kimmel better than Fallon, who never shuts up and rarely asks his guests a good question, but his age-related bias has started to offend me, which is new: I never noticed it before. I must be getting old (ha). Meanwhile, the World Health Organization draws the line at retirement age (sixty or sixty-five) and, in developing countries, "when active contribution is no longer possible."

The only thing everyone knows for certain is that there are a lot of us standing on the brink of the unknowable nightmare. According to a study prepared by the government of Ontario, where I live, there were 1,878,325 Ontarians aged sixty-five or older in 2011—about 14.6 percent of the provincial population. But because the baby boomers started turning sixty-five in 2010, the number will double over the next twenty years, to about 25 percent of the population. Almost half the health-related spending in the province is devoted to that 14.6 percent of the population. I know people in their thirties who are driven to distraction by this fact; it seems to offend their sense of fairness. I try to help out by exercising and staying as fit as I can, and therefore out of the hospital for as long as I can, but the fact is: old age is when people start to decline, when they most often need medical attention. If we didn't spend half our health budget on that 15 percent of the population, something would be radically wrong.

But even these numbers are misleading. According to the Canadian Institute for Health Information, the growth in medical spending since 1975 is due mostly to price increases—the cost of physicians and drugs—and not to the care of the elderly. From what I can figure out, Canada spends an average of about $6,000 per person per year on health care. By one estimate, we spend roughly the OECD developed-world average, or more than $12,000 a student, on education. I don't begrudge paying taxes to the public education system, though my children are well out of it. But many of my young friends are less willing to extend such generosity toward my (aging) health. "I object to spending all that money to satisfy my parents and their generation's neurotic obsession with not dying," a thirty-fiveish pal, a former Ontario provincial government adviser, said to me a while ago. He sees me, the older man, as a wasted cause with no value to his future; since he has more life left, he thinks his life is more valuable than mine. I don't doubt that it's true, but measuring the value of someone's life in such a technocratic way is a new development, at least in a country that has a charter of rights. Primate societies that eject their eldest do so either because the elder is a drag on resources and can't make a contribution, or because the elder is hogging all the young, impregnable females. But this isn't a society of primates. My pal is a very decent guy. Naturally, he does not see his anger toward me as an unconscious manifestation of his own obsession with not dying.

How long am I going to be pissing him off? According to the journal *Gerontologist*, the life expectancy of a Canadian male is 81, fourth highest in the world. At age 65—five years from now, for me—my life expectancy will be 17.4 more years, on average (give or take habits, lifestyle, and genetics. Women of 65 can expect an average of 20.8 more years). That means I have, on average, about 23 years to keep writing. A lot happened to me between the ages of 23 and 46. That is my fantasy—a second go-round. I suspect I have lots of company in that fantasy.

Next year, in 2015, for the first time in Canadian history, there will be more of us older than 65 than there are under 15.

JULY 17

Trudging up the stairs to the Banff Centre from downtown, gasping for breath. But: there's a twenty year old, also gasping! Fuck him! Then some fifty-year-old *runs* past me, while talking to a pal. Fuck me.

It turns out there are some common factors affecting longevity. The things to avoid are oxidative stress, lack of exercise, and chronic inflammation (brought on by a weak immune system). The things to promote in oneself are calm and focus; exercise; and steady attention to anti-immune thingies. Oh, and cognitive engagement: people with an education were shown to shrink less in a 2013 study on bone loss. There you have it. Drugs and drinking and smoking are out; they just hasten the end.

The breakdown of the body seems to happen part by part, overseen by a central cellular authority that governs the aging of cells. Cells, it turns out, can divide only a limited number of times. Give or take the effects of sunlight, chemicals, and free radicals, which do direct damage to cells, the number of times a cell can divide is programmed by the genes, and specifically by the length of the telomeres, the sequences at the end of each chromosome. Once a cell reaches the not so magic number, it lives a little while longer and then dies. This is called apoptosis, a cheery little word. This is not what Shakespeare meant by fate, but it is what fate actually is, at its most predictable: a telomere, a thing over which I have little to no control. I am in the hands of my telomeres. My eventual death is inevitable, but not entirely my fault. The length of my life is mostly in the hands of the genetic gods. Strangely comforting, most of the time.

JULY 25

I'm now obsessed with the physiology of aging. As a general

rule, the eyes go first, then the ears. Then the internal functions. Generation Xers should stop feeling so cocky about their eternal youthfulness (as I felt cocky about mine until, um, two years ago): body functions begin to decline at the age of thirty. Yes. Thirty. Take that, you little shits.

This scientific stuff makes for harrowing reading. Example: the bones. Every bone in the human skeleton is replaced every ten years—until you hit thirty. Then the amount of bone deposited with each recycling declines. Bone is a composite of crystals of mineral bound to protein, or collagen. (Entirely mineral bones would be too brittle; all protein would be too soft.) As I get older, the mineral level in my bones increases, for complex and abstruse reasons that I have tried to understand but can't quite grasp, with the result that I develop stiffer, more brittle bones. People over eighty-five, for instance, are as much as fifteen times more likely to fracture a bone than a spring chicken of ten. The mineral component of bone is known as its "ash content." Of course it is! The older you are, the higher your ash content. The most vulnerable sticks in the body are the femur at the hip, vertebrae (especially at the top of the spine), the radius, and the ulna. I now (since the age of 55 or so) have what my doctor calls "a nasty neck," a stenosis of the nerve canal in my vertebrae between the third and fifth discs. That could eventually cause my head to droop, which will compress the throat, which will make it harder to breathe. And so on. A bunch of economists at USC, Harvard, and Peking universities published a study in 2013 of more than seventeen thousand Chinese adults over the age of forty-five. They discovered that aging men—over forty-five!—shrink an average of 1.3 inches; women lose more, an average of 1.5 inches. City people shrink less than country folk, and people who finish high school keep a centimeter more than those who don't—less manual labor, presumably. Height loss is thought to be associated with a decline in cognitive health. I'll be short and stupid. The solution—a point culled from much confusing and contra-dictory reading—is to take vitamin D. Nearly 90 percent of elderly patients who are hospitalized for long stretches have vitamin D deficiencies.

And that's the optimistic take from China. Other studies have revealed far worse findings: that most indi-viduals lose a centimeter a decade after forty, which means that at eighty men and women are about an inch and a half shorter than they were in their prime. So my plantar fasciitis is right on schedule.

Rebecca, however—who loves to gossip about the town and its ways, is slightly conservative in the way young Western mothers can be conservative, and is someone, it just hit me, who *doesn't make me feel like a fossil because I am sixty*—has given me exercises, and she has encased my feet in plaster to make a pair of orthopedic inserts that I can wear while exercising. She also tells me to tape my foot at a ninety-degree angle to my leg at night by running a wide piece of tape or three along the sole of my foot from heel to big toe, and then up over the big toe, to my shin below the knee, where I fasten this hypotenuse of tape with more tape. The trick is to keep the tension on the tape without cutting off the circulation to the lower leg. It's ungainly and it makes me sleep poorly, but my foot is getting better. Rebecca says I will be 100 percent. I believe Rebecca. In fact, I adore her, though I am not as abject and drooling in my appreciation as, say, the eighty-years-olds who see her, who need her even more than I do. Still, Rebecca is a small highlight of my non-hiking week. She promises me a future, even at my age. But she is the only light. The research shows that in addition to our stature, our hearts, brains, facial bones, and sex organs all shrink with age. That is not good news.

JULY 30

I have started doing the old Royal Canadian Air Force exercise regime, the 5BX plan, for eleven minutes every morning:

- 22 toe touches
- 16 sit-ups
- 23 leg lifts, lying on my front
- 15 push-ups
- 440 running-on-the-spot steps, each 4 inches high, with 10 stride jumps every 75 steps

You do all this in 9.5 minutes. Easy, except for the push-ups. At thirty-five I could do thirty of them at a drop. This morning fifteen made me think I was going to spring apart like a cheap toy.

My father did this daily and religiously, running around his little patio every morning in knee socks. I thought he was nuts. But it makes me feel better, and I am slightly pleased that I am operating above my age group's pathetic recommended level (C+ on the third lowest of six charts, on which I am a proud B. It's not much, I admit, but it's something, and I am craven enough about my age to mention it). This is an interesting fact about muscle loss: growth hormone doesn't help. Resistance exercises do.

The Banff literary journalism program ends tomorrow, and I'm heading back to Toronto in two days. I've led the program for five years now, and have imparted everything I know about reporting and writing long-form non-fiction: use scenes, use details, use point of view, use dialogue, report endlessly and rewrite ruthlessly, and write about what you care about, regardless of whether it's considered officially important. I would say more people are better writers today, thanks to our incessant online output. But every year the students change while I say the same things, and that in turn makes me want to move on. They've asked me to do it for another year, and I've agreed, but after that, I want July to myself.

I can finally hike, and have been making my way up Tunnel Mountain with the aid of my new orthotic inserts. They are things of genius. And I have been biking. In fact, I just bought a second-hand all-carbon Orbea from Joe Lunn, the husband of my doctor in Banff. (Yes, I have a doctor in Banff, as well as the physiotherapist. I have been coming for five summers, and I hike a lot, and I need a doctor, okay?) The bike weighs nothing. In certain gears on the flats I can move forward with almost no exertion. I can accelerate up hills. On the bike I'm in my twenties again—at least until some guys in their twenties blow past me on their own carbon-fiber bikes as if I were a standing tableau behind glass in a museum: OLDER CANADIAN ON BIKE, CIRCA 2015. If I average about fifteen and a half miles an hour for ninety minutes—a fast outing for me—they must outpace me by nine miles and change an hour. They are competitive bikers, true, and they are in their twenties. I am not. I wish I were, but only physically: I wouldn't want to be younger in any other way. That stretch was too painful, too floundering, too callow, too anxious.

The eyes! Have I mentioned the things that can happen to my eyes as I grow older? A sixty-year-old needs three times more light than a twenty-year-old to see detail. No wonder my mother kept replacing soft sixty-watt bulbs with hundred watters that fried your skin off. A game of rummy with my late, eighty-three-year-old father-in-law? Like playing cards in an operating theater. The lens of the eyeball stiffens and becomes denser, making focusing on close objects harder—I know that too well—but the lens also yellows, changing the way you perceive color. This is why old painters use so much blue, to counteract their yellowed lenses, and why blue letters are harder to see as you get older. The number of nerve cells in the eye declines, making depth and fine shades harder to see. The iris gets smaller and less reactive too, which is why the world appears even dimmer, or why bright lights on the highway begin to be vaguely alarming after sixty—years, I mean, not miles per hour, though I now drive slower than I did. A change in vision is the first undeniable sign of aging, and starts at forty. The eyes then get dryer; floaters increase. It's external as well as internal. As the facial muscles around the eye weaken and stretch, the eyelids hang away from the eyeball (ectropion, it's called), an effect enhanced by the fact that as the amount of fat around the eye decreases, the eyeball seems to sink further into the skull. Alas, poor Yorick, he is us.

In fact, that's the general surface problem all around, according to a paper from the National Institutes of Health: "Gradual tissue atrophy [occurs] as the mesodermal content of the body begins to shrink; the envelope of the ectoderm becomes too large, and redundant skin folds and wrinkles appear." As for the gradual deepening of lines around the eyes and between the brows, that can be corrected by relaxing the muscles. Hence Botox.

AUGUST 6, 2014

I have decided to grow a beard. My plan is not to shave it off until I turn sixty-one. My wife is against the plan. "It makes you look older," she says, which in turn makes her look younger, or at least as if she is with an even older man. But a beard, I feel, has the charm of stating the truth, of purveying no false advertising on this human package. In any event, the beard is coming in white and grizzled. It does make me look older.

I am on my way to Rockport, Massachusetts, on Cape Ann, north of Boston, to spend two weeks at my brother's house by the sea. I plan to read and write and swim.

On the way, I have stopped in the Adirondacks for a couple of nights to visit Tecca and Al at their place here (Tecca is turning sixty herself this month). They seemed very happy to see me, which I took as a compliment. The last time I saw Al, in the Cotswolds, he was still trying to understand what had caused him to pass out on that bike ride, and why his eyelid wouldn't quite open. Within three minutes of my arrival today, he told me that he has been diagnosed with an autoimmune disease, myasthenia gravis—a chronic (not good) autoimmune (not good) neuromuscular disorder characterized by fluctuating weakness of the voluntary muscle groups (i.e., that eyelid). The incidence is 20 out of 100,000 people, which speaks to the bad luck that can beset you after sixty—eventually it besets us all—but which seems graver in the young. But luck is relative: Tecca mentions an old pal from high school who has been dead ten years from breast cancer. Al is unlucky, statistically, but the friend was unluckier.

The good news is that myasthenia gravis is not fatal, and that it can be managed, even suppressed; that is what I wanted to know first and foremost. Myasthenia gravis occurs in all races, both genders, and at any age, though onset at fifty to sixty is commoner among men. (Al almost made it out of the danger zone.) When a nerve sends an impulse to a muscle telling it to move, a chemical in one's synaptic fluid called acetylcholine travels across the space from the nerve ending to the muscle fiber side of the neuromuscular junction, where it attaches to many receptor sites. The muscle contracts when enough of the receptor sites have been activated by the acetylcholine. But someone with myasthenia gravis can have 80 percent fewer receptor sites because of the presence of an antibody that blocks or destroys them (and which, in an uncompromised body, would attack viruses and foreign proteins like, say, Ebola, which has just landed in New York City as I write this. Is the world coming to a fucking end?). There are a number of treatment options—including plasma exchange and the removal of the thymus, which sound, respectively, futuristic and extreme. The most common treatment is steroids such as prednisone.

"I was on flucloxacillin for my eye, and it actually made things better, but then I took myself off, because I don't want to be on steroids and get all puffy. I need to look into all that," Al said, as if we'd been talking about steroids for the past four hours, when in fact I haven't seen him in nearly two months. I listened as he laid out his plan. I hadn't known what to expect. I had already imagined what I would say at his funeral, as I was driving down. This is the way I honor my friends; this is the way I come to know what I feel for them, and how much I love them, by imagining that they are no longer here. It's the only way I can do it.

I had dinner my first night here with the two of them and RL, a local wilderness guide, and his wife, whose name I immediately forgot, forcing me to refer to her as "my friend" and "you" whenever I spoke to her. If she had been even a little more flirtatious, I probably would have remembered; that is the kind of asshole I am, sometimes, even at my age. The other day Keddy, my old pal in Berkeley, told me on the phone that he had been struggling with a cold for a month, and had been to visit an acupuncturist. "She gave me the treatment, and then said, 'Did I give you the discount last time?' I didn't know what she was talking about." I immediately assumed that she then offered him a sexual favor, that "discount" was code for a happier ending. "Then she handed me the bill and I saw she had dropped her fee by 10 percent for the seniors' discount."

Seriously. I'm sixty years old. What is wrong with me? Though, having been away in Banff, I haven't had sex for a month. A month! I still remember the days of being fifty-seven, when going a week was too much. But now I can stand it for a month. I am not sure this is good news.

Before the guests arrived, Tecca and I had had a one-on-one about Al's condition, and not knowing what to say, not knowing how to bridge the gulf of his illness, I referred to something I had read in an essay in Banff, about the way people react to fatal health news—how some people are able to use the time to make every moment count, whereas others become depressed and can't get over the fact that they are going to die. The trick, according to the story, was to remember that the end is nigh—"We're all terminal, in a way," I said to Tecca—and yet relax about it enough to use every minute we have left, to full effect. Tecca agreed, wholeheartedly. She is surprisingly unsentimental about some issues, and a ball of much about others. But living with illness is obviously easier said than done.

The real question is, what does it mean to live to full effect? How do you know if you are fulfilling your time, or wasting it? How do you know if the novel you try to finish is worth the effort? Would it be better to hang around with your kids, your wife, your friends? Maybe it would be better to work for others? And this is the thing: no one knows. Dr. Johnson knew this. What did I read about Johnson the other day, in Boswell's London journals, I think . . . ? I can still remember what I've read, just not always where. What was his line about sorrow, or grief? Sorrow is the rust of the soul. And regret is the oxygen that makes it.

This is what I think about for hours on end now: how do I make my life mean something? The horizon looms closer now, I don't know how long I've got. None of us do. None of us have much control over our lives, over where they will end up, over how they will end. This is why we are afraid of uncertainty, of the disabled, the frail, the fragile, the needy: they remind us of our own disabilities, uncertainty, frailty. Al apparently told Tecca that if his new affliction cripples him, he'll consider assisted suicide, as many rational people would. I tell myself I would do the same. But in the pinch, who knows? I may hang on to every gram of life I get. Because that is the other part of life at sixty: how you turn cranky when other people waste the little time you have left, like that idiot in the Escalade (a stupid car) who is so desperate to get into the line for the beach parking that she has blocked the road access going the other way, so you have to sit there, and you want to tell her that she is a selfish cow, cutting off your life because she can't stand to wait for any part of her own. Or when I hear the sobering news about Al, how there is also a part of me, a subterranean, nematodean side, the reptilian survivor side, that thinks, amid all the what-can-I-do-and-what-can-I-say thoughts: thank God it's not me.

Al and I drank at least two bottles of wine and most of a bottle of Scotch last night. The next day, recovering, Al read Alan Bennett's memoir of his Yorkshire upbringing until mid-afternoon. I had recommended it and was gratified that he liked it. I mean, look, if we're going to get old, let's do it in full view of one another, and share each other's tricks and pleasures. My father discovered spy novels at ninety-five, thanks to a kind friend. I can't imagine how thrilling that was, what a boon it must have been.

The sum total of my own hangover day's exertions—I'm moving on tomorrow morning, first thing—was a rained-out attempt at kayaking, and a walk to the top of Hurricane Mountain with Al and Tecca's dog, Stanley. At the top I thought I was having a stroke. It turned out to be a panic attack. Not sure why. Maybe it was the hangover.

Tecca said something interesting at dinner tonight, when it was just the three of us: that everyone grows up the same way, more or less, with a few obvious exceptions (my disabled son, Walker, being one), but everyone gets old in their own way—no one's old age is the same as anyone else's. And so we all end our lives with a maiden voyage, a first time at bat. Will you be lucky? Will your health hold through the last quarter of your life? *The Last Quarter*: not a bad title. "It's a window through which you can then see the rest of your life," Tecca said.

It's all a crapshoot, so what crap are you going to aim for? You cannot expect victory. You can only hope for engagement.

AUGUST 8

I had two pieces of toast and a cup of coffee and some yogurt with Tecca and Al in the fresh air of the new clear morning (it had rained heavily the day before) on their screened-in porch. I took a shower in my neatly framed and planked guest cabin, where the day before, lying hungover on the bed, I had studied the timbering, wondering if I could ever copy it.

It was cold in the morning. I could see my breath forming in the air in front of me, just as I could see Mount Marcy in the distance to the far south, where Jackrabbit Johannsen skied so far and so quickly at such an advanced age. (He has been a hero for a long time.) The warmth of the shower water on my shoulders felt so perfect, I tensed my stomach and back to feel it more, to feel it go right into my core, to attempt to save some of that warmth to get me through drying and dressing in the cold, fresh mountain air. I felt lonely and alive and indescribably happy: I was about to drive through an interesting part of the world, going to a place I have visited most summers since I was a child, and known intimately, and therefore loved. My brother, my dear old ally, was going to be there, and so was the Atlantic Ocean, and we were going to swim in it together, as we have done all our lives. Not all my best times have been in a close bond to others, but most qualify.

I drove carefully, but as quickly as I could, across Vermont, through Middlebury, where I saw the glistening grey limestone college, the hope and the future of America, swaddled in money. (Hayley applied there, but said the obvious and overwhelming wealth of the place made her nervous. I felt the same way going to boarding school as a scholarship student, but didn't have the gumption to say so.)

I arrived in Rockport at two-thirty, and immediately went for a swim. The water was sharp and clear and welcoming, semi-rough. Frank and I then drove into Boston to pick Tim up at the train station. Dinner followed. I felt the automatic acceptance I always feel in their company, as well as in this part of the world: I feel that I belong here. Maybe this is just memory, but I am happy to feel it. Robert Macfarlane has convinced me, in the course of my slow progress through his book *The Old Ways*, that when a people follow the same paths for thousands of years, they develop an almost genetic affinity for those paths. My emotional response to the energy of the Atlantic comes to me via the Scots and Danes and Vikings who traveled up and down the coasts of Great Britain, over to Ireland and Greenland, to Iceland, to France and Holland and Spain. But maybe it is my brother's eager embrace of my presence that does it as well, the warmth of a shared life that began with our mutual pact against the physical fury and violence of our mother and the kind but beaten refuge of our father. Then you spend a lifetime trying to escape the pattern of that upbringing. We made that alliance: that has to mean something in the accounting of our lives, doesn't it? I desperately want it to.

I went to bed as soon as we came back. The sheets in my bedroom in the far ground-floor sunroom felt cold and smooth, but they warmed up.

The sun starts to light the sky over the Atlantic shortly after 4 AM. I got up an hour later and wrote a three-thousand-word letter to Hayley. We'd had a slight argument before I left Toronto, about spanking: I only ever spanked Hayley once, a single pat, when she ran into some traffic as a little girl of three, and maintained I had broken the pattern of my mother and her father. But Hayley had memories of fierce verbal reprimands. I was appalled, and so made like a Victorian, and wrote it all out to her.

When the letter was finished I went for a swim in the ocean off the rocks in front of the house. It's a private but tricky place to swim: the pink granite shield of the shore cracks and breaks and boulders down to the water, in a jumble of ledges and ramps and hidden crevices that below the high-tide line are covered with slippery seaweed. The challenge is to get into the water—usually diving off a submerged rock at the precise moment when the waves sweep in, without hitting another rock—and swim out to sea, and then swim back on a wave and climb out again, using the seaweed as a mooring, without getting slammed into the rocks. It's exciting. It requires nerve and a cool head. Going in off the rocks has been my ancient routine with my brother since we were boys.

It was sunny and the ocean looked flat, but the swells were deceptively strong and short, little bullies, and I scraped my right shin badly hauling myself out of the water. I tried too hard. That was my mistake: you have to let the water do the work. But when the waves tried to carry me back into the water, as sometimes happens, I resisted and clung to a rock, and the sea swept my leg across some barnacles. I could spend a lot of time writing about those rocky sea entries, and the times we have done it, and the people we have taught to do it (my daughter and my late father included), and the debates we've had about the best points of entry and exit.

It amazes me how afraid I am these days of stuff I never used to give a second thought to. I stood on the rocks for a long, long time, ten minutes at least, thinking: how will I get back out of the water today, what will my escape plan be if Plan A goes awry? Even moving on the rocks is different now, and Tim confirms this: I used to hop from boulder to boulder in full command of my balance. I used to move like a bird, but now I am a crab.

I swabbed the scrapes with alcohol, to kill the possibility of infection from the barnacles, and then wiped them with witch hazel, to cool things down, and then I took a picture of them with my phone to send to my wife, which last part, it turned out, I could not do (a technical glitch, let's not get started on my incompetence there). Then Tim and I headed off to do some grocery shopping. We got caught in Saturday traffic, waiting for the drawbridge back onto the mainland, after we asked a guy in his fifties in a black golf shirt for directions to the farmers' market and he kept elaborating on landmarks that we knew perfectly well. Finally Tim said, rather irritably, "I know where that is." Afterward, he chastised himself, as I knew he would: "What's wrong with me?"

He thinks he's getting old because he can't remember details, but he lives in Manhattan and works for an investment firm and his mind is full of details and stresses and expectations and pressure, none of which is good for remembering things. His train of thought does wander, and there are details he can't pull up as quickly as he used to. I remember that stage, even at the not too distant remove of two years older: you are still trying to do all the I'm-on-top-of-it things with a body and a spirit that are beginning to understand what it means not to be entirely on top of things. Whereas, even two years on from there, you have no such illusions. You aren't trying to dominate the world anymore, because it has started to dominate you (Getting into the water! How?!). My experience is that once you admit this, you start remembering stuff again.

We had to go all the way to Magnolia to get the groceries because it was impossible to get back to Rockport on the roads full of beach-goers. Tim was clearly checking out his old territory as he drove: he lived here full-time before he moved to Manhattan. This is the happy land where we took holidays every summer as kids, the place where we all came into focus. We stopped in Gloucester at Destino's for subs, the same sandwich shop where our mother used to buy them as a rare treat for lunch on the beach. While we waited for our subs, I watched another family going through much the same formative routine. There are things that don't change for generations, even though the people doing them change.

Then it was back to the house, where I tried to remember how to unfold my folding Klepper kayak. The sailing rig still defeats me. Then another swim before a meal of the striped bass we had picked up at Connolly's fish market. On this second swim of the day, I made it in and out successfully, but took a new route up-rock to get back to the house and wiped out, a complete ass-up-in-the-air alley-oop, onto my back on the granite. But I wasn't hurt. I felt invincible. Invincible! Who knew? Who expected that rogue thought, on this day, at this time?

Afterward, in the outdoor shower that looks out over the ocean at the distant passing boats, I was very proud of my cock, its girth and size. A man again, recovered from my errors and fear of the morning. I tell myself I will never forget this day, and I hope that is true. The shower was part of its sublimity. Sharon Olds wrote a spectacular poem about outdoor showers:

> Crusted with dried brack, dusted with
> sand, shaking from the cold Atlantic,
> hair gristled with crystals, tangled with the
> jellied palps of wrack—just step on this
> slatted rack, pull the iron
> handle of the forged world toward you.
> The sluice courses, down your shin,
> in a swirling motion, milk smoke, the
> silky rush of fresh water, supple and alkaline.
> Lids clenched, you reach for the small
> oil torso of soap, run it
> along your limbs and whirl it over the points of the
> three-point shower star of sex:
> arm-pit, arm-pit, sex. Then the gritty
> dial of your face, lather it, bring it
> under the coursing, and open your mouth,
> stone-sweet well-water,
> and then the head,
> delve it in so the sand around the scalp
> dances like the ions at the edges of matter,

and the shampoo, mild soldier,
take her by the shoulders and pour the pale eel on your head.
   Then feel them going:
salp, chitin, diatom, dulse, the
blind ones of the ocean. Rinse until
it pours down your head like water, the dark
descendant pelf of the land. Now open your eyes—
green lawn, silver pond,
grey dune, blue Atlantic,
the simple fields of God, liquid and solid.
Turn and turn in hot water,
column of heat in the cool wind
and sunny air, squeeze your eyes and then
open them again—look, it is still there,
the world as heaven, your body at the edge of it.

I love that poem. I think of it every time I step under
that hard water in that shower at that house by that ocean.
I am glad I can still remember it, am glad I got to read it.
Maybe this is what part of being alive is about, and why I
can never regret that I was, even if it has to end one day.

AUGUST 11

My morning ritual is always the same. Out of bed, kettle
on, shower, shave, breakfast, newspaper, hearing aids. I've
had the hearing aids for two years, to fix a familial pattern of hearing loss that makes it harder for me to hear
high frequency speech—women's voices, for instance, and

consonants, which define words from one another. (The problem is that the tiny hair cells, called stereocilia, which move up and down in my inner ear to pick up sound waves and change them into the nerve signals the brain interprets as sound, are either damaged or dying. They never regrow.) The hearing aids cost me nearly $4,000: I can Bluetooth them into the TV or my cellphone, I can adjust the volume or redirect their little microphones forward and backward. I still hate the fact that I have to wear them, but they restore my hearing to the point where it is not at all necessary for people who see I am wearing a hearing aid to RAISE THEIR VOICES WHEN SPEAKING TO ME. I want to say, "Look, with the hearing aid, my hearing is probably better than yours."

The devices work, but they are appallingly unsexy. The other day I gave someone at a cocktail party a double cheek kiss, and my hearing aids howled on both sides. I feel like some kind of slightly handicapped dog. But presbycusis, or age-related hearing loss, is everywhere. One in three people between the ages of sixty-five and seventy-four have difficulty hearing; after seventy-five, it's half the freaking population. It runs in families, but can also be caused by long-term exposure to loud noise, by changes in the inner ear, by impacted ear wax and high blood pressure and diabetes, and even by some medications that are poisonous to the sensory cells in the ears.

It turns out the ears, unlike the penis, never stop growing. This is why the heads of so many elderly look like Greek urns, with massive side handles. Then there is the hair growing out of the ears. In my case it seems to be on steroids.

AUGUST 12

Wrote another letter to Hayley this morning. I invited her to come down and visit me, but she is working for the summer and probably can't find the time. I never wanted to spend much time with my parents when I was twenty-one; why would she? Although I have, at least, a slightly more honest and open relationship with Hayley than I did with my own parents. I want to think of my relationship with my daughter as an accomplishment, a real one, something I actually did right, but what are the odds of that? Parental failure is probably an evolutionary necessity, as Hayley pointed out the last time we spoke, to perpetuate the efforts of the human race to become more compassionate. I quoted the Philip Larkin poem "This Be the Verse" ("They fuck you up, your mum and dad/They may not mean to, but they do") and mentioned D.W. Winnicott, the British psychoanalyst who had a humane view of a parent's inevitable failure. Someone once asked him to lay out the responsibilities of a father to his children. Winnicott replied that there are only two. One is to stay alive long enough to get your kids on their feet; and the second is to fail them, because failure, for a parent, is inevitable. A parent's failures are what drive their offspring to try harder, to do better, to figure things out more, and also what drive them to leave their parents and start their own lives and careers and even families. The only trick, Winnicott added, is to fail your children naturally, to enact the inevitable slow decline, to become less and less capable and interesting and compelling, so that they can leave you, and "fail"—if that is what we insist on calling it—on their own. The thing to *avoid*, he said, is failing them by dropping them off an emotional cliff—by crushing them or disappointing them or alarming them in ways they should never expect to be crushed or disappointed or alarmed. Because those sorts of failures are sometimes impossible to get out from under.

Last night at dinner, one of Tim's neighbors said I looked fifty-eight. At sixty, I consider this a compliment. At fifty, I would have been happy if someone had mistaken me for forty, but a mere two years off wouldn't have cut it as a compliment. But now I'm desperate for anything I get. Speaking of which, I have started wearing my pink pants. I've had them since Walker was a baby. I don't know why I have started to wear them now. Because I want more attention? Because I don't give a damn anymore (hence go-to-hell pants)? Because I figure I need colorful clothes to make bystanders realize I am still alive, given the often dark state on the inside? I think brightness is fine, unless people start to mistake me for a stoplight.

And of course there is my handwriting, which is ever more illegible; and my lack of dexterity and balance, a notable decline (I can't do the one-legged thing in yoga class anymore, at all). In solidarity, Tim says it's like his spelling has had a stroke. We were discussing all this while watching Luke, the nine-year-old son of their neighbor, prance over the shoreline rocks. "I've gone from gazelle to blind gazelle," Tim said. He claims he is weaker at the gym, even since his doctor prescribed a testosterone pump to make up for the drop-off in testosterone that occurs about now, chronologically. "But only one spritz a day, on the shoulder," the doctor had warned. "Some guys like it so much, they're up to six spritzes a day in no time."

"How does it make you feel?" I asked. I wanted some myself.

"My, God, I had so much energy! Who needs speed? I was surging along on four and a half hours of sleep a night." He eventually stopped taking it. A few years earlier his doctor prescribed the steroid prednisone to repair a thumb he injured doing burpees. (My brother is the Jerry Lewis of human injury.) "But here's the problem with prednisone: I'd be standing in line at the deli and see the salami in the case and burst out crying. It was the emotional Alps." Last night, on our way back from dinner, he missed his exit on the highway. Par for the course.

Thanks to the letters to Hayley, I now can't stop reading Larkin. I started with "Aubade," his infamous ode to the dark night of the soul, fearing his own "unresting death,/a whole day nearer now,/Making all thought impossible but how?" Larkin isn't thrown by the remorse that the prospect of death brings on ("The job not done, the love not given, time/torn off unused"—a deadly phrase) so much as the "total emptiness forever . . . the sure extinction that we travel to." He thinks it's the nothingness of death that makes us backpedal so furiously away from the prospect of aging, "the anaesthetic from which none come round." But death itself, the actual blackout, will feel like nothing. It's the prospect of missing life I can't bear, and I think the poem actually agrees. On this subject, Larkin was the Shakespeare of his time.

AUGUST 13

Woke up this morning and discovered it was half past nine. Then I realized I had put my watch on backwards, and that it was a quarter to three in the morning. You'd think I might have noticed it was still dark. Then I checked my phone because, after all, I was awake, and discovered Robin Williams had died at sixty-three, having hanged himself by his belt in the doorway of his bedroom. He had been seen last at ten the night before, and according to his publicist had been suffering from depression.

Sixty-three is three years from now, for me. It is impossible to think that I might be dead then, but impossible not to consider the possibility. If it is hard to understand how someone that successful and wealthy (he had had financial difficulties in the past, but according to his lawyer and financial adviser had not been struggling of late) could take his life, remember the intense pain and torture of depression. But his death felt personal, as it seemed to feel for thousands of people who immediately took to Twitter. It was his mental versatility that was so impressive, that and his daring, his willingness to connect any two disparate things that came to mind. His humor seemed to suggest that everything is relevant. Janet Maslin, the *New York Times* writer, once chronicled a single Williams riff that went all the way from an impression of Jacques Cousteau to an invented "Truman Capote Jr." at "the Kindergarten of the Stars," which is a riff on a riff on a riff. He had a movie coming out, one that by all reports featured one of his best performances yet. He had recently checked into a sobriety renewal program.

I still remember the story Keddy told me about being in a newly popular restaurant in San Francisco sometime in the late seventies, I think, back when the Palestine Liberation Organization had organized a refugee camp for 1,500 homeless Palestinians. Suddenly, Robin Williams popped his head in the door of the crowded restaurant and shouted, "Yasser Arafat, table for 1,500!" That says it all for me.

The scripts for *Mork & Mindy* were fifteen pages shorter than the scripts for *Happy Days*, where the Mork character first showed up; the show's writers would simply type in "Robin will do something here" to make up the slack. "He was uncontainable in this unusual way," Henry Winkler was quoted as saying today in *The New York Times*, which seems like an admirable legacy (I can't remember the word for . . . oh, wait, there it is now: *epithet*. Er, I mean *epitaph*. You see what I mean). Sometimes Mork's associations worked, Winkler said, and sometimes they didn't, "but it was always better than anything you've ever done."

I spent an hour or two scrolling through the tributes to his talents—the famous *Mork & Mindy* scene where he thinks eggs in a basket in a fridge are fellow aliens, and sends one into the air to fly away, and then gives it a burial at sea (down the sink) when the egg splatters on the kitchen counter; the scene in *Dead Poets Society* where he urges his students to seize the day ("Because we are food for worms, lads. Because believe it or not each and every one of us in this room is one day going to stop breathing, turn cold, and die"), which is the same scene where he tells them that their sense of being immortal will not last, and shows them the pictures of old boys on the school walls. The photographs are there to suggest that glory is ageless, but Williams's character sees through that: he says that the old boys in the pictures feel "invincible, just like you feel," they too feel they were destined for greatness, just as the new batch maybe feel. And then came the stuff that stopped me: "Did they wait till it was too late to make their lives have one iota of what they were capable?"

So much of what Williams did was admirable, liberating. He seemed to exist to tell us that we should use everything, every scrap we can get our minds and mouths around. *Yasser Arafat, table for 1,500!* Garry Marshall, the producer of *Mork & Mindy*, put a camera on Williams exclusively, in addition to the usual sitcom three, because he didn't want to miss any of his improvisations. He later said four cameras weren't enough, that he should have had five. When Williams came in for his audition, he stood on his head in Marshall's office chair and pretended to drink a glass of water using his finger as a straw.

There are only a few people at a time on the globe who can stand out like that, who can do what comes to mind. Most of them have featured in the world consciousness in the same role: barely moored madman. Before Williams, there was Jonathan Winters. Williams often spent his lunchtimes with Jonathan Winters at the studio's restaurant (no, what's the right word, starts with a *c*? Wait. *Commissary? Canteen?*). Before Winters, there was Oscar Levant, a television hypochondriac who played the piano and complained for a living on the Jack Paar show. ("Good night, Oscar, wherever you are," Paar used to say, after he died.) Levant once claimed the American Pharmaceutical Association had voted him Pill of the Year. All three of them served as our Fool, in the Shakespearean sense, the embodiment of reasoned unreason and unreasoned reason, the pre-rational, pre-Enlightenment, pre-Descartian being who in the Middle Ages was often allowed into the city only once a year, but who was watched closely in case he gave away some sign of the future, of a meaning to existence that the rest of the city's inhabitants, in their narrow, goal-oriented tunneling, had missed.

Williams's background was fairly ordinary. He grew up in a wealthy family in Chicago. He became a comedian because he wanted to make his mother laugh—like John Updike, like Nicholson Baker, that old story. Like the brilliant David Foster Wallace, a writer I could read all day long,

Williams succumbed to depression (he also had Parkinson's), and depression is its own tunnel, its own logic. Their fans measure both men's lives by their accomplishments, and consider them successes. But the expectations of their fans were probably half the problem. As much as I want to judge people by a more compassionate yardstick, the firm and unyielding standards of the doing, accomplishing world are always seductive. But the standards of Williams's fans are not reliable, because Robin is a genius, but also a cokehead; a genius, but a lousy husband. Did his depression mean he was unable to ignore the changeable standards of others? But then what do you rely on to measure your progress? Maybe you have to stop thinking of your life in terms of progress, and simply let it be what it is?

He died at 12:02 PM in a neighborhood called Paradise Cay, a waterfront enclave in the town of Tiburon. Evidently not as advertised, in his case. Strangely—or not so strangely—all the photos in the tributes are headshots. That was where all the action was, after all. That's what we wanted from him: his mind, quicksilvering along.

This morning I helped Tim take the recyclables and the trash to the transfer station, as the dump is known in pristine Rockport. We watched the oldsters maintain order in their lives, hauling their segregated leftovers; they all seem so much older than us, though of course they are only seventy. Then we headed into Bearskin Neck, a narrow strip along the sea in the center of the town, intending to grab a coffee; found a parking spot; briefly discussed the latest trend in Rockport art (copies of old-style Rockport scenes); chatted with a garrulous woman in a shop selling items with Provençal patterns; admired some woven market bags; shopped for a necklace for Hayley in a bead store; and ran into Tim's old postman, a guy who has since bid for a walkable downtown route rather than the driving-centered territory of the South End. "I walk everywhere now, 9.2 miles a day. First thing I did was lose twenty pounds," he said.

"You did not," Tim replied.

"I did. I lost twenty pounds. My doctor, he's younger than me, he told me, if you keep that route, you'll outlive me. And he's forty. I had a woman on my old route, she turned one hundred, and on her birthday I brought her a letter from the president. From Bill Clinton. Because they do that, right? I said, 'You got a special letter today, from the president.' And she said, 'Now, why would he do that, he must have better things to do than that.' And I said, 'Well, it's not every day someone turns a hundred.' And so I think that if my doctor's right and I live to be a hundred, I'll get to buy everyone a drink."

"Oh," I said, "at a hundred you don't have to buy anyone a drink. In fact, after ninety-five, everyone buys your drinks for you." I'm not sure he realized I meant it as a joke.

There was some more chat and then we shook hands, and he said, "Well, I look forward to buying you that drink at a hundred."

"And I look forward to accepting it," I said, only then realizing that he was fifteen years younger than me, that he was humoring me, the older man. "But that's the prerogative of an older man," I said gracelessly, to cover up my undeniable vanity.

We moved on down the Neck while Tim shopped for a belt. I looked at a black leather one, but it was overly Western for my taste, a little too what-the-hell-I'm-sixty-I-can-do-what-I-like-because-no-one's-looking-at-me-there-anymore-anyway, with a buckle the size of a pie plate. You should buy a belt two inches bigger than your waist, and I was pleased to discover that a thirty-eight was too big for me. I even looked at a new leather briefcase, but as with every purchase I make now, I had to do the math. Not the elementary math (your belt size should be two inches longer than your waist: "You want to feel comfortable on the third hole," said the shopgirl, a talkative brunette in her mid-twenties, I guessed, pleasant demeanor, someone I briefly and academically imagined sleeping with—would she? wouldn't she?—until I realized what was going through my head and came back to earth. Even at sixty, the first step of the stairway into hell or heaven, I am deluded enough to be attracted to a saleswoman trying to sell me a fucking belt!). I mean the advanced-class math of *will I make sufficient use of this item in the unpredictable amount of time I have left?* After sixty, that calculation underlies everything you do, whispers away whether I pay direct attention or not. Should I cull my books? Which volumes won't I read before I die?

I wonder if that's what has been making me so nervous: that the unadmitted possibility of death lurks in the atmosphere, undermining everything I attempt? The statistical precariousness of life after sixty is a bit like reading something online: the links in the text are always there, tempting you away from the main story, all those possible exits and byways and roads taken or not taken, hollowing out the confidence of your progress. I find reading online is much more exhausting than reading a physical book, and I can't keep at it for as long, because something is always going on somewhere else in the wings or in the hypertextual background, and so my escape into the story itself is never entirely complete or carefree. Life after sixty may be so nervous-making because something is always ticking away in the background, threatening to take over the story.

So at last we bought that coffee in Tim's favorite coffee shop (latte for Tim, large red-eye for me, which is a coffee plus a shot of espresso, delicious, but also a disaster later for shitting incessantly; as Tim says, "After sixty it's not a question of whether you are going to shit your pants, it's just a question of 'have I?'"). There was the usual cast of summer denizens in the café, including a schlubby guy in his forties in one corner evidently trying to write something, and another, thinner, sleeker guy, hair combed back, sockless and wearing a black linen shirt and white pants, late fifties—the very last, uppermost stop at which any sort of physical arrogance is possible, before one's physical self starts failing and falling and drooping and creasing and shaking and blurring. There was also a woman in her ... probably early forties, very slim and graceful, with high cheekbones and pouty lips and dark, curly hair, and maybe one or two too many tassels on her clothes, bespeaking a neediness—someone who definitely gave me a second look, though what the second glance actually meant was debatable (it barely qualified as visual contact, but hey). Was it because I kept glancing (discreetly) at her? Then I thought, "Oh, maybe it's because you're wearing rubber boots and shorts and an old T-shirt and haven't shaved in two weeks, you tit." Still, it is possible, at sixty, to desire someone in a coffee shop, to want what you see with a sharp pang. It's not that I want anything to happen; as my brother says, it's just reassuring to know that you still experience desire, that you can still think that way. The pang is decisive, and decisiveness of any kind gets rarer, more valuable, like a bar of gold. It is getting rarer as I type.

Which is also a liberation. Doesn't Roth say, somewhere, that that was why he married? Because he was tired of pangs, and just wanted to read the newspaper over breakfast?

I had a dream last night, no, the night before last, that an elegant older woman (older than me by eight years, specifically) wanted to have sex with me, but for some reason, even though we were in bed together, I held back. She was slender and had freckles. Then I had a dream that I was supposed to take part in a public debate but ran out of time to prepare, and showed up late in my underpants and a shirt, pretending to have fallen asleep. I thought, "Well, they won't really care, I wouldn't care that much if someone missed a debate," but then I thought, "Maybe you have a responsibility to people who expect things of you." But the debate was to be held before a group of men, exclusively, including the hapless head prefect from my boarding school the year before I became a senior. I realized that, with an all-male audience, the debate didn't really matter: I didn't want to debate a purely intellectual topic, though I figured I might have something to say, and had even worked out a line of chat, one I suddenly forgot. Afterward (afterward in the dream, that is) I thought, "You should have winged it, moving from topic to topic, as Robin Williams might have." It was an active night.

Johanna maintains that as men and women get older, men start to look more like women, whereas women start to look more like men. That is the illusion, but the truth is that both genders devolve toward the middle, into genderless physical collapse. I find Johanna lastingly attractive, and admire her skin, which is a good thing, because I doubt I will ever touch new, unknown skin again, in an intimate way, now that I am no longer chronologically viable. I could be wrong, but I doubt it. And here's the kicker: many days I am not broken-hearted that I won't.

I tell myself that if my own marriage ended, I would not marry again, as I've said: I tried that. But there's no predicting. Afraid of dying, of what's coming down the road, I feel I ought to hedge my bets and behave, but there are no set rules, no matter what the self-help books say, and posterity doesn't give a shit how you live. Everyone over sixty feels the public prejudice against them, feels vaguely compelled to be sedate and proper, but everyone wants to smash the prejudice as well.

In any event we finished our coffees and left the café and drove home in our separate cars (there had been two loads to take to the dump). It was raining, and the weather was getting worse, with floods all over Boston. Safely back at the house, I could see spray off the crashing waves from my window. Tim took a nap and then read his detective novel (he's on holiday). Later we went to dinner and a movie (*Guardians of the Galaxy*). On the way home, we stopped for a drink, and ran into a gay friend of Tim's who confessed his sexual proclivities are becoming more and more specific, in his case nipple-related. Half an hour of mutual nipple gazing, nipple licking, and nipple tweaking is nothing (I was prudishly shocked and fascinated by his account), because nipple play actually works, is surefire. It's the only erogenous zone left that never fails him, the corner store that never closes. These tactics are just as arousing as ever, he says, "but it's not exactly intimate." That may qualify as the understatement of the millennium. I would guess he was in his late sixties.

"Not tender?" I said.

"Yes. Not tender."

That's what I fear: that over time, newness and tenderness will evaporate. But why should that be so?

AUGUST 14

I'm still addicted to websites that list people who are turning or have turned sixty this year. The first site I ended up at today turned out to be an outdated version, which claimed that Bill Murray, the actor, had just turned sixty. From his photo he had lost a lot of weight, and seemed closer to seventy-five. I admire Murray, I admire the way he has chosen to do strange movies, and follow his own eccentric route through celebrity and wealth and even decay, and yet the fact that I looked younger than someone my age whom I admire was . . . *extremely uplifting*. But then I discovered he's not sixty at all, he's sixty-four if he's a day, and decided that it was uplifting, instead, to be younger than Bill Murray, because those crucial four years mean that *there is still time*.

Jay Leno is sixty-four, and is the lead photograph in the online list of famous people over sixty. His skin is clear but the color of my dining room table, and he has the sense of humor of a tractor. His humor has always struck me as a comedic form of porn: the old reliables, over and over again, for a quick spurt and nothing lasting. I would not include Leno in my Sgt. Pepper's Lonely Hearts Club of people I want standing behind me, and so his agedness is of no interest to me. I would include Letterman in my club, for his daring: he's sixty-seven.

Cybill Shepherd is a bit heavier, still resolutely blond, and she is not ashamed of her body, judging from the picture, in which she reveals both her lifted cleavage and her slightly heavier underarms. She's sixty. I still remember her on the diving board in *The Last Picture Show*, in which she played a spoiled Texas teenager. This makes me feel better.

Morgan Fairchild at sixty has very large breasts and a face that looks forty. Morgan Fairchild has no effect on me, so the news that she is my age has no effect on me, beyond some bewilderment that anyone would be willing to use that much filler in their face. I used to disdain plastic surgery as undignified, but my views have softened since I realized how much the younger world wants to deny the older world any longing or lust or vanity—in other words, since I turned sixty. Still, Morgan Fairchild looks like a genetically modified nectarine on two genetically modified grapefruit. She's the entire fruit basket.

Ed Harris, sixty, a good if disorganized actor, looks more weathered than I do.

Stevie Wonder could be seventy, or thirty-five. He's sixty-four. Not comparable.

Richard Branson is sixty-four too, and looks younger, but he is worth billions, and so I don't really count him as a real person. I could never be what Richard Branson has made of himself, so the comparison is irrelevant.

Tom Petty, sixty-three, like most of the musicians on the list, looks younger and more relaxed than I do. They all look as though they are having a dashing time: Petty,

Peter Gabriel, Huey Lewis (who looks stupider than he did when he was younger), Peter Frampton (whom I associate with never having grown up), David Cassidy (who still looks thirteen). I envy all the musicians. Okay, not Cassidy.

William H. Macy Jr. is sixty this year. He looks about as old as I do. He also looks smart, and is smart, and a great actor, so the comparison is reassuring. Bill Hurt is also sixty. I was his age when he appeared in *Body Heat* and *The Big Chill* and ninety-one other movies; I thought he was older than me for sure. But Hurt is an alcoholic; I am not—at least not entirely. He looks lost. From this I salvage a twig of nasty superiority.

And Dr. Phil, aka Dr. Phil McGraw, is sixty. He looks like a well-tanned hedgehog. He is not in my basket of mental friends and heroes and examples I want to admire.

But this is the thing about these lists: they're everywhere, and they've been going on for years. On the Internet, the machine of eternal life, you can find last year's list, and the list from the year before that: John Goodman (sixty-two, looks younger), Christine Baranski (the boss lawyer on *The Good Wife*, sixty-two, looks fifty), Roseanne Barr (looks seventy, is sixty-two), Liam Neeson (sixty-one, but looks ninety, strangely), General David Petraeus (forty-five, and we know why, heh heh), Mickey Rourke (Jesus!). Putin—mad Vlad, deranged horse-riding nipple freak—is sixty! I didn't think of him as such a strong man after that (thinking to myself, "Hitler was only forty-nine when he invaded Poland"). John Tesh (who at sixty-two looks like a Malibu Barbie of fifty) and, of course, David Hasselhoff, from *Baywatch* (who looks twelve or ninety, depending on the angle).

I think of most of these people as existing entirely at the behest of the public eye, as being the product of the perceptions of others, almost nonexistent without an audience to make them manifest and real. I'm content to be an introvert, and find some satisfaction in private pleasures—in writing and reading and drawing. I wish I could make music (my most lasting artistic regret).

I just don't want the daily, hourly, moment-by-moment reminders (pain, sag, creak, ache, wrinkle, weakness, put-downs, exclusions based on age) that I am getting older. If not for that constant chorus, I could exist nicely, on my own, working and reading away. I'm not saying I want to be alone—hermits have nothing to write about—but I think I have the capacity to survive it. Getting older does actually seem to be a matter of becoming more and more solitary, until you are finally completely alone for the final implosion. I keep coming back to this.

Johanna has arrived for the weekend. It's a miracle she is here, because we (three sixtyish men) all misread her twenty-four-hour itinerary, thinking she was *arriving* here at four-thirty, instead of *taking off* at that time in Toronto, which was the actual case. We went to dinner at the Market on the shore of the Annisquam River, the tidal estuary that makes Cape Ann a cape. I can think of few more pleasant places to live. My wife would like to live on a river. I wish I could give her that dream.

Later, as we arranged ourselves in bed, I asked if she wanted to have sex, but she was tired from traveling; we read for an hour instead. I didn't hold it against her, as she doesn't either when the shoe is on the other foot. The sexual dance becomes more delicate after sixty; it's more susceptible to offense. But it endures anyway. The ease of our connection is its charm, the comfort and the familiarity. That thought didn't often cross my mind as a young man; now it's a mantra. Age doesn't matter when you know each other. Johanna's mother has a nice phrase: when you close your eyes, you're all the ages you've ever been.

Twenty-six years, as of September 9, we will have been married. A sturdy round of applause is in order, especially given what we went through with Walker. "It's such a year of milestones," Johanna said, as we lay in the dark. She sounded astonished. "You scattered your father's ashes. Your sixtieth birthday. Our twenty-fifth wedding anniversary, and our thirtieth since we met. Hayley's twenty-one, her imminent departure. Walker's eighteen. Cathrin and John getting divorced."

Their split still isn't formalized, but last weekend, Cathrin and John and John's family gathered to divide up the contents of their 160-year-old cottage. *Cottage* doesn't do the vast original structure justice, and certainly doesn't do justice to the way John's mother made it unlike any other place, with her discerning, adventuresome eye. Cathrin had laid it all out on Facebook, which is where I saw it: the bed where Johanna and I took turns sleeping with Walker (in that gorgeous place, where his silent appreciation of silence and a clean breeze and cool, fresh water were so obvious), the screened-in porch, the cabin by the water where the kids spent the night, talking to one another in their sleep, the daybed, the tin cut-out lampshades imported from Mexico, the birch-bark canoe hanging from the ceiling (I helped mount that). The smooth old table where I drank so much coffee and ate so many meals and read so many newspapers and talked, talked about everything, thinking it would last forever. Cathrin asked me what I wanted as a keepsake, and I said the little yellow painted metal jug, but one of the sisters wanted that to add to her stockpile. In the end, I got the corkscrew. It's a big, wooden, sturdy corkscrew that always got the cork out. I like it.

As I write this on the rocks of Rockport, the sun is going down and a large storm cloud is gathering to the southwest. The bugs are coming out. One just bit my foot. It itches. At the cottage in Muskoka, there was always a tube of anti-itch cream. Cathrin was the queen of anti-itch creams. I have these details stuffed into my head. What did I do with them? I wrote them down. I have at least done some form of duty to them. This is what it was like: this, and this, and this.

When I was younger, I never thought these phases would end. But the cottage is gone, that stage is finished. A new stage has to begin.

SIXTY

I forgot the other step in my morning routine of daily preparations for the shrinking stretch of time I have left: sunblock. I managed to scorch the back of my neck yesterday, and my nose is always ready to turn an ever deeper shade of red.

Incidentally, the nose doesn't stop growing either. But as one's muscles shrink and one's skin loosens, the tip gets bigger and the rest of it droops. This in turn encourages rhinitis, steady sinus drainage, and the need to clear one's throat. The taste buds, nine thousand in all, begin to atrophy, along with one's sense of taste; salt and sweet go first, and that begins at sixty. The sense of smell begins to diminish, on average, at seventy. Have I mentioned dry mouth? Receding gums?

Have I noticed my voice rising? On occasion. That's because, as I rush into my seventh decade, I am losing muscle mass in my throat. Paradoxically, women's voices deepen as they age, for the same reason. Then of course there is the skin. I have new wrinkles at the corners of my eyes, under my ass, on my ass, on my cheeks (my cheeks! there were no wrinkles there, no vertical striations, a year ago!), on my forearms and at the crook of my elbows, on my neck where it joins my chest, under my ears, and, of course—my inheritance from my mother—under my eyes, where I have more bags than I know what to do with, an entire matched set of luggage. I could carry my groceries home in those bags. My skin is beginning to soften and thin, yet at the same time stiffen: the surface of my flesh, the stationery of the soul, the main advertisement of who I am, the billboard of how old I am. Sometimes, with enough moisturizer, I can shave a year or two off my face, but I can't hide the backs of my hands, where new age spots show up like lost cousins, suddenly and in their entirety and with no warning at all.

There are many reasons for all this. The body produces less collagen and elastin as one ages: collagen makes your skin tough, and elastin makes it flexible. To make matters wrinklier, the fat layer under the skin decreases. Sweat glands decrease in number; heat gets trapped, one overheats—except when the decline in subcutaneous fat makes one cold and prone to turning the thermometer to ninety. And then of course there are the traitorous pigment cells, the melanocytes, which drop in number but increase in size, causing my skin (this started happening to me a few years ago) to look both more translucent and more covered in brown spots (which get larger and larger, in a process of hyperpigmentation) or white spots (hypopigmentation, due to a breakdown in all the sun-exposed areas), to say nothing of purpura, which are the bloodshot veiny stretches. I don't even like to look at the flanges of my nostrils, which have become a public gauge displaying the number of glasses of wine I have consumed in the previous decade. And let's not talk about skin tags. In that regard, I resemble a well-traveled steamer trunk (in body shape, too). Who the hell knows what causes them?

Out-of-control cell production? They seem to attract one another.

All of this, of course, is displayed on the largest organ of the body, the skin, which has a surface of about five to six and a half square feet, and which regulates the excretion of metabolic waste.

In women the metamorphosis is, if anything, even more dramatic, as the decline in production of the hormone estrogen represents a decline in the rate of cellular renewal. The skin of both genders suffers a reduction in capillary blood circulation velocity—even my fucking blood is moving more slowly!—which in turn makes it harder for the skin to maintain its hydration, its strength, its elasticity. All of this comes about as a result of the bad boy, oxidative stress, brought on by exposure to UV radiation and environmental pollution, which in turn induces the production of free radicals that make the skin cells age, become blotchy, lose their pigmentation, and swell. Depending on one's lifestyle—and I have yet to stop drinking—the normal physiological functions of the skin can decline by 50 percent *by middle age*. In other words, there is no need for anyone beyond the age of thirty to feel any superiority in this regard.

AUGUST 16

The world is in a dire state, and I am leaving it to my children. Gaza; Ebola; that asshole in Russia, and his unconscionable support of those other assholes in eastern (or western)

Ukraine who unintentionally (?) blew a passenger plane out of the sky and then intentionally covered it up (unforgivable). All of this I am leaving to Hayley and Walker.

I have had no response to my letter to Hayley re the failures of my fathering, as of yet, though she says she is "drafting a reply." Drafting a reply! Fantastic. She is also in a dither about which computer to buy, now that hers has blown a gasket, three years after we bought it. My ten-year-old SLR Pentax camera is irreparable because the Ricoh corporation doesn't want to store the parts. Age is unpopular on all fronts these days.

I worked yesterday morning for five hours, then took a break for a swim with Tim at Cape Hedge beach. Yesterday's storm had abated, and the day was as clear as a diagram. But the water was so cold I had to get out after two submersions. This has never happened to me before. My legs lost their feeling, my balls were going to drop off, my head ached every time I went below the surface. I must have made some noise in response to all this. "That was very entertaining," two middle-aged mothers said, laughing, as Tim and I hobbled back up the shiny, low-tide mirror of the beach.

Then Tim reprimanded the lifeguard for being on his phone while two kids played in the admittedly big waves. "I'm just texting my father," the lifeguard said. "Great," Tim said to me afterward. "I can see the headline now: *Two children die while lifeguard texts his father.*"

Cranks, aging cranks. Although I have to say, Putin and his ilk have been pissing me off for years.

This morning I spent a few hours reading through articles that have been written for the *Huffington Post* blog about the turning point, the great age turnstile, of sixty. Let me repeat that. The *HuffPost*. Blog. About Turning Sixty. The main case against talking about getting older is that everyone does it, and a lot of it sounds alike.

There were dozens of posts in the file, and they were all more or less the same, and all tagged with the same delusional keywords: *Aging Gracefully, Feeling Fabulous, Older Middle Age.* "The sun pours in over my shoulder as I write this," began the best one, written by Claudia Ricci, a professor of journalism and literature at SUNY Albany. She aimed straight away, as so many of us do when we're writing about getting older, to demonstrate that she was still extant, still in the experiential here and now, which is obviously the best thing aging has going for it: what's the alternative? To her greater credit, Professor Ricci then asked herself why she felt she had to say something profound, given that sixty was just a number. She recommended meditation, and I found myself nodding to that point, too. "In the midst of mental chaos the breath is the steady and single reminder that we are here today, and if we're lucky, maybe tomorrow." But there's an even starker question beyond that: is there something more interesting to look forward to in the course of aging than meditation and passive being-in-the-world? Hardly anyone takes that one on, at least in the *HuffPost*. Because that answer might be more discouraging, or at least more unpredictable.

A woman named Annie Stein, a self-described "Author" in Los Angeles, according to the rigorous labeling system of the *HuffPost*, pointed out that—apart from her plans to throw herself a big-assed party, which seems to be the most profound thing many *HuffPost* writers do when they turn sixty, because *they deserve it*—"there is something about knowing that if you are blessed . . . in 10 fast-flying years you will be 70. That, my friends, is shocking because, let's face it, no matter how many times we say that 60 is the new 40, 70 is old no matter how you slice it."

A lot of the sixty-year-olds in the *HuffPost* approached the milepost with the thought of eating well. We've been eating well here, albeit plentifully: soft-boiled eggs with avocado and sautéed habanero peppers with an English muffin for breakfast; watermelon and feta salad for lunch, with a little olive oil and balsamic; grilled skirt steak marinated in olive oil and tarragon sauce for dinner, a bottle of wine I had given Tim in 1994. (It turned out to be a little thin, as we still were in 1994.)

All of which makes me realize how old we are not. Because eventually, making the present memorable matters less and less, and you have to confront what has faded away. It all does fade, and that terrifies me. I remember the afternoon my father resigned himself to the fact that he could not beat the decay of his end. He was sitting in an emergency department, hooked up to an oxygen tank for the first time in his life, because he'd been short of breath during a visit to a doctor who'd been dressing a wound on his leg that wouldn't heal, and the doctor had sent him to Emergency and then called me. When I found my old man, he was chilly, so I lent him my parka and the toque I was wearing. It was all an accidental thing, and then it was no accident at all. He never came off the oxygen. I saw his resignation in the sag of his shoulders the moment I walked into his berth in the ER, in the hang of his head and especially in the look of fear and hopelessness in his eyes. I took a photograph of him then, but I threw it out; I couldn't bear to see that strange desolation on his long, kind face. But the darkness of getting old is never the message of *HuffPost*'s sixty-is-great! crowd. They don't want to upset anyone, because that wouldn't sell, and their relentless exclusion of all but their most optimistic thoughts makes their prose read as if it were written by imbeciles.

In the last *HuffPost* blog I read, "60 Perfect Reasons You Should Be Psyched about Turning 60," the first reason was: "You can enjoy the freedom to dress down when you want." Number 30 was: "You appreciate a good laugh and seek them out." I was afraid to read beyond that, in case Number 31 was "You can also make a good argument for blowing your brains out the back of your skull."

This is the level of discourse at which we approach the existential conundrum of age. What that discourse lacks is any respect for the state of being old, and a blind and foolish faith that if we just keep living as we were living, everything'll be fine. I am as guilty of this as anyone.

Eventually, I shut the laptop and took a walk down the rocks to the sea. The Atlantic Ocean was still there, regardless of how old I was, and it was a lot older. You can watch it for a long time. The tide comes in, goes out, and the swells hit the rocks harder or more gently. The sea keeps doing this while we live and die and live and die and live and die. It exists and lasts, but we never do. The sea insists a life is not much, a passing speck in time. But it also says, because a life is just a passing speck in time next to the sea, a life should try whatever it is it wants to try. Because it doesn't matter, because a life is at one level just some particle that washes in and washes away, so you should give it a go anyway. You might as well write whatever you want to write. You might as well try.

AUGUST 17

I go swimming in the salty sea, and then shower and forget to put some flattening goo on my hair when I go out, with the result that the chiffon of disappearing hair across the top of my head stands straight up in the air, as if I'm sitting on a live high-tension wire. Which is never far from the truth. The hair: it's a sad, sad story. Yes, I have already chronicled my bald spot, my fringe, and my haircutter's efforts to maximize what's left, but time alters hair. I am among the three-quarters of men who do not display significant baldness until the age of thirty; unfortunately,

I am among the two-thirds of men who have significant baldness by the time they are sixty. And of course I am almost entirely grey, but a lot of people are: the chances of going grey increase 10 to 20 percent with each decade beyond thirty. I know at least two sixty-plus men who dye their hair shoe-polish brown.

The heart changes too. My aging heart has a harder time speeding up than it did when younger, and it can't pump as fast as it did (hence my maximum heart rate, roughly 160 beats per minutes, which was 200 beats per minute when I was twenty). The walls of my arteries are thicker and less flexible, while the space within the arteries has expanded slightly as well. As a result, they can't relax as well while the heart pumps, which in turn leads to increased blood pressure. One way to measure stress is to measure how fast your heart pumps prior to exercise; this is not good news for me, given that I feel stress when I open the fridge door and the mayonnaise isn't on the top shelf. Perhaps I should stop worrying about that shit. Tell me how. In any event, the heart pumps a million barrels of blood in a lifetime, three supertankers' worth. I wish I hadn't given mine such a hard time. About 40 percent of deaths of people over sixty-five are heart related. By the age of eighty, men are nine times more likely to die of chronic heart failure than we were at fifty.

AUGUST 18

Gorgeous crisp day: everything is lethally clear, there is no haze to gauze up the view. The shore of Thacher Island, half a mile out to sea, with its two granite lighthouses, one dating to before the Civil War, the water (that silver blue), the boats—sailboats, two-masters, like fresh laundry hung in a stiff breeze across the blue water—are as clear as they can be. Lobster boats, working men.

Tim left early this morning. I cried, privately, as his car disappeared down the driveway. Pathetic. Then I drove Johanna to the airport, getting lost both ways. Before we left, standing in front of the hallway mirror, Johanna said, "I'm the least attractive person I know." It's her new ultra-short haircut that made her say it, and it's the opposite of true, but the fact that she sometimes believes it upsets me, because I don't know how to convince her otherwise.

At sixty, I'm both more compassionate, more aware, more tolerant, and less so, because I have less time.

Then she put on her Birkenstocks and we were off. I call them her "German farting sandals," which makes her laugh. I can still make her laugh, really laugh, and that is still the highest compliment she can pay me. "Lose the beard," she said as we said good-bye at the airport—that solid hug, that three-decade-long embrace, which could be hotter, but could be colder too. "Then you can have sex." A joke. I laughed. But I was tempted.

Panicked by my sudden solitude, I wasted the morning answering email. In the afternoon I went roller skiing—7.5 miles along the shore to town and across town and back up the shore. It's a beautiful way to see the sights.

SIXTY

Unfortunately, the brakes fell off the skis, so I skied sans brakes. I realize I looked like a complete lunatic—aging, bearded, beet-red, sweaty face, checked boarder shorts, black cross-country ski boots, tape on three fingers, poling away at the asphalt on three-foot-long wheeled skis in the sweltering middle of August in a seaside town.

There is something about the sheer endurance of keeping at it—pole, pole, pole, pole, hurry up a hill, turn carefully down, pick up the pace, hit a stride, realize that you could be going faster, and push yourself to go faster, until you have to slow down again. It's never simple, this confrontation with the physical self. Half the time I hate it. My father must have had a different, less judgmental approach, because I think he actually enjoyed physical exercise. "I suppose it does me some good?" he once said to me, of his daily calisthenics, not quite asking a question. "I'm sure it's essential," I said.

Afterward, I went swimming off the rocks by myself for the first time this trip. Even if the tide is low and the ingress is easier, you have to be more careful than you would naturally be, deliberately, painstakingly, almost fussily careful, because you are alone, and no one can save you but yourself. You have to grasp the rocks by hand as well as place your feet carefully, because the consequences of an accident could be serious, even fatal. One slip, bang your head, fall into a roughish sea: that could be the end. But I make it in and out, and then I stay out for only ten minutes before going back, two and three times, into the deeper water, because I have to—because I cannot waste this chance to be self-sufficient.

AUGUST 19

I have been reading Winnicott, the late British psychoanalyst, on solitude, by way of Adam Phillips, the still-extant British psychoanalyst. The great thing about Winnicott's view of solitude is that he sees it as a virtue, sees the capacity for solitude as a positive trait, not as loneliness or a shortcoming. This is training for the oncoming solitude, right? I mean, it has to be: that's what aging is, a gradual thinning of the crowd.

Winnicott says that to be able to handle solitude, you have to have been mothered by someone who lets you be alone, without requiring that you be aware of their needs at the same time; they neither abandon you, and make you afraid, nor hold the gift of solitude over your head, reminding you of their own.

But how often does that happen, as a child or as an adult? Because we internalize our early relationships, we carry the flaws of them with us for the rest of our lives. As a result, we're confused and stymied and panicked by our own solitude—asking either, Where is Mummy, why is she not here? or How is Mummy, is she upset that I've gone? What you want instead is to be alone in her company, safe but not indentured. That has to be the primary responsibility of a parent: to create a form of sanctuary where the child can be him- or herself, alone but not terrified, alone but not obligated for the gift of that aloneness. A place where the child doesn't have to respond to anything else but what he or she is thinking about.

Later on, in adolescence, some psychoanalysts believe, this relationship with the self and the mother-figure is transferred to the teenaged body, but the problem is the same: how can one live with oneself, with the solitude of one's being, without freaking out or feeling obligated? When I was a teenager and a young man, I relied on my body for my sense of self: it told me what to do, who to be, who I was, what I could be. But then what happens when you get old, when your body starts to break down? What sort of a self do you have then? You get old, your body starts to dissolve. In bits, in parts, joint by joint, rocks grinding themselves against one another. Suddenly your old companion, your body, your original watchful but forgiving mother, abandons you. Then what do you do? In what safe and contained space, in what sanctuary, do you enact the third unlinking, the third solitude? That's the question. I suspect it has to take place in the sanctuary of one's own mind.

AUGUST 20

Can we speak briefly of the urge to pee? I realize that the bladder becomes less elastic and stretchy over time, that its maximum volume may decrease; frequent urination is not, as the writer Henry Miller once opined, a sign of higher intelligence. The more wretched your bladder is, the more likely you are to suffer from kidney disease.

My father was down to 25 percent of his kidney function by the time he died; it was probably kidney failure that killed him, given the slow but steady pace at which everything else was slagging him. I probably have that to look forward to, this solid knowledge that it is not going to end well. How does one handle that? Be thankful that it hasn't happened yet, and hope for the best?

And this is the thing: the decay all starts way, way, way earlier than anyone realizes. In two-thirds of us, the weight of the kidneys starts to decline in our thirties, which in turn affects their filtration rate. The changes are first noticeable in women: their urethras shorten, and the bladder's lining become thinner, which decreases the ability of the urinary sphincter to close fully, thereby increasing the risk of incontinence. Pregnancy (muscular stress) and menopause (loss of estrogen) don't help. In men, neither does the enlargement of the prostate gland, which can block the flow of urine and lead to kidney problems. A waterfall of badness erupts once these systems start to misfire and lose discipline: lack of estrogen leads to atrophy of the vaginal mucosae (hence the dreaded dry intercourse of later life). Things start to even out, and men and women become at least more physically equal in our breakdowns: the risk of cardiovascular disease is lower in premenopausal women than it is in men, but after menopause the risk balances out. Not that I wish this upon any woman. But at last, in gradual mutual weakness, we really are in it together. Testosterone decreases, probably because of changes in pituitary function; the drop in testosterone means decreased hemoglobin, leaner body and bone mass, possible memory changes. You pee yourself, baby, but I can't remember that you did.

I know how I feel about other people's wrinkling skin (it doesn't make me like anyone less), but I know how I feel about someone seeing my own: terrified. Lots of older women of my acquaintance get irrationally breathy at the sight of a younger man's unsagging chest, visibly lighten in the presence of young confidence. We seem to need to see elasticity, unless we can find our way to not seeing it, to hiding it with tenderness or experience. But we are wired to describe our declines as declines, as wanings from perfection, and that's a recipe for unhappiness. If you doubt me, read the National Institutes of Health's descriptions of the aging body, written for the general public: they are all couched in terms of decline, not in terms of change; it is all wrapped up in the chains of less, not in the ribbon of natural functional alteration. We keep trying to be perfect, and we keep failing, and aging is the readiest and most available manifestation of the decline, and of our own resistance to it, and thus the easiest thing to blame. So we focus on the decline. So the breasts become more *fibrous*, and *sag*; so the blood flow to the penis *slackens*, decreasing the lastingness and reliability and even hardness of the erection, making it harder to ejaculate a second or third time. People have sex into their nineties anyway.

Some guy in a bar the other night asked me how often men masturbate at sixty. I said four times a week, hypothetically. "I cannot tell you how heartening I find that answer," he said. He was in his late thirties.

"But do you fantasize about a sixty-year-old woman?" his pal asked.

"Not always," I said. "But it can happen. It's often people from my past."

"And how often can you have sex, theoretically?" he asked.

Ah, I replied: that's a harder question to answer. How many partners are we talking about? How many sessions, or how many penetrations? Are we talking about how many times *do* you have sex, or how many times *could* you have sex, if the person you are with was available and willing? At my best or my worst? Rested or tired? Are you including the sessions of masturbation as well as intercourse? Finally I said four. Times a week. Hypothetically. A sixty-one-year-old friend of mine told me he recently made love to his new girlfriend seven times in twenty-four hours. That seemed healthy. But it was the beginning of the relationship.

Some studies suggest that frequency doesn't decline until about seventy-four years of age, although older people do start to complain about "painful sexual positions." Of course, that's provided you have someone to have sex with: in one study, 78 percent of men aged seventy-five to eighty-five reported having a spousal or other intimate relationship; only 40 percent of women did. But a recent multi-generational survey of men and women between the ages of forty and eighty reported women more likely to rate sex as an unimportant part of life, and more likely to report it unpleasurable. (I'm not suggesting this is their fault.) There are lots of surveys in which respondents claim they have sex into their nineties. A study of healthy residents of a California retirement home found that 62 percent of the men and 30 percent of the women over eighty had had "recent" sexual intercourse; among a group of Swedes, 46 percent of men between the ages of seventy and eighty reported orgasm at least once a month. My guess is that was all the opportunity they had.

There have always been outliers, as far as humping oldies go. Chateaubriand, the great French statesman, so loathed his aging face after sixty that he refused to sit for his portrait, and repulsed the amorous advances of a young woman when he was sixty-one because he couldn't trust why she loved him: if she wanted a father, he was filled with horror, and if she wanted a lover, he couldn't believe her. He was a very unhappy dude, a master of the universe who couldn't bear his own decline, and so blamed the world for its decadence.

But the Duc de Richelieu, who was born to a seventyish father, himself had a mistress, and spent his evenings with whores, at the age of seventy-eight. He made no apologies for the wizened stick he was by then: he liked hearing the prostitutes' secrets. He married again when he was eighty-four, and got his wife pregnant, and then cheated on her. He was still having sex when he pegged out at ninety-two.

Victor Hugo was an enthusiastic voyeur well into his later life. He had only half a dozen sexual encounters a year between the ages of sixty-three and sixty-eight, but after that he loosened up: he still rarely carried out an entire sexual act, but loved looking, fondling and kissing women's body parts. His notebooks from the summer of 1870 list twenty separate encounters—sometimes three a day. At ninety, the cellist Pablo Casals was still taking a morning walk every day, playing the piano for an hour and a half and the cello for three. By then he'd been married for ten years to one of his students, a girl he met when she was twenty and he was eighty. Picasso (two kids when he was past sixty), Rodin (no time for women until he was seventy), Henry Miller (married a twenty-nine-year-old Japanese woman when he was seventy-five), Tolstoy (liked a romp with his wife after a morning of riding, at the age of seventy): all dogs. The writer Edmond de Goncourt was one as well, but it tormented him, even at the age of seventy-one, when he decried his powerlessness over "the spermatic beast" within him.

We know more about male artists, but there have been lots of female writers and artists and scientists who defied the sexual expectations of their age as well. The point is, sex, health, and mental activity seem to go hand in hand. I think that's good news.

Sure, there is the possibility that sex will mean less as I age, that I will simply want and need it less, that I will be liberated from its clutches. But that will also mean giving up on its lively democracy, its reassuring equalizing, the way it makes us all the same. I'll miss that.

It's Thursday. This morning I went swimming at a local quarry with three fourteen-year-old girls and their nine-year-old brother, the children of N., a friend of Tim's here in Rockport. She told me to show up with a car at eight-thirty in the morning. I thought I was the driver for her and her kids. When I drove up, N. said, "I have a phone call to make." I was babysitting on my own.

But there are worse companions. It was a hazy, warm day; the kids wanted to go swimming at Steel Derrick, a private quarry on Cape Ann. You have to be a member, and to be a member you have to be a resident of Rockport. As summer residents forty-eight years ago, we used to swim there and get kicked out, like clockwork. You still get kicked out, but this potential rejection did not bother the kids, so I pretended it did not bother me. "The trick is to get in and out before the guard arrives," they said. Fresh intelligence to me.

We drove in silence broken only by my inane questions: what grade are you in (all but Luke heading to high school), where are you going to high school (private Catholic girls' school), and so on. We had to pick up one of the girls at her house; her dad is a partner at a private equity firm, and owns more than one house on the water, reportedly for tax reasons. Private equity firms have entire departments dedicated to minimizing the taxes of their partners. I wonder if this is why Mitt Romney had no feel for the middle class.

We parked the car by the side of the road in a wooded lane at the top of a hill, then took a path through the forest.

There were signs everywhere indicating that we were tres-passing: *Maybe you assholes will now understand This Isn't Yours* STAY OUT. But the path was well worn. We made our way to the back end of the pit and slipped into the water.

It was gorgeous. The girls immediately began jump-ing off a succession of higher and higher ledges: eight feet, twenty-five feet, thirty feet. In between were long swims across a seventy-foot-deep quarry filled with rain-water. "You're all good swimmers, I presume?" I'd asked. Luke wore a life vest, but he paddled along. He wouldn't jump, though I tried. "It only looks scary," I said. Then I climbed up the second cliff and looked down and decided against the second jump. It looked scary. "Come on, just do it!" Sophie shouted, but I didn't have the nerve. I felt like their father but realize I must have looked more like their grandfather, especially with my beard. This did not offend me so much as it made me feel altered. I'd like to be a grandfather. Johanna and most of her female friends can barely wait.

The girls paid a great deal of attention, all their non-talking time, in fact, to adjusting their bikinis, making sure everything was covered. They seemed to inhabit varying stages of innocence and knowingness, and spoke quietly in a clutch, so as not to be overheard. Mysteri-ous. They got cold quickly, and we decided to leave. I was ashamed of not having taken the leap, and was ashamed of my excuses no less: oh, it might hurt my back, oh, it might reinjure my plantar fascia. Oh, it might frighten me. Jesus.

This too is what I despise about aging, this caution, this flurry against the world's possibility, the wings of safety enfolding every chance, removing it from consideration. Everything cooling off.

But you can still take kids swimming. On the way back through the woods, along the green-mossed path, Luke began to talk. He has a guileless, endless curiosity, but wrapped in the manner of a sophisticate, a kind of smooth patter he seems to have picked up somewhere, though no one knows where. The other night he and his mother and sister had come to dinner with Tim and me. Tim was out grilling the steak, while Luke bounded from rock to rock to rock like a spaceman in zero gravity. "When you're finished grilling, why don't you join me on the rocks?" Luke said to Tim, and I thought, "How old are you—forty-two?"

On the path in the woods, he had other things on his mind. "So," he said, "how do I put this—are you, ah, gay like your brother?"

"No," I said, "I'm not. Just Tim and Frank." Pause. "I'm married." (So are they.) I felt a bit defensive, having spent six weeks pretty much on my own.

"Ah," Luke said. "I wondered. Because when you said an old girlfriend of yours used to go to St. Joseph's, I wondered." Pause. "Did Tim ever date girls?"

"Yes," I said, "he dated a few." Pause. "But he always kind of knew he was gay, from the beginning."

"Ah." The world was still new to Luke, still the exploding ball of memorable details and strange human behavior and inexplicable longings and sometimes lovely physical sensations, like swimming in soft quarry water. I had noticed he had started to suck his thumb when he didn't go off the cliff. He was never going to go off the cliff today; he is too young for that, as I am too old. I like that bond.

"It's just the way Tim is, like I'm the way I am, and you are the way you are." I was trying to be truthful without sounding like it was a big deal. Whereupon Luke launched into a long and complicated explanation of how he and the girls all knew each other. "It all goes back to when my mother was pregnant on the beach with Tristan, my brother."

"No, with me," Sophie shouted back. She was ahead of us with her friends, but had been listening.

"I'll show you the pit we go to, that has no guard," I said as we drove home through the hazy air, and took them to the pond up Landmark Lane, where I went with Johanna and Tim last Sunday, where I found I do not swim with quite the knifing ease I used to, though I can still go a long way. None of the kids even turned to look at it, so benign was it compared with their great leaping quarry. They're at the other end of time. They should make me sad, but I was inexplicably thrilled to be in their company.

In the middle of rereading David Foster Wallace's commencement speech to the 2005 graduating class of Kenyon College, "This Is Water"; it has been republished as a book by Little, Brown, one of those little texts with a sentence or two per page that stores put by the register. I'm a little embarrassed to be rereading it: it was a bit of an anomaly for DFW, a speech rather than a piece of writing, and has become immensely popular and oft-quoted, occasionally by imbeciles, which in turn makes me ashamed of my persistent affection for the essay. I found it on the bedside table of my room here at Tim's, as if I were living at a hotel, with a lip gloss and some face cream in a tube beside the bed, and everything in working order. That's the great thing about his place: everything actually works. Being sixty, I like it that everything actually works.

While I'm in the middle of reading the essay, Tim calls. He's back in New York, at his job (stockbroker), full of dread. He has been engaged in an email war with a competing broker, with whom he is supposed to be sharing an account, but he fears the new guy is trying to grab it all. This is Tim's interpretation. "He probably resents having to share an account with someone in his late fifties who's in 'harvesting mode.'" He means someone who is heading toward retirement, reaping the benefits of a life's work of building contacts.

"What do they call the other guy's end of things?"

"The seeding phase."

Emails had flown back and forth; there were accusations of poaching, denials, backstabbing. Standard corporate practice. Tim called a friend, a former broker, and she said, "Tim, you're just making the transition to nongrabbing," which wasn't putting a particularly fine point on it.

"I want to transition to non-grabbing," he said now, on the phone to me. "Grabbing doesn't help society and it doesn't help with your life as a human being. It insulates you, but it doesn't provide any meaning. On my deathbed, grabbing isn't going to help much."

I almost, but do not, say, "on your deathbed, nothing is going to help much." His fracas reminds me of the passage in "This Is Water" in which Foster Wallace points out the foolishness of worshipping material gain—and pretty much anything else, as well. "If you worship money and things—if they are where you tap real meaning in life—then you will never have enough. Never feel you have enough." The same is true for revering power or youth or intellect—not insidious in themselves, but deeply and dangerously unconscious, as DFW points out, "default settings," in his now-famous phrase—

> . . . the kind of worship you just gradually slip into, day after day, getting more and more selective about what you see and how you measure value without ever being fully aware that that's what you're doing. And the so-called "real world" will not discourage you from operating on your default settings, because the so-called "real world" of men and money and power hums along quite nicely on the fuel of fear and contempt and frustration and craving and the worship of self. Our own present culture has harnessed these forces in ways that have yielded extraordinary wealth and comfort and personal freedom. The freedom of all to be lords of our tiny skull-sized kingdoms, alone at the center of all creation.

A year after he wrote those words he took his own life.

I don't know if that was the world DFW couldn't escape, that Robin Williams couldn't get out of. (I realize they both suffered from depression, which is a world that doesn't need reasons.) It has been my world, the world of my brother's co-workers, and it has a lot going for it— smart people and an attention to detail and comfort and pleasure and great food, for starters. It's a lovely place to have visited. But I don't want to live there for the rest of my time, because nothing compels you to get free of it, and it is in trying to get free of the prison of the self that life gets interesting, at least at this late stage. I hope I have explained as much to my daughter. Have I? Something for her to consider.

I have been reading *Benediction* by Kent Haruf, an excellent and readable book in the transparent style of Hemingway and Cormac McCarthy, about an old guy who has been told he does not have long to live. To my relief, Haruf believes there is no escaping being obsessed with the end of your life. In Italy, at the end of June, Bob King, my mother-in-law's boyfriend, tried to make the world conform to what he believed would make it happy. He insisted Joanne drink Campari, even though she doesn't like Campari; she wanted what her daughters were drinking, the more contemporary and delicious Aperol and prosecco, but prosecco and Aperol did not reflect Bob's conception of the dolce vita in Italy, circa 1973, back when he was in the pink, rather than the grey and the white. Made me feel for him, to want that much to be right—a hopeless cause for anyone. He was uncomfortable in the van: he couldn't sit on the left side, because his arm got sunburned; he couldn't sit on the right, because his face got sunburned; he didn't want to sit in the middle, because he didn't like the middle. I can hear your objections now: "C'mon! He's ninety-four! He's allowed!" Which is true. But I bet he would rather be allowed to be what he can be, rather than what he is supposed to be, if he could convince himself to make that choice. That's the big default setting, the real rat race—"the constant, gnawing sense of having had and lost some infinite thing," as David Foster Wallace so beautifully put it. Maybe the infinite thing is the chance to be who you actually are, in all its complications, in full fragile need, without regret or apology or even complaint.

All this is racing through my brain in the upstairs bar of Short and Main, a restaurant in Gloucester, Massachusetts, where I am waiting for a table for one. I prefer eating at the bar, especially when I am alone and have no intention of talking to anyone. I make a little introductory conversation with the woman next to me at the bar, purely out of politeness. She had ordered white wine and bourbon.

"Is that good?" I ask.

"It's supposed to be," she says. "I've never tried it."

"I have a friend whose mother drinks white wine and Coke, swears by it. Probably the same principle."

"I'll let you know."

"Please do. You never know when you'll need to switch from gin."

She laughs. Then her boyfriend glides up, gives me the sort of look you see on faces when someone's infant fills its diaper on a plane. A stiff competitive puff blew through me and waned. "I might be old," I thought to myself, "but at least I am not the guy who can't stand his girlfriend making small talk at the bar with an older guy." I turn back to reading DFW and taking notes, fretting vainly that people will think I am a pretentious git for doing this in a busy bar. I'm just waiting for a table. The place is crowded mostly with younger people in their late twenties, but upstairs, in the so-called jazz bar, the cadre is older. I notice that sort of detail all the time now.

The younger crowd seem to think they have all the time in the world. I keep thinking of what Johanna said last spring, about how, in her thirties, she thought her fifties would be her heyday, a time of coasting. "It's not coasting at all," she said a while ago. "It's knife-edge all the time." Her heyday, as noted, was her thirties, "when I was interviewing celebrities and traveling to LA, but I never noticed because I had to be back to look after Walker's appointment with the physiotherapist." Live your heyday when you can. Life may not slow down into a becalmed and lovely retirement, into a pool of torpor and gentle fellow feeling. It may just keep racing by, and leave you breathless.

I eventually get a table downstairs, at the kitchen counter, looking into the inferno where my dinner is being cooked. I chat with my waitresses, a Portuguese woman in an elegant red chiffon floor-length skirt and a black top, and a thinner American in a short print dress and black sneakers. I consume half a dozen Damariscotta oysters, two glasses of Verdicchio, a radicchio and endive salad with pecorino, shrimp baked in a wood oven in a white bean sauce, and some ginger ice cream. Excellent. *You choose what to worship in the world.* As I leave, I hand the woman next to me her orange jacket, which had slipped to the floor. A last act of chivalry, and then into the night! These are my adventures at sixty.

But coming down the stairs, the young busboy, laden with dishes—eighteen at most—offers to let me go through the door first. I demur: God knows why, that's an old man thing to do. Then I say, "Age before beauty." I now realize someone once said it to me when I was a young man.

"That's a good one," he responds.

"It's an old one," I reply. "Maybe too old to use."

"And there you are, not looking a day over thirty," he says, to which I reply, "Shut up," mock irritated. Yes, that's definitely an old man thing to say. I must stop saying it.

AUGUST 23

Back from a long, fast ride around the Cape and Eastern Point on my new second-hand all-carbon Orbea. I traced the remnants of East Coast American vacation capitalism— enormous houses, vast fortunes. I don't think those mansions have as nice a view as Tim's place, where I am looking at the tide racing in to the right. It moves so fast some days, reminding me of how quickly I must move now. But I passed some gorgeous gardens, and a lot of snobs. People actually gave me shitty looks for being so presumptuous as to ride on their seldom-traveled roads.

I biked up to what I was pretty sure was the Eastern Point Yacht Club and asked some woman, "Excuse me, but what is this place?"

"It's a club," she said. Preserving the mystery, I guess.

"Oh," I said. "Like the Eastern Point Yacht Club?"

"Yes," she admitted, somewhat shamefacedly. It was the high point of my day.

I used to sail there, go to dances as a teenager. Pretty girls, girls with money. They didn't have much time for me.

Then I passed through Brace Bay, which is . . . private? There are signs everywhere that say private, private road, but are they really private? Privately owned? Private-equity private? Gated neighborhood private? Or just we-say-this-is-private-to-keep-codswallops-like-you-out-of-here private? I biked down all the roads marked PRIVATE, but no one said anything, they just looked at me like I was the Ebola virus on a bike.

Now I'm back, cooking leftover chicken and drinking rosé. Tomorrow I'm buying some cod. My brother lived alone here for twelve years, winters included. I don't know how he did it. By 10 PM, I have locked all the doors. But every night the rumbling automatic ice-making machine in the freezer scares the crap out of me, when it drops a new load of ice. It sounds like someone forcing the screen door open.

AUGUST 24

Spent a few hours at the beach reading the Sunday *New York Times* and sketching in between refresher dips in the surprisingly warm Atlantic. It's impossible to describe how completely satisfying it was, reading, a little eye work, some physical exercise. Luke's parents were on the beach too, but I was just as happy not to have to talk. I was drawing my feet when Luke walked up and asked me if I was drawing my feet. "You really should come over and join us," he said in his nine-year-old Park Avenue manner. I said I would before I left, and he took off, distracted by his sisters.

Earlier, I had been sketching an old woman on the beach, an entire generation older than me. She was eighty-eight, her daughter informed me, proud of the fact that her mother still walked into the water on her own. Her skin had zero collagen left: in her eye-encasing glaucoma goggles, she resembled a sack of skin that would burst through its bottom if it got wet. All her mass was hanging low off her bones, and every striation, every one of a bezillion soft, fine, adjacent wrinkles were arranged in the same direction. Not ugly; fascinating. Lucian Freud would have painted that skin.

I had lunch with Emily G., a Radcliffe publishing course graduate I taught for a summer in 1983. I was twenty-nine.

She was twenty-two. We weren't romantically involved; I simply respected her judgment, even then. I noticed she was on Facebook about two weeks ago, and that she happened to be near Rockport. We met in town for lobster rolls, and she immediately informed me that she had been separated from her husband, a failed musician, for three years—an act that had cost her half her savings and half her pension from working twenty-five years at a big famous corporation. She's fifty-three. "I do feel that the men I meet who are in the same position I am seem more lost, more drifting. They have always been one thing, and now they can't be that thing." Whereas, she says, women like her have had to reinvent themselves all along, and so are better prepared for big changes such as divorce and getting older. She's dating three men currently—one for sex, but he's a Republican and therefore politically undesirable; another, a scholar and physicist, with whom she wants to sleep but who has never been married, and is therefore emotionally suspect; and a third guy, whose insurance business, alas, is being undermined by the Internet.

"Which one has the most money?" I asked.

"Well, that's the problem with all of them," she said. "None of them really has any money."

After lunch, we ran into a bad busker on Bearskin Neck, and she said, "I have to get away from this music."

AUGUST 25

As I'm pruning Tim and Frank's roses, with my head in the

thorns, a branch manages to pickpocket one of my hearing aids. Where it is now is anyone's guess. It's strangely upsetting—the potential cost (they may still be covered by the warranty against loss), but mostly the loss of detail, that connection to the hear (pardon me) and now.

On the beach this afternoon, as the day winds down, as the last sun-worshippers play out their time—it's like an Eric Fischl painting—I finish Haruf's *Benediction*. A line at the end reaches into me, about the dying old man: *They swabbed his mouth with water and spread balm on his lips.* Instantly, I wish I had been able to do that for my father, but I was in Argentina, and missed his death, as noted. I can hear my mother's voice, her exact tone: "All you ever think of is yourself." Her most powerful cudgel. Now he is gone, and I can't make it up to him. He's gone. I miss him—not emotionally, not grieving anymore, just physically: I miss his presence in a room, his physical company. Sometimes, when the robin in our yard comes back in spring, I wonder if it could be him. Or perhaps it would be more accurate to say I wish it were him. I don't have anything I need to say to him. I just wish he were here, wish I could show him one more time that I am here with him. I imagine this is love.

It would be unbearable, of course, all these losses—my father, Tecca's father (he was a good guy), Al's mother, Cathrin's aunt, the children growing up and away, the dog aging, our habits crisping into age-hardened rinds—but then I look down the beach and see some kids crouched on the sand by the edge of the sea. That ancient scene, where we got our evolutionary start, where the human race ate oysters and clams and grew a forebrain, the act of discovery enacted over and over again by the water that threw us up onto the world. Those brown bodies against that pale sand and that blue water and that bluer sky: always there, every year, every day, trying to find again what brought us there, what keeps us there, what we leave there. I felt a bit better. The sea and the kids and the roll of it all, the gulls dipping down into the sand, reeling up, screeching; parents on their cellphones, walking in circles; the small girl with the yellow sweater and her sandals in her hand, staring at the water, hunched over like someone thinking, a statue of a human thinking; and the glisten of the wet sand reflecting the sky and the brown rocks; and the tongue of the sea reaching out to taste us; and the venturing ships so far out on the horizon, bringing us God knows what that we need and don't need; and Luke, I can see him, crouched Vietnamese-style, knees akimbo, digging in the sand, shaping the sand, shaping whatever he can. This is what childhood should be: the children safely under the eye of their parents, sitting at the top of the beach, but free to explore, without feeling guilty, down to the water, down to the edge of adventure. It's only later that the stakes get more serious. The squat military sand fort, low and flat and bombproof, of another little boy, and two stout women with old Rockport legs, that quivering, massy, bewildering flesh, admiring it. "Made by Matthew," written in the sand with a twig beside it. Luke's orange bathing suit. His blond hair. The young woman with the blithe figure in the green bikini top and the pink bottom—separates, they fetchingly call them. And of course the waves on a continuous break at various levels across the entire mile-long beach, not crash by crash anymore but a constant passage, the sound of time leaking out steadily. The boy who built the fort is wearing a white golf shirt and red and blue board shorts, and is taking two steps and a skip along the beach, two steps and a skip. Don't we all?

All this goes away. It breaks my heart. But at least I saw this: I knew this. I wonder if I will be able to remember it. I have to draw it, write it, describe it, somehow put it into my hand and my fingers and my brain and my body. Maybe that way I can keep it with me until I don't need it anymore.

AUGUST 26

On my last day, David Wilcox drives up from Arlington for a visit. I haven't seen him in ten years. He's fifty-eight now, retired from teaching psychiatry at Harvard and a string of hospitals in Boston, cataloging his late brother John's brilliant paintings, a lifetime of work. John and David Wilcox grew up in Dennison, Texas, and so it is to Texas that David is now returning more and more, first to create a museum for his brother's work. He tells me he spends most of the rest of his time reading. Lately, he's been working through Pliny the Elder, the *Naturalis Historia*—thirty-seven volumes of observations and information about the world, the precursor of the modern encyclopedia. "What I have always loved about Pliny's work, and I've only read selections," Wilcox says—we bought some eggplant Parmesan subs from Destino's, and we're eating them in the kitchen of Tim's place, looking out at the water—"is it has its own bias. The Heisenberg Principle prevents any observer from not creating some effect on what is observed. And yet at the same time it is this earnest—albeit from a Roman Empire grand view—attempt to report on the world."

In the dedication, he tells me, Pliny lays out what turned out to be his motto: *Vita vigilia est*. "To be alive is to be watchful." He wrote the thirty-seven volumes at night, after days spent reading and observing. It was in the details that he found the divine.

Then Wilcox had to leave. We made plans to hook up again before another ten years passed. You have to pay attention.

I leave tomorrow at 6 AM. A straight shot home.

AUGUST 28

In Montreal to help Hayley move into her new apartment for her last year of university. Terrance the Boyfriend is helping (they aren't living together), as are Ben and Iain, the two males among her four roommates. Such an arrangement would have been impossible in my day, in the allegedly liberated 1970s:

someone would have slept with someone else and ruined the karma. Iain is a geographer and data-mapper, enrolled in Canadian studies. Ben, a talented pen-and-ink artist who graduates in the spring with a degree in East Asian studies, is on his second reading of David Foster Wallace's *Infinite Jest*. *Infinite Jest* is a brilliant novel, a modern work of genius. But at sixty you seriously debate reading it: is the dwindling time you have left worth expending on such a novel? Even a brilliant novel? *War and Peace* is more established, definitely proven goods. But Ben makes me want to read *Infinite Jest* again anyway. If it can move him to that much commitment, it might move me to the same. And that's what I long for, something to commit to, something to make me feel that the time I have left is not being wasted.

Hayley offers me a room for the night (one of her female roommates has yet to arrive, and the whole flat is spacious and clear and organized), but I decline: I don't want to impose and, frankly, I feel out of place even among these gracious young men and women. I don't process information quickly enough, I feel too established, too parental, too *old*. Not that I don't admire the apartment: it's a classic third-floor Montreal walk-up, with lots of light and new appliances and space (also unlike the 1970s). We haul furniture from Hayley's old flat—which has now been diagnosed with black mold, and is occupied by friends with ultra-cool names such as—I'm sure I have these wrong—Asia and Tsara and Bazarra: congenial, studious, scholarly, sexy. Very nice company. But I fear I try too hard to be approachable, friendly, Dadlike (or is it non-Dadlike?)—being "awkward," as they would say: a concession to age, to time, to their natural grace and my flapping, gradual collapse. Then Terrance and Iain and Ben and I haul giant spring-loaded couches up the two flights of steep stairs to the new third-floor apartment. I can hold my own strength-wise, but I am puffing like a calliope. Naturally, I think it's lung cancer.

I booked a hotel room, and then headed back to have dinner with them all, and then decided to stay in the apartment after all. How often will I have the gift of the company of so many bright young men and women?

Anyway, Hayley and I had had a great talk on the way to Montreal as the broken rear-door alarm on the car beeped for five hours straight. We discussed her growing sense of the narrowness of most ideologies, whether they are political or sexual. There are ideas, and then there are realities. Sometimes they are not the same thing. I'm pleased she came to this on her own. We talk about Terrance, and his plans—he's studying abroad for his second semester—and gingerly, ever so gingerly, as if I am swallowing hot coals, I inquire about their plans as a couple, of which there are none, though they are fond of each other. I realize none of this is my business anymore. I never had such a conversation with my parents; it was unthinkable, given my mother's habit of viewing any interaction I had with women as basic criminal activity that would lead to a) masturbation and b) the instant pollution of my soul.

IAN BROWN

220

We also talk about my beard, which Hayley thinks makes me look gaunt. "I don't know why a beard would make you look thinner," she said as we listened to the Dixie Chicks.

"Probably because it makes my face look longer," I said.

She encouraged my efforts to keep a diary of turning sixty. The way to write it, she said, is to write true things, and forget about trying for the *HuffPost*-style self-help manual, "which would probably be more commercial." But since she deemed it a good idea, I was encouraged. Then she curled up into an impossible pretzel of long brown limbs and fell asleep in the passenger seat, despite the relentless beeping. I think this might be heaven.

Back from Montreal. Within a day of moving in, Hayley has fixed up her room more than I ever have one of mine in sixty years of life on earth. She has the great talent of being well organized. The older I get, the more I understand how crucial that talent is.

I headed home, but not before brunch at a hip place on Saint-Laurent that specialized in traditional Quebec breakfasts (I had kedgeree) with Hayley and Terrance and tall, leggy Lauren (one of Hayley's roommates and close friends) and Lauren's tall, large-headed, and very nice boyfriend, Nick. Nick and Lauren are aiming for different cities, and so are breaking up after this weekend; it's rational but sad, yet again unlike the 1970s. Terrance's parents are slightly younger than me. His dad, though balder, is a young-looking fifty-eight, just retired from teaching gym in Sainte-Agathe; his mother is the head of infection control for a Laurentian hospital and looks to be the same age. But in spirit they are more youthful: they had been to an Alouettes game the night before, and were attending an

Arcade Fire concert that evening. I can't understand the lyrics of Arcade Fire, even when I can make them out.

It broke my heart to leave Hayley behind: I miss her presence, and I miss the effect her presence has on me. In Montreal, I got up early each morning and walked the neighborhood, reading the paper, drinking coffee, sometimes even writing (as I am now), waiting for her and her roommates to wake up. Alone, basically, but sustained emotionally (in this case by my encounters with my daughter) until the next bout of solitude. (This is the pattern that has always worked best for me—a revelation that finally penetrated my basalt skull in my late fifties. For years I fought it, thinking I had to be more social, and less naturally introverted, until I was too tired to fight it anymore. So aging has its upside.) Not to say that raising children is not a harrowing and thrilling adventure, but maybe a grown and now-independent child, like a grandchild, is an ideal amount of love and loving. She does not need me in any crucial way anymore, and so I have the cherished status of the much-appreciated extra helper—a guy who is around if she needs me. I am happy to play that part. It's one of the best in the play, if you ask me—generous but not coercive, needed but not needy. She has her own life now, which is why being with her pals made me feel not unwanted so much as optional. I might have offended Iain when I remarked how confusing and somewhat repressive I find sexual politics these days—that while the endless rules about what is and what is not consent protect young

women, they also remove the need for any personal judgment and integrity on the part of both parties.

I averaged eighty miles an hour on the way home, frus-
trated by the inconsistent pace of the other cars on the
highway. I bought a bag of Pep mints, ate half of it, until
nauseated (I fear I have diabetes), which in turn necessitated
twenty minutes in a gas station bathroom. Get used to this.

When I reached home at six, I found Johanna working at the dining-room table. She was welcoming but
distracted by the upcoming Toronto International Film
Festival, which is throwing her life as a film journalist into
its annual tunnel-visioned tizzy, and by a gruesome deadline on a book she has agreed to write, as a named ghost,
with Mark Towhey, Rob Ford's former chief of staff, which
is due in a month. I don't know why time seems to pass
so quickly, to be in such short supply. We thought about
going out to dinner, but after a glass of wine I was much
too tired, and we ordered takeout Indian and watched television. It's one of my favorite things to do with Johanna.
We take our dinner up, and we watch good television, of
which she is an excellent judge, and we talk about what we
see, and how it's written, and why. I sometimes fear the
habit is deadly for the writers in us, that *Breaking Bad*, as
good as it is, will never be *War and Peace*. That doesn't stop
me from watching *Breaking Bad*.

Then the routine of life as a couple kicked into gear.
Johanna asked if I was mad. "You seem mad," she said. I

didn't think I was, but you never know who you'll end up resenting because time keeps passing faster than you can manage it.

SEPTEMBER 4

The hearing aid clinic. The usual baffling wait for an audiologist; nobody ever speaks in the waiting room, probably because we're all there to have our aids adjusted so we can hear clearly again. I report the aid stolen by the rose bush, and it turns out I'm still covered for the loss. Two weeks to replace it. They give me a loaner, a less sensitive earpiece than my original. I'm shocked by how much less I can hear with it. My hearing is not improving—why did I think it would?—but neither is the rest of me.

Recently I had my photograph taken at the newspaper, to be positioned at the top of any columns I write: I look like an aging Soviet boxer. A deaf Soviet boxer. Not helped by having returned at lunch to see Howard, my barber. Howard said it is still too soon to cut the tuft on my upper forehead. So it still looks like I have a small tropical oasis above my eyes in the vast desert of my balding skull.

SEPTEMBER 8

And then the dentist. But also a drink with someone who wants to be my agent. Someone new. A new agent at sixty? Extricating myself from the old one would kill me, of course, so it will never happen. But it's nice to be pursued.

I can tell what sort of a day it will be, for the most part, as I round the landing from the second floor on my way down to make coffee at six in the morning. Through the front hall, out the window beside the front door, across the street and down the way, I can see the light from the rising sun in the trees. If the upper limbs are lit, the weather is fine. This is the first thing that gets me out of bed.

Email is no way to start the day, and neither is reading the newspaper anymore. The one makes me homicidal, the other suicidal. Poetry helps, if it's good poetry. A few paragraphs of a good book. Today it's a piece in *The New Yorker* by Nathan Heller, the short story writer, about whether elite universities are good for the soul. It makes me wish I had taken my own university career more seriously, or had been more independent in my studies, or had been less scattered; in other words, the piece has exactly the opposite, de-inspirational effect of the one I had hoped for.

Last night, I spent a couple of hours or more talking to an ambitious feature writer from the *Toronto Star*, who'd asked me for a drink to talk about starting a non-fiction book club, but who actually wanted to know "how to learn" to be a better writer. I felt like a fraud. I told her to write about anything that made her afraid, so she would have something personal at stake. Much easier to say than do.

Now that I can see into the trees, it doesn't look like this is going to be a particularly nice day.

Today, on the way to work, I started thinking about G., who once tried to steal L., an old girlfriend. This was more than thirty years ago. I was driving down Spadina, imagining him berating me to a group of colleagues at work. Such a thing never happened, but it seemed real enough, because pretty soon I was kicking his head in, in my mind. I did not do it unprovoked, of course; he started it. In my fantasies, I am still a gentleman.

I thought these mini-psychoses, these fully imagined fantasy slights, would fade with age. Apparently not. However, I did almost throw my neck out, twitching and pulsing in the driver's seat. I am sure I am not the only person in the city working out a thirty-year-old insult as he drives, but it feels as if I am. That's the brain for you.

I've been reading about the brain as it ages. But because my brain is aging, I can understand very little of what the neuroscientists are trying to say.

Reading the neuroscience of getting older is like consulting the oracle at Delphi: the outcome is set, there is nothing you can do, beyond not smoking and eating properly and exercising and having sex. Oh, and avoiding stress, which is not good news for me.

One of the most prominent theoretical schools of thought on brain development—and they are all fairly theoretical, given that we know virtually nothing about the brain on a neuron-by-neuron basis—rests on a multi-year study done in

Scotland. The study found that the overall outlook for the state of your brain in later life depends on how healthy and active your brain was when you were eleven. I'm not making this up. That would be, what, grade five? Miss Wilkie's class? I loved Miss Wilkie's class. I discovered books and writing and learning in a new way. I also developed a crush on Miss Hugman, who became Miss Wilkie's sister-in-law, with the result that Clark Stevens and I went out to Fairview Mall (alone) and bought Miss Hugman a service of the china pattern for which she was registered, with money we raised from the class. It was all quite an adventure. I felt alive, mentally.

In any event, if you were good at eleven, brain-wise, chances are you'll be pretty good in later life, or at least that your brain will last longer before it fades away, as most brains eventually do. And what determines how good you were at eleven? "A favorable early life environment." Well, great. If you have a screaming, violent, alcoholic, and otherwise traumatizing parent who caused all-round stress, thereby boosting your brain-shriveling cortisol levels? Not so good for your grey cells later on, old buddy. But maybe Miss Wilkie was the antidote to that.

It's a perfect day: sunny but cool, my favorite state. My neighbors, renters, are puttering in the garden. The dog is asleep on the sofa. The Norway maples, sometimes called Schwedleri maples, are coppery brown now; I can see one filling up the upper half of the dining room window, above the honeysuckle.

The neuroscientists are such stark perfectionists. The brain, they never tire of telling you with a sniff of I-told-you-so, finishes developing—are you ready for this?—at twenty-two. It manages to stay at that peak of function for about six years, then begins to careen downhill, picking up speed as it goes, for the rest of one's life. I am not exaggerating.

The parts of the brain that begin to deteriorate first are those involved with "executive control," oh Jesus save me, functions such as planning for the oncoming future and "task coordination." This is stuff that seems to happen in the prefrontal cortex, which was the last part of the human brain to evolve, the part that let us plan for the future, thus distinguishing us from, as a geneticist once told me, dogs. But it's the first to go! Hilarious, really—nature's ultimate revenge on the shithead humans. The executive control functions are also the last to develop. The human brain, in other words, is a sadist, taking away what it had just given to you. Which seems to be the pattern of life itself, in many cases.

Then there is the sad story of episodic memory. Episodic memory is the system, if in fact it is a system, we use to recall events, to place them in space and time, to give them shape and details and scenery. I still remember Miss Wilkie in class, for instance: tall (I would say six feet, but I was four foot eight at the time), slim, dark brown Olive Oyl haircut, forthright but merry voice, a quick sense of humor, and an unparalleled ability to explain things clearly and kindly. She was *kind*. That was new. She called on me, and I was an enthusiastic-enough student that I longed to be called on. I read *The Yearling* in her class. Miss Hugman was shorter than Miss Wilkie but less aunt-like as well. Mr. Walsh, who was even shorter and ginger-haired, was always flirting with her, but she had chosen another man, and this gave me secret pleasure. I still remember the way Miss Hugman reacted to that wedding gift: her hand to her always-smiling mouth, her faint proud shock that her students (she taught us geography, in French) had figured out how to buy a registered wedding present, on our own. Two boys, at that.

That's episodic memory. I still remember the play-room at the back of our house in Montreal. If I wait long enough, I can bring back the bright orange Naugahyde seat cushions on the stools at the counter on the playroom side of the pass-through from the kitchen, and the matching armchair. I can still recall the bright colors of the linoleum floor tiles in the kitchen, and the lighter, more pastel-ish tiles in the playroom. I can still remember the clock over the door to the dining room, and the black rotary-dial wall phone beside the door, and its phone number, Oxford 5-5382, and the playroom, when it was still a summer storeroom, and I can remember climbing up on the work table and hammering at the window that was there before they built the pass-through, because my mother had banned me that day from the kitchen for making too much noise (drumming on some saucepans while she spoke on the telephone. She spoke for ages on the telephone. I guess she was lonely). I must have been . . . four? Three? Then I fell backwards off the table. Knocked myself out, I think. Not good. Never good. I don't remember that.

This is episodic memory, the memory that creates the stories that make you who you are, narratively. But episodic memory begins to decline at the average age of twenty-seven. (The research is always that precise, though of course reality never is.) In other words, that diminishment already afflicts the people who think of me as over the hill, though not as much as it afflicts me.

I was on FaceTime with Hayley this morning when Johanna wanted to show her some flowers in the backyard, via my laptop camera. I said I wanted to disconnect my backup hard drive first. I could hear one of Hayley's friends saying, "Why does he have to do that?"

And someone else in the background said, "They're old people."

We are. But even Hayley, who is twenty-one, is getting closer to the age when her brain will begin to stabilize, and stop growing . . . a thought that for some reasons upsets me more than my own decline does: I want her storehouse to be even fuller than mine was; I want her to be more confident about the usefulness of its contents. (Because it's all useful; you just have to have the confidence to use it. Did I remember to pass that along?)

I keep thinking of the way Simone de Beauvoir begins *Old Age*, her brilliant and interminable book on the subject, by quoting Buddha, when he was still Prince Siddhartha, and liked to sneak out of the palace his father had locked him inside. The first time Siddhartha went out, he saw an old man hobbling along the side of a road with a cane. Siddhartha was astonished. He recognized the old man instantly as his own future. "It is the world's pity that weak and ignorant beings, drunk with the vanity of youth, do not behold old age! Let us hurry back to the palace," he tells his charioteer. "What is the use of pleasures and delights, since I myself am the future dwelling-place of old age?"

Which, if you ask me, is a little fatalistic, but I am not Buddha. But if we are all in this slide together, eventually, perhaps there is some way of accepting the slide—of not mocking it in youth and of rolling with its good side when we are the sliders. I keep thinking of how much I gained by slowing down and taking my father as he was, rather than as I wanted him to be, as was also true with Walker, my disabled son. But until it actually happened, I was mere impatience.

SEPTEMBER 17

On the train to Ottawa, for the opening night of a play Emil Sher has written based on *The Boy in the Moon*, my book about Walker. It promises to be a rather bizarre experience, watching someone's enactment of our lives based on words I wrote and interviews that Johanna and Hayley gave to the playwright.

I'm still reading about the brain. It's frightening. From our mid-twenties on, we begin to lose up to a point a decade on something called the "mini-mental state examination." It's a thirty-point test—arithmetic, motor skills, language—the kind of test they use (later) to assess dementia. A three-to-four-point decline is considered clinically significant. So the forty years between twenty-five and sixty-five are a serious slide, no matter who you are and how well you're doing.

Instead of fearing it, and therefore denying it, and belittling it, maybe this inevitable decline is worth our compassion, or at least worth taking into account as we get older. Of course, I never did: I was in full denial too. Everyone knows it happens, and we all express our impatience as people get slower. Now, if I miss a word, people actually slow down and speak louder, as if I am a mental cripple. But I treated my elders the same way. I couldn't help but think I was smarter, faster, more with it. And I was.

But that's just processing speed, which is what the young have that we aging fools are losing. It's sometimes known as fluid intelligence. What doesn't wane, at least until the sixties and seventies, is crystallized intelligence—what's sometimes called "wisdom" (I hate that word, it makes me feel so old), and which seems to be an amalgam of experience and perspective and the ability to zoom out and in, an ability not to mentally panic if the answer doesn't immediately appear. There is at least one theory that this happens because the brain, when it starts to slow at twenty-seven, compensates: the older you get, the more your brain relies on other parts of itself to do jobs that were once site-specific. It's not as fast, but it enriches the experience, sort of. In any event, crystallized intelligence can actually grow, even canceling out or at least distracting from one's declining processing speed, into one's seventies, depending how much you exercise, how healthfully you eat, how much you don't drink, and even how much you have sex. (I am conflating various bits of research here.) I almost fell to my knees weeping when I discovered this. At the same time, I wonder if that's why amphetamines are so appealing in one's forties and fifties—cocaine and Dexedrine and the other speed-up drugs that seem to become popular again at that age, judging from the wastrels I know. Maybe it's a way of warding off the beginning of the big slowdown.

And the sad news? After sixty, and especially after seventy, most brain studies seem to say, decline is unavoidable, or at least too severe to be compensated. It's all very well to say sixty is the new fifty, but after sixty there's not a hell of a lot you can do about it. The die is cast, comrade. In other words, it is going to show up in my life any fucking day now. You can compensate, you can rely on notes and memos and cues and reminders, but the brain doesn't stop shrinking and cracking and drying up like an old piece of ginger. It's old age that's the problem, that I still have to look forward to; death (as de Beauvoir pointed out) is a breeze next to old age. For all the metaphysical dizziness my nonexistence in the future causes me today, I won't be here to experience it. But my ignorance of what old age will be like (if I make it there: always that proviso) is also what saves me from doing myself in. Compared with old age—what I have heard, what I have read, what my father showed me—sixty is a gorgeous springtime. (Surely I'm not yet as bad as him. Or him. Or her. Or him.)

I met a guy the other day, a friend of Al's, married to a younger Brazilian woman. He's a wealthy man, someone who has had money all his life, with all the self-confidence that type carries. Nice guy despite that, or maybe because of it. He owns a horse farm. Two years ago, at fifty-nine, he had a stroke. He recovered—I certainly would never have known he had been so blighted. At breakfast at Al's, before we headed out for a bike ride up the river, he told me that he had been complaining that very week to his doctor about his sex life—or, to be more specific, about his inability to respond sexually as vigorously as he had been able to. (The erections still occur, but you never know how serious a particular erection intends to be: is it a keeper, or a passing fancy? A lasting friend, or a stranger?) In any event, his doctor had some advice: "Your sex life is as good today as it is ever going to be." Sobering. Also a goad to action.

Where was I? Oh, yes, the decline of the brain. Hilarious.

In advanced old age, you lose brain cells steadily, and in critical areas such as the hippocampus, one of the regions where memories are processed. My father made it to the end of his nineties, but as he got older he couldn't remember the details of the stuff that had been his stock-in-trade at the age of seventy-five or even eighty. He could remember the outline of the war, for instance, and parts of his service as a commando in Norway, but the details had faded. The name of the red-haired Cockney who insisted on slitting Nazi soldiers' throats instead of taking them prisoner, the name of the fellow he is laughing with, both shirtless, in the officers' club in Calcutta—both gone, forever. This is why many writers stop writing as they get older, because as you get older, you skip over detail. It's almost self-imposed, this forgetting. I feel myself slowing down, and in a panic of thinking I have to cover more ground, I start speeding up, zooming past stuff. Whereas—this is important—the trick is actually to slow down more, to stop moving as fast, and pay attention more, and remember what it is you see, regardless of whether it is what you are supposed to see, or what you think you are supposed to be remembering.

I remember, for instance, last spring, when that rusty Norway maple I can see from the dining-room window was just in leaf: how it filled the sky of the dining-room window on that gorgeous day in Toronto, and the way it rallied over the pink honeysuckle blossoms flowering around the strut of the second-floor porch. I could hear the voices of my neighbors, indistinct as they were, people gardening in the sun; the tree moved me more than the honeysuckle did, as if it was a bigger, more important world beyond the smaller, personal one. The window was open and I could smell the spring. The lattice of the fence rose into view below the honeysuckle. Below the window, inside, was the marriage chest Ernest Hillen had given us as a present. For luck. Who am I to say it didn't work?

I don't think I will be able to stand the loss of detail. Even thinking about this makes me want to shoot myself now, before it happens, if it happens, when it happens, because it will happen, it always happens. Maybe that's why so many people over the age of sixty post pictures of flowers on Facebook: those are details, of a sort. I don't mind turning around and looking backwards at the age I am now, instead of rushing into the future the way Hayley sometimes wants to, but when I can't do that, will I want to stick around? Who knows? The end may come and all I will want to do is hang on for the last few sparks within me. I don't think it's predictable, and I think everyone experiences the exfoliation of the remembered soul at a different rate, and in a different way. None of them is the right way—or more accurately, the wrong way, as long as someone takes the trouble to honor it. I saw the urge to fight back, to hang on, in my old man, the desire to get better, to improve, until he realized that all the exercise in the world wasn't going to make him puff any less going up the stairs. Once he realized he wouldn't improve, he wanted to die even faster than he did. "Even in old age the brain is flexible enough to compensate," a study pointed out to me the other day. "But at some point the losses start to make themselves felt." Then what?

To stave off that helplessness, all the experts say, you must exercise regularly, as my old Da did, prancing on his patio. And it was worth it for the longest time: targeting motor control and balance with exercise improves cognitive function for sixty-to-eighty-year-olds. (I'm still agog when I remember that bracket now includes me.) Even a few regular sessions on a Nintendo Wii can help. From what I can see, as much as I disdain it, even brain training works. "Importantly," some study I read observed, "these changes [following brain training] were large enough that participants reported significant improvements in everyday activities, such as remembering names or following conversations in noisy restaurants." Jesus wept. Those difficulties are already afflicting me, on occasion. And so I have taken up the *New York Times* crossword, at least when I can sneak it in before Johanna zooms through it. I often watch her as she works it. It's kind of thrilling.

The last time I left the ophthalmologist's (after he had told me my eyeball pressures were steady at 14; after we had talked about how many years we have left—"How old were your parents when they died?" "Ninety-eight and ninety-five." "Oh, well, you're gonna be in trouble, you'll hit a hundred." "No, I didn't live the same clean life." "You abused yourself enough? Still, I think you'll make it longer than you think. Me, I figure I have another twenty years or so"), I was racing to get back to my car, and in the parking lot lapped a woman I presume was in her early eighties. The guy ahead of me at the payment machine and I had both paid for our parking before she even found her ticket. She had to rest her purse on a low wall, and then she was into it up to her elbows. She had soft white hair and good posture, despite the mattress-like orthopedic soles on her white sneakers (they're a dead fucking giveaway, I must never wear them). Every movement she made was considered and reconsidered before it was enacted, and then reviewed. It was like watching history take shape. I cannot imagine being that slow, though I dislike myself for not being able to imagine it, because I will one day be slower. I dread that oncoming step-by-step-by-step-by-step-by-step progression, the ever-approaching deceleration, like a record play-e-r d-y-y-y-i-i-i-n-g, to use an outdated simile.

But after I paid and began the trudge up the parking garage ramp to my car, I realized I had no idea what floor I was parked on, because I could not recall a moment of the walk, half an hour earlier, from my car down the ramp to the lobby of the ophthalmologist's building, passing the buttressed pillars and sagging walls of the fucking collapsing parking garage, i.e., my life. I must have been distracted or thinking about something. This, in other words, is the beginning of the end.

On the other hand, as the brain scientists never tire of pointing out, by way of compensation, by sixty-five the brain prefers to remember positive emotion rather than bad news. True. This too is a function of the brain's compensatory abilities: the good news is easier to handle, and probably requires less speed and focus, so it prefers to ignore the horror and the tragedies. Cathrin was saying the last time I saw her that she feels she is becoming wiser, because her outlook is becoming more positive. I didn't have the heart to say, "It's just your fading brain, your oncoming, babbling, bubbling optimism." As of yet, I find the bad news unavoidable; it feels dishonest to look away, even though the laid-back are less likely to develop dementia than the stressed. Much less likely: people who are socially active but calm have a 50 percent lower risk of dementia than isolated, stressed types.

SEPTEMBER 22

Strange to watch a play of one's life, with a few hundred people sitting next to you. Johanna and I snuck into a preview of *The Boy in the Moon*, unannounced. I was secretly terrified and thrilled, if only to see this thing we pulled through together made real. Johanna was exceptionally nervous, too, and wanted to see what she was in for before the formal opening night we are both supposed to attend. "I thought we might be opening ourselves up to judgment," she said. "And I wanted it to be good, not bad. Of course, it helps a lot that the woman playing me"—someone named Manon St-Jules—"is young and gorgeous." I was worried the play would be too nailed to the floor of the real to work as drama. I kept thinking of Shaw's remark, about the crudeness of reality making the world unbearable. The actor who played me—Peter Haworth—seemed to capture my incessant twitching and self-involved intellectualizing quite well. The overall effect of having someone depict your life is that it makes you think your life is over—that it is done, and that the way you come across is beyond your control. I wish I had known this when I was younger; it might have had a freeing effect.

But why think of a life that way? Why not think as David Hockney thinks? "I'm not sure there actually is any such thing as failure," he once told the writer Lawrence Weschler (I am paraphrasing wildly: I can't find the original interview, but the quote has stuck with me for what must be nearly twenty years.). "You just do your work, learn from it, and move on." He once said he traveled to get away from the influence of others, to find the peace and isolation necessary to make his art. Whenever he felt lonely, he set to work, and the loneliness went away. He started to go deaf at the age of fifty, so he began to paint more spatially, because hearing is all about space. But implicit in the genius of Hockney's confidence, his inspired resistance to judgment from self or others, is his understanding of his work and life as the thing it is, lived to the best of his abilities and skills and temperament and luck, to no one's standard but his own. Hard to do, and a mark of genius. Still, a life that stifles itself because of relentless self-judgment is a dark, demeaning, depressed, not to mention boring (because nothing is ever a surprise) life. And this is the way we live now, in constant comparison, made worse by social media, the world where everyone thinks of him- or herself as a critic, as some genius of discernment. I am not surprised the most common student psychiatric complaint on campuses today is anxiety.

I always hesitate to think that everything is relative, because everything ought not to be—I doubt that cruelty or genocide, for instance, can be justified on the ground of relativity—but there's a lot of evidence that most things are, especially aging. When Susan Orlean was worried that Charlie Kaufman, the screenwriter, was transforming her into a coke-snorting nightmare in *Adaptation*, the semi-fictional film (in which Orlean was played by Meryl Streep) based on Orlean's nonfiction book *The Orchid Thief*, the producer took her aside. He pointed out that Kaufman (who was played in the movie by Nic Cage) had depicted himself as a compulsive masturbator. Orlean later told an interviewer, "You know, he's got a point there. What am I complaining about?" The point is, we're all more knowable than we think. I wonder why we hesitate to admit it.

My favorite part of the play was the woman who played Walker, who is never seen onstage: he is represented by clapping. It's the one language we all speak, Walker included. We all know how to clap. It doesn't seem like much, but at times it seems like everything.

SEPTEMBER 26

A column I wrote about Ray Rice, the NFL player who knocked his wife Janay out in an elevator, has led to my being assigned to a nightmare of a bigger story. In the column, I quoted a local domestic abuse counselor who said, "Why do you journalists always ask, 'Why does she stay?' The question no one asks is, 'Why does he hit the woman he loves?'"

So then I opened my mouth to say that her question was a really good one to follow up on, and now I'm looking at a pig of a story, which is going to take at least three months to research and write, which has no known answer, and which is going to please no one, least of all me. First I must find some men who hit women, who are willing (rare) and able (rarer) to talk about their habit. It's an impossibly complicated story that almost defies a calm, rational, readable telling. Maybe that's why I felt compelled to take it on. Maybe old school is the only way to do something like this.

In Keene, New York, with Kling, Mitchell, and Randall. (We all went to boarding school, we all use our last names, because that lets us display our affection for one another by switching to first names, sometimes.) We've spent a week or two of every winter for the past thirty years looking after each other as we ski mountaineer on glaciers and avalanche slopes, but as we've grown older, other, safer pursuits look a little more appealing, hence this holiday. We golf for three days (their choice, and I come round, sustained by my drives, then destroyed by my short game), are rained out for another day, bike another, hike a sixth. We're very fond of each other.

The random possibility of death by cancer/stroke/heart attack/some other shit is now a daily fact of our lives. Its probability follows us everywhere, a heavy, long-proven math. I have a blemish of some kind on my nose that has been there a month—is it melanoma? The specter of that statistical probability hangs over us like some giant party pooper; its presence sparks either panic or full-on denial.

To stave off the specter, we are all madly trying to stay fit. I take secret pride in the fact, for instance, that I am probably the best biker in the group. Talk about tiny triumphs.

The statistical probabilities make us dour, more intentional, and yet more passive too. *You never know.* That phrase is suddenly resonant. Time, diminishing, multiplied by choices, divided by the product of interest and opportunity (sub-factored by available savings and cash flow, itself a product of a complex equation encompassing carefulness, foresight, discipline, and the capacity for boredom) together yield the sum of what might be accomplished in the time that is left.

We talk about it a lot: how do you decide, in the unquantifiable but finite time you have left, what to read (this one has just hit Mitchell), where to travel, what to do (kids, writing, reading, pleasure?), how much golf to play (it seems like both the perfect and the least perfect hedge against the rapidly shutting future: trying to perfect what is not perfectible). Mitchell doesn't like being sixty (and he's an extraordinarily fit sixty) because "it lets me say, well, I can't do that, I'm sixty!" For that matter, should I be spending a week in the company of three guys in the woods in the Adirondacks, when I should be . . . what? Working to make money to save for later when I can't move and might be dead? What will end up being more important than non-stop conversations about golf, the non-stop making of coffee, the non-stop peeing and hyper-regular shitting, and of course the nonstop conversation about systems—how to improve the plumbing/heating/solar panel/water supply/gas mileage? It's like a creed. We spend an hour on an iPad comparing video of Ernie Els and then ourselves, swinging golf clubs on some quasi-scientific program Mitchell has rigged up. The conclusion? None of us are Ernie Els. We talk about going to Bhutan. It sounds expensive. They are three of my closest friends. I probably have something more important to do. But I have nothing to do that is anywhere near as important as this. Because I will remember this.

What else did we do? We drove into town, ate a frozen lasagna, went to bed—early. We were all up by six-thirty every morning; that's common at sixty. We hit some practice balls and played a round of golf on a long course on a snapping fall day in the Adirondack Mountains. We cooked steaks and traveled to a farmers' market, arranged to buy some pot (two of our foursome are inveterate vacation potheads), went for an eight-mile hike up a brook to Indian Head and Fish Hawk; traveled to another town to buy the pot from a local businessman and his fierce, unsmiling wife, who is both a welder and a butcher (there's a crime novel in that combination); then to another hamlet to meet another young guy making a subsistence living with a brand new microbrewery, over which he seems to dwell. It was as if we had wandered into the twelfth century: the low light, the haphazardly rubber-booted men and women at the bar, the branch-handled beer pulls. There were three young men and women in the bar as customers, including a very beautiful dairy worker, whom Kling seemed to know, who was herself being embraced by another young woman. Youth is like a foreign country to me now, a strange land I love to tour, gazing intently at the sights. Afterward, we drove back through the pitch-black mountains, the high beams of the car transforming the curves ahead into friendly caves of light. Later still, somewhat uncharacteristically, I smoked some of the pot before retiring. When will I learn not to do that? For five hours I lay awake in my bed, quivering with worry about work, cancer, finances, deadlines, and what, if anything, was left of my soul. I would have masturbated, but I was too worried to summon an erection, which launched another waterfall of worry. What if that stops working too?

The next day, we had salmon (anti-cancer!) and golfed again at the august Ausable Club, a shorter but even prettier and trickier course, my game resizing itself hole by hole, my drive failing me, my chipping improving only marginally. 109. I beat Kling, but no one else.

We ate dinner at Baxter Mountain Tavern, and were served by a charming young woman named Aleisha. Tall, dark, thrilling smile, lively presence, neither bored nor cowed by our aged beings. She talked about her plans (to get married) and her life as a teacher; she is in despair for her kindergarten kids who live on their iPads, and have poor attention spans, poor manual skills (they cannot draw), and no short-term memory. That was interesting. We were all charmed and captivated by her. As usual, we jockeyed

SIXTY

for her attention, a gaggle of aging idiots. Five years ago we would each have been secretly convinced (incorrectly) that Aleisha could be ours, given the right circumstances. But now we know we're dreaming, and are just happy for whatever attention she beams our way. Randall tipped her 20 percent.

OCTOBER 11

Back from Keene, back into the newsroom at the *Globe and Mail*, back into the humming, anxious, imminent failure of my life. Today on the street I ran into a guy I know from another newspaper.

"What are you working on?" I asked.

"I've retired," he replied.

"Are you enjoying it?" I asked.

"Loving it."

My heart sank. He was a very good writer, but said other things mattered to him more. I keep meeting people who have retired at fifty-five, who are proud and relieved to be out of the game. I keep meeting people who say, as someone did the other day, "I don't worry so much, now that I'm sixty." I envy them. Meanwhile, my bank account hasn't been in the black for an entire month. I have to economize.

This morning, I went to buy the fixings for our Thanksgiving meal. Unusually, no one has invited us and we have invited no one, and Hayley's staying in Montreal, so it's down to Johanna and me. Period. I bought a turkey breast rather than a turkey, and a tiny ham, the tiniest ham I have ever seen. When I asked a young counterman where the turkey breasts were, he looked at me as if he had never heard of such a thing. I actually said, "This is pathetic," to myself as I picked the turkey breast off the display. I almost bought a turkey anyway, just to make the act of Thanksgiving seem less pro forma, or maybe I mean more pro forma. But I thought better of it. Why not embrace not having to eat half a monstrous *dinde*? The pressure of tradition is strong, strong, strong. I don't even like turkey that much. Why not embrace the independence of age and isolation? This is my new theory, anyway. Having made a turkey dinner thirty-five times, it is now liberating not to have to do so. Yeah! I'm catching the *HuffPost* vibe, honey. Sexy sixty can't be far behind. Fuck the turkey, free the man.

Fine. I will. But that doesn't change the fact that our Thanksgiving dinner, the two of us over a single turkey breast and a mini-ham, could be a scene from the opening of an Ian McEwan novel, in which an aging couple snacks on leftovers (while the world burns). In fact, our dinner was hilarious and almost touching. We kept making jokes about the abundance of our cranberry sauce.

OCTOBER 26

I've spent three weeks interviewing men who beat women, women who were beaten by men, therapists who help both, academics who study them, social workers who work with batterers, advocates who support battered women. I have never worked on a more contentious story, especially with these shocking allegations of sexual and other kinds of assault committed by Jian Ghomeshi, the famous host of the CBC Radio program Q, bubbling up in the background.

That scandal is brand new and it's already toxic. I happened to tweet that it might be a good idea for Ghomeshi's victims to go to the cops and was buried in a barrage of invective insisting I must believe the victims. I do believe them, and understand the criticism. But I would still urge any friend of mine who was sexually assaulted to go to the police, even though it would be her right not to. Several accusers claimed women's names can't be kept out of court proceedings, but they can, and by law. Others insisted the police are at the center of an adversarial court system that shames women in rape trials; in fact, the Toronto police, at least, now go to extra-serious lengths to gather evidence and protect women who have been raped or abused domestically, following precise, formal, official directives that run to tens of pages. The women's movement forced solid reforms in that regard, starting twenty-five years ago. But the victim-blaming adversarial courts will never change unless more women go to court without feeling ashamed, and without being shamed, which won't happen unless they go to court and we don't shame them. The alternative—being tried out on Twitter and Facebook—is public shaming, this bitter online sharia we indulge in at regular intervals (Ray Rice, Rob Ford, Hillary Clinton, name your target). I guess it's effective, until the attack shifts to someone who doesn't deserve it, and then it feels like mob justice. I prefer the clarity of the law, which can be upheld or changed and upheld again. But I feel like a very old rhinoceros for even having these doubts; with the Ghomeshi fracas in full voice, a female feminist friend fumed at me yesterday, they are "unhelpful." As facts, they feel like old men: cranky, obstructive, and standing in the way of everyone's happiness. It would be helpful to forget them.

OCTOBER 28

Shaved my beard off today, in stages: first down to mutton chops and a Fu Manchu, then a goatee, a Vandyke, a Colonel Sanders soul patch, a Hitlerian toothbrush mustache, then sideburns alone. None of them suited me. I think it is pretty incontestable that I look younger without it, but more importantly, I look more vital. Buzzing the beard down then scraping it off, I felt suddenly lighter, and freer. I wore the beard because I wanted to make a public statement about my age, because I wanted to be perceived as older, more serious, more grave, more gaunt, closer to death, less distractable, as if there was something on my mind (and face) that would not go away. I wanted to be *hors de combat*. A beard provides that exclusion, that barrier to intimacy. Or so I found.

What did it gain me? Some breathing room or, more seriously, some feeling room. I looked like a hermit alone with his thoughts, and so people left me alone, and so I was a hermit. I wanted the freedom to go off on my own. The urge seemed to correspond with a feeling that comes and goes with regularity: that I am at the end of the line in everything—career, strength, hope. That's certainly the public rap against age. In my experience of my sixty-first year, I have found it only occasionally true, but the public expectation that it is true still weighs heavily on one's sense of potential. Sixty may or may not be the age you can start to feel old. But it is certainly the age others begin to think of you as old.

And then I cut the beard off and the sun shone in again. I guess I was over some kind of sadness, or perhaps I'd been rehearsing for death. People look at my face again, and I welcome that. Suddenly, three-quarters of the way through my sixty-first year, I don't mind being seen as I am.

I read a new poem by the aging, dying Clive James. It's all the news in the literary pages, James's last poem as he slowly withers from leukemia. A funeral poem, a kick at the can of immortality. He was diagnosed in 2010, and has spent four years staring down death. His death is reportedly imminent, but James's brain and eyesight are intact—"Enhanced, in fact. When did you ever see/So much sweet beauty as when fine rain falls/On that small tree . . ." The tree, a Japanese maple, was chosen by his daughter; in the fall, "its leaves will turn to flame." Which produces his resolution: "What I must do/is live to see that. That will end the game." A way of taking love with you as you go. Will that make death bearable?

NOVEMBER 9

Interviewed John Cleese onstage last night as part of his book tour for his new autobiography, which is getting mixed to positive reviews. He's a good storyteller, but he doesn't exactly linger in search of greater meaning in the book. Completely charming man. Ten minutes before we went on, he decided how many excerpts he would read as part of our conversation, deferring to my wishes (which were to have him read whatever he wanted, though he took my advice on the selections); he wanted to close with us doing a sketch together. He wore jeans and a golf shirt and a jacket and white loafers with no socks onstage, and had none of the self-important, me-first-and-always attitude of many celebrated actors. Cleese thinks of himself as a writer, first and foremost.

He's a zesty seventy-five years old, which gave me courage. Cleese is proof that life does not end until it ends. In 2008, when he was sixty-nine, he divorced his third wife (a California psychotherapist), a split that cost him twenty million (American!) dollars—forcing him to earn a million a year extra for the next seven years to pay off his divorce settlement. This he somehow managed, starting with the Pythons' Alimony Tour. He used to have a mansion in Highland Park, mortgage-free; now he lives in a smallish apartment with a mortgage and his fourth wife, a younger Englishwoman who seems to believe in vortices and their woo-woo ilk. His fourth wife. One would think he might have figured out the simple rule—No More Marriages, John—by the time he turned seventy, but apparently even comic geniuses are optimists. Admittedly, he is John Cleese, the inventor of the Silly Walk and some of the most inspired scenes of sublimated fury in the history of entertainment, but his personal life is a bit of a disaster.

IAN BROWN

Yet I forgive him, as does everyone else.

We are less generous with ourselves in moments of summing up. It makes me think that summing up, weighing a life on a set of scales, is not an especially productive idea. It's a bourgeois notion that serves no one but the system. De Beauvoir noticed that, as well. Which reminds me of Cleese's brilliant Mrs. Premise and Mrs. Conclusion sketch, starring two aging middle-class British ladies in a coin laundry debating whether the masterwork of Jean-Paul Sartre (or Mr. de Beauvoir, as he was not known) is an allegory of man's search for commitment.

Cleese's autobiography is an account of his life up to Python—or, to put it another way, a chronicle of the evolution of his sense of humor. But it ends in mystery on that account: the most middle-middle-middle-class upbringing in Britain, which he experienced in Weston-super-Mare, can't explain the uncompromising rule-breaking originality of his humor. Partly it was the sixties, when he came of age, and partly it was that he had no inner censor: if something was politically incorrect, Cleese aimed straight at it. Perhaps he was so thoroughly, deeply, fundamentally, almost autistically intimidated by class that he had no choice but to put his domed head down and ram straight into it, like a bull. He doesn't actually say. People claim he could not get away with it today, but I think that is wrong: you can say whatever you want if you say it well enough. Cleese aimed to produce, still aims to produce, four pages of script a day. He has even voiced a set of directions for

TomTom, the in-car GPS device. "My daughter downloaded it, started using it," he said in our onstage interview. "She said it was impossible for her to actually do what I say." He has that kind of wit. I was beside myself with joy.

I eventually asked him about all his marriages, and he said, "It's quite nice to know that at the age of sixty-nine you could meet the love of your life. Particularly when you've had as many expensive disappointments as I have." This I found naive but charming, and recalled from his memoir that he was a virgin until he was well into his twenties. He claimed not to have made that much money, which I find even more difficult to believe. Allegedly, his initial salary as a Python was four thousand pounds a season, the equivalent of a regional bank manager's salary. His aim as a writer, he said, was to be "really funny." Not "pretty funny" or "charming." He knew he had hit the mark when Graham Chapman, his Python writing partner, laughed. (Chapman decided he was gay about halfway through the Python shows. Then he drank himself into the grave.)

Toward the end of the conversation—it lasted ninety minutes, and he only seemed to flag toward the end—I asked why, in his opinion, people responded so enormously to Monty Python—in fact to all his work, because *Fawlty Towers* and *A Fish Called Wanda* are among the comic masterpieces of the past century.

"You always feel affection for people who make you laugh, even if it's just a good friend who makes you laugh,"

Cleese said. "But it's more than that. Somebody once said to me that what they loved about Monty Python was that, after they'd finished watching it, they could not watch the news anymore. Because it was pointing out that nobody knows what they're doing."

Maybe this is the kind of insouciance you need to survive aging in one piece. After sixty, the pressure to conform, to behave, to be a polite and respectable, "wise," even "cute" human being without any troubling signs of humanity (lust, anger, principles, disagreeableness, inconvenient truth-telling), is unending; our obedience is the price society wants for paying attention to us, for not shunting us off to the end-of-life stockyards. Cleese figured out how to escape that pressure by paying attention to what struck him as absurd, ridiculous, and funny, as opposed to what was supposed to be amusing, and then making it absurd and ridiculous and funny. Louis C.K. does the same thing. Larry David does it at the age of sixty-eight. You have to be brave and stick to the truth.

Although maybe I'm just being cantankerous. There have been workmen outside all day, making so much noise it could have been a war: a jackhammer, a concrete saw, a radio, one of them even singing opera, in Italian. A neighbor is renovating his house. A few months ago, he casually mentioned making some kind of restitution for putting us out with the renovation, which will affect our ability to get into our own house for about a month. I mentioned this to Johanna. Then, a few weeks ago, when I mentioned that we might have to split the cost of re-pouring the concrete in the laneway between our houses, Johanna cleverly reminded me of the offer of compensation, and the thought hit me: maybe the guy next door, who is a very nice guy, could pay for the whole re-pour, to make up for the summer of hell. Except that he hadn't mentioned the compensation offer in a while. All that was going through my teeming little Machiavellian brain when I encountered my neighbor leaving the house today, and he asked me if the noise was bothering us. "Well," I said, "it's certainly loud." Which was not a complaint, merely an observation to let him know that I was monitoring the degree to which the renovation was putting us out, in case it came up in the future. It was a sixty-year-old man thing to say.

Hayley had been standing beside me, and she was appalled. I was being grasping and cranky. I in turn was chastened and irritated. After some discussion, she said, "Maybe it's just that when you're young, you don't care about that stuff; when you're old [there it is again], you want to be comfortable."

I'm not sure about that. When I think of the appalling stunts my own parents pulled—my mother in high dudgeon dragging me to the grocery store to return a half-eaten roast of beef to the butcher because it was "full of fat and inedibly tough" (he wisely gave her a fresh one: my old lady was the Marie Antoinette of Pointe-Claire); my father churlishly giving a parking attendant a hard time for charging so much to store a car—it was what I perceived as their sense of entitlement that offended me. I did not understand then that my mother desperately needed to please her children and husband with her cooking, and would go to any lengths to eliminate whatever stood in the way of that appreciation, and that her fierceness in this regard was one of the few proofs of love she could allow us. I did not understand then how hard my father worked for how little money, and how much that exorbitant parking charge took out of him. I was too young.

Hayley was right: it was sneaky and political of me to tell our neighbor the work was noisy. But—apart from the fact that my wife is expecting me to keep an eye on our interests—I *am* worried about keeping the house in shape as an investment for the kids' sake, especially in the wake of next door's improvement, and so I fear that I have to resort to almost any lengths to make that happen. And of course I do see that Hayley wants me to be a good and decent and above-board guy, so that she can trust my advice. The house and the noise and what I said to my neighbor about the noise have nothing to do with it. We're dealing with hidden fears, secret shame.

We all live inside our secret fears. I cannot help but notice that every time I pretend mine don't exist, I deny someone else's as well. I should have said out loud to my neighbor, "Yes, it's noisy, but I'm hoping that when the blood starts to trickle out of my ears, you'll be moved to make it up to me by renovating my basement, so it can be as nice as yours." And he would have laughed, and I would have tactfully reminded him of his offer. Maybe next time. Because this is what I long to be, as I head into the late innings: less hidden, less afraid, more naked, less ashamed. I want to wear my fragility on my body—not just my so-called need, but my intentions, and my doubts about my intentions, and my doubts about those doubts, and the laughable wobbliness of my progress in all things. I want to be human and complex more than I want to be right and clear—because if I can be those things, others can be those things too. We can be those things together, which strikes me as an intelligent formation in which to approach the unknown, toward the end of the road. I do not have to be a bearded, white-haired, cranky, desperate, wrinkled cliché to others, and they do not have to become clichés (young, callous, selfish, judgmental, impatient) to me. I do not want to have to pretend to know the answer, as keen as I might be to find one. And I would like company, sometimes. My wife, my friends, my kids, my colleagues, my elders, my youngers.

All this from a passing remark. I will say this for getting older: if you can calm down about the decline, you can think your way into feeling freer. At sixty, I think I may finally recognize love.

NOVEMBER 17

Snow fell during the night, and stayed: heavy on the ground, the backyard fence, the trees, the yellow leaves. I had managed to get most of the leaves up this fall—five bagfuls—and to clean up the garden in the most basic way, but never got around to trimming the hostas or the white astilbes in the front yard. The astilbes turned rust brown overnight, and the hostas are now flattened gold stars in the snow, as if they managed to make it back to the front yard after a raucous night out, but no farther. They look like KO'd boxers, like drunks.

NOVEMBER 18

And today is freezing cold, minus-seven. It's as if the world is a different place, another planet: the cold is so intense it feels like a separate state of being, sharp and unyielding. I confess I feel the cold more now; or at least I am aware when it is cold. Five years ago, the temperature barely registered. Still, I have a long way to go before I am as sensitive as my father was in his eighties and nineties: he wore a down jacket from morning to night, and kept the thermostat at a wilting eighty-five.

My parents were in their forties before they had me and my siblings, which meant that my mother was fifty when I was ten. One of my main childhood memories is of my hot-flashing mother screaming, "Who turned down the heat? Leave the bloody thermostat alone!"—only to explode ten minutes later about how the house was now bloody boiling. That went on for a decade.

I can't convince the Arts section to take more than 1,500 words of my Cleese interview, despite what I consider to be its many charms. Is it too old school? Old hat? I don't think people have stopped laughing at his work, but maybe I am *out of touch*? This is paranoia, steeped for sixty years. I have also written another piece about our shockingly bad post-digital manners, brought on by technological entitlement. On the day it snowed, for the first time in years, people actually stopped looking at their phones as they walked down the sidewalk: they were afraid of falling on the ice. Driving was so hard, drivers forewent the newfangled habit of sitting in a much-needed parking space and checking their email.

But without the snow, we return to the regular fuck-you parade of people pretending to have face-to-face conversations while they check their messages or text. There is no pretense about this: it's full-on, in-your-face not looking at your face. They make human noises at you (it happens incessantly at the *Globe*)—"Huh. Uh-huh. Right"—but they don't quite treat you as another human. Apart from not understanding how people can do two things at once (and two things that entail detail and interacting with other human beings, at that) and pay attention to all the subtle notes we should pay attention to—and I have had a cellphone and a computer as long as anyone, and am at ease, technologically—I find the nose-in-the-phone habit . . . not just rude, but mechanical. I can't bring myself to do it even when I want to; it seems disrespectful of the other person's very existence. According to a survey I saw, the average North American spends up to two and a half hours a day on some hand-held device, and checks it an average of 110 times. That's nearly thirty-eight days a year—about eight years, over a lifetime.

I am not spending eight years of my increasingly precious life looking into an electronic devotional device. And yet if I mention my repugnance, I am branded as an old man who can't keep up. But—as I pointed out to some twenty-five-year-old the other day—I've been using "her" technology for a decade longer than she has been alive. She knows how to navigate faster than I do, but I know where it has taken me, and where it seems to be going.

And then, watching one of my bosses peck at his keyboard like a hungry bird at the same time as he was asking me what I had been thinking about—which should have been a terrific conversation—I remembered what D. said. The only people who do this to others are people who have authority or power over them. Bosses do it (hence its occasional name: "boss pose.") "If I'm the senior boss in the room, I can message on my cell," D. explained. "Whereas if I am in a meeting with my boss, I would never go on my phone, even though he can be on his."

I am often told that I should get over being offended. But I wonder if we all shouldn't be less willing to be subservient, to be put in our places, by technology and the people it profits most. Common decency is always a rogue entity, because it's free; it hasn't yet been monetized, because it confers no quantifiable advantage.

One of those dark November days, no sunlight, no prospects. Can't seem to stop sighing. Drove to Hamilton yesterday for the launch of Stephen Brunt's new book with Jordin Tootoo, the Inuk hockey player. The usual clever crowd were there. The writer, I can't remember his name, and I know him, the guy who—Joseph Boyden! Joseph Boyden persuaded Brunt to do it, to transpose Tootoo's oral history to the page. In his speech and brief reading, Brunt talked about the thrill of appearing in a book with an introduction by Boyden and about how much he appreciated going up north with his eldest son, Nat. An impressive modesty, and an evocative reading of the chapter in which he visits Rankin Inlet and the environs—a brutal place described beautifully. Brunt has organized his life well.

Today, in the city, I ran into V., a friend who is a Jungian therapist, who tells me he hasn't managed to rake up his leaves yet, which makes me feel better as I have finished mine—and his are oak leaves, and toxic, which makes me feel even better. Still, I hate days that are comparative.

I've discovered that one of the side effects of writing about men who hit women is that people automatically presume you're drawn to the subject because you hit women too. I do not.

That's not my guilt. My guilt is the seeping sense that I missed something, that I haven't lived up to my promise. It's a form of regret that seems to surround everyone to some extent, for all the popular wisdom about not having any. Regret seems like a flood that is going to strand me, alone.

Jean Vanier—whose work on disability I started to read when Walker was a baby, when I was desperate for someone to make any sense at all of his handicapped life—thinks that purgatory is the stretch just before death where you regret all the chances you missed to be human, when you could have chosen to be the equal of another but for one reason or another—shyness, fear, insecurity, the relative ease of doing nothing, competitiveness—did not. As I was driving to Hamilton yesterday, I found myself imagining (talking out loud!) the speech I would give on my eventual departure from the *Globe*. It was a very pompous speech, one that spoke of the yearning in us all to do work that has never been done before, and how hard it is to convince a corporation with a reputation to protect that it should let you do that work. I would say that I have been very lucky at the *Globe*, left alone to do what I could. In my little Mittyesque fantasy, people at the *Globe* spoke of the speech for decades to come. Honestly, I am three as much as I am sixty. But that is a fantasy about wanting to do things differently.

I hate having regrets, but at sixty they show up, sharp and aggressive, like nasty dogs. Regrets, and a fog of guilt, for not having put myself on the line more—for not having made more of an effort with my mother, despite her incessant guilt-mongering and threats and physical abusiveness, for not having seen how terrified she must have been. For not having loved Johanna more unreservedly. For not having committed more wholeheartedly to the project of making something of this short slip of time that is my life. Just now, making my breakfast—a poached egg on a crumpet spread with a slice of avocado, with some salt and fresh pepper—I was thinking about how much pleasure it would give me to be able to serve soft-boiled eggs and avocado to some friends in (okay, it was a weird thought) a cabin by the sea; but even that lovely dream never came to pass because I never thought I could make it come to pass, because I was always distracted by more immediate obligations. I was afraid of the long haul. The greatest gift turning sixty has given me is that it has made me aware of that fear. I can do something about it now, as long as it is not too late, which is the other main fear.

DECEMBER 1, 2014

Woke up this morning, in the middle of beginning to write this nightmare story on domestic abuse, thinking: "Well, all I can do is do what I can do. Why should I expect any more of myself, if expecting more is so exhausting? I am who I am, as Popeye said." Except that this is exactly the kind of sixtyism that Mitchell dreads has beset him: this idea that, now that I am sixty, I can be content with merely being here. No transformation is required any longer. This is also the first time in my life that I can recall waking up this way.

DECEMBER 11

Snow. Everywhere. Didn't realize it had fallen, but there is four inches on everything, and another ten to come today, as if the world can't stop weeping. I feel the same excitement I felt as a boy, that I have felt with every heavy snowfall I have ever experienced: outside, great beauty and softness, an impediment to the obligations of the day, a day when you can't get around, so you can take time to look round; an adventure. And freedom, of course, from the dark clutches of that house, because my mother would send us outside to toboggan. I spent a very happy twenty minutes shoveling snow off my front path, the sidewalk, steps, and back passageway. I almost skied to work, then decided against it. That's not bad: almost skiing to work at sixty. It's not Jackrabbit Johannsen. But it's not bad.

DECEMBER 12

My sisters' birthday. They're twins, and fifty-five. I'm old enough that I remember the day they were born, as my father and brother and I toasted bread in the living-room fireplace on Golf Avenue, in the middle of the famous 1960 eastern Canadian ice storm. We were without power for nearly two weeks. Maudie was so small she was in an incubator, and had to stay at the hospital. That fact is still part of my understanding of her. And then one morning my father and a neighbor hooked up a generator as I was in the front closet, looking for a pair of mitts. I flicked the light switch without thinking, and the light went on, and I realized I had assumed it would, when for so long it hadn't. I felt slightly disappointed that the adventure was over.

The girls came home a week later. I was fascinated by their tininess: they were the babies, and needed protecting. I've probably treated them that way all their lives, to their irritation. Born in a storm. I find it impossible to think of them as old.

Yesterday was the Christmas lunch, the annual holiday gathering of a few guys from my class at boarding school. It was sparsely attended, and didn't last long: Austin, me, Young, Bermingham, Larkin, Parker, Hanbury, in the Harry Potter room at the Fynn's of Temple pub. Had the turkey club without eating much of the bread. A nine-ounce glass of wine; the others drank beer. Hanbury had Scotch. These details never change.

Bermingham has retired, is still being paid by Blake's as partner emeritus, is still teaching yoga, taking photographs, and traveling; he has just been in France. Austin was beside himself because a young woman had offered him her seat on the streetcar. "Do I look like I want to sit?" he said he thought but did not say. The woman had referred to him as "sir." Bermingham, the yoga teacher, had the same thing happen to him recently; he claims he wanted to say, "No, but would you like me to show you how to put your legs behind your head?" None of them seem to be going to any of the school's rah-rah events—the golf tournaments, the alumni cricket games. I never think of us as sixtyish, but the slow collapses are obvious. I confess to looking around at the company and wondering who would be the first to die. And of course there are the tiny details, the ones no one wants anyone to notice, such as when Larkin said, "Nice to meet you," when he was leaving—not what he meant, but it was already in the chamber, loaded by rote, and his brain fired anyway.

I walked back to work, to my desk at the newspaper in the feature-writing department, up on the third floor away from the hubbub of the news desk—though it has plenty of its own—and, after my nine-ounce glass of wine, genuinely thought I was having a stroke. I couldn't remember anything. Austin's father has Alzheimer's, the decline all packed into the last year. When he and his wife moved into the Belmont retirement home a year ago, he had scored twenty-four out of twenty-five on the Alzheimer's test (the subject of the last Christmas lunch). The other day, he scored five. Austin says it's a terrible experience, and a common one. And so, back in the office, as my brain was racking itself for words and getting them on the fifth try, I vowed to quit drinking. It took me the rest of the afternoon to write two paragraphs. Admittedly, they were important paragraphs, but still.

When that was over, I headed home, after a brief dither about whether to walk or drive to the Christmas party of White Pine Pictures, Peter Raymont's company. When I got there (I walked), I had another glass of wine and met Raymont's money trader, the risk analyst woman who is dealing with the multi-million-dollar check he just received from France for his *Cracked* series, which the CBC canceled after two seasons but which Europe went crazy for. Just hearing the word "cracked" reminded me that I wanted to write about fracking ages ago, before it hit the public consciousness. Same was true of hedge funds. *No one to blame for this but myself*, I thought, followed by *never thought big enough*. Followed by *the old man all over again*. The usual landslide.

Twice today, I thought to myself: "If I can't write, I may have to kill myself. How do I do that, without leaving Hayley out in the cold?"

DECEMBER 22

Spent the day yesterday trying to get to Crested Butte, Colorado, where—it must be said, given the trough of a day that followed—I am looking forward to spending Christmas with my wife and daughter and sisters and brother and nephew and in-laws. But the connecting flight from Denver to Gunnison was canceled due to weather, and instead of leaving at 11:30 AM, we waited through three delays until they finally canceled the flight at three. We then waited to see if a flight to not so nearby Montrose would take us, and it did, which in turn required my brother-in-law Matt to drive two hours to pick us up. Then they lost our luggage. Or at least my luggage. No ski gear.

So I'd spent the day in the Denver airport, time and life ticking by, watching bubble-butted blonds of various ages and genders, wearing what Hayley informed me are doubly appropriated Native designs, lope by, and young moms adoring their children, and all sorts of young men wearing shorts, of all things, in the middle of winter. Plus eating, let's not forget eating: a falafel (flannel wrapped around catsick), part of Hayley's falafel, diet Snapple, two pieces of a Wolfgang Puck roasted mushroom pizza, some of Hayley's salad, and then US$50 worth of Denver airport

Chinese food. Airport boredom. But cruising around DEN with Hayley—Johanna was nailed to her computer in the waiting room, finishing a column—chatting about her future and trying to persuade her to come skiing, that didn't feel like a waste of anything.

DECEMBER 23

Spent the day skiing in Crested Butte: icy, with a small accumulation of snow on the sides of the runs. I'm pretty rusty, and treat the entire adventure cautiously. Because United Airlines lost my bags, I am skiing in Matt's long underwear—dating from an era when both he and I were thinner—a pair of rented brown ski pants, rented boots and skis and poles, Remy's gloves, one of Matt's hats, my puffy jacket, and Matt's twenty-year-old shell, dating from his arrival in Canada, when he worked at Whistler. He seems more outgoing than usual, and is between construction contracts; maybe that's why. My sisters seem remotely young to me, despite the mere five-and-a-half-year gap between us: Maudie's son is only fifteen, a nice guy, hockey mad. He has taken up the position of goalie. Hayley seems impossibly sophisticated: she is off to New York for a week after our return, with her boyfriend (staying in Tim's apartment), and she is returning directly to Montreal from there, a fact that upsets Johanna openly and me secretly. There is the usual tension between them, the battle of the ovaries, Johanna's fading, Hayley's freshening. Johanna also has a hacking cold, and spends the night coughing, which means I spend the night listening to her cough, and feeling bad for her, and also wanting to throttle her. She stays at my sister's pretty house while we ski, having foresworn downhill several years ago. Tim arrives later in the afternoon, and is quite ill too: a busy schedule, an extensive meal and drinking the night before in Provincetown, and the altitude on arrival (somewhere around eight thousand feet). So he's gone to bed as well. It's a house full of invalids. Everyone has flown to Colorado to sleep all day. Of course, I take some secret pleasure in not being laid low.

But by the evening, everyone is feeling a little better, and so, in the endless shuttling between the tiny town of Crested Butte, where the ski hill is located and where Maude works, where the town is so heritage sensitive that you can't replace old single-pane glass with the double-paned version, and South Crested Butte, fifteen minutes away (to the south!), where Maude and Matt and Remy live, we stop by the pot store. Marijuana is legal in Colorado, and my brother, especially, is keen to check it out. He hardly ever smokes pot; I can't remember the last time he told me he had. This idea is greeted with the usual burbling of disapproval from Maude and Daisy, and the usual professions of ignorance from me. I'm a quite timorous and only occasional user, mainly because when I do, I always seem to end up dancing on a table and twirling my underpants over my head. That might be a slight exaggeration, but it doesn't feel like an exaggeration when I'm high. I do become extremely voluble, and often shout. Not in anger, but in eagerness. My notes from any night I have been stoned are completely useless, my notebook full of illegible rantings, usually about some random guy's posture, or snatches of conversation about how badly someone has been treated by someone they thought loved them, or about some girl I saw in a bar (because when I smoke pot, I drink), and the elbow-high gloves she was wearing, or the way she treated the man she was with—some note I tell myself I am making for some potential future story that will never, ever happen. That's the change, you see: In the old days, when I was younger, I could pretend that I would get around to everything I dreamt of, eventually. But I have come to the horribly late recognition that, to paraphrase Larkin, "most things won't happen; this one [death] will." I've run out of time, and now I have to pick and choose what book to read, which vacation to take, which story to write, which conversation to have. Not that I can control all of that either, but that doesn't stop me from thinking I should be trying to control it. Isn't that what all these effing books about aging are promising? That I can control it all? In fact, with every passing day, I see how little any of us can control; that even in deciding the purpose one puts a life to—I'm still deciding—it isn't seizing control (which I keep trying to do) that matters, but surrendering to what controls and matters to me, whatever it is. "Hard to believe that death is just around the corner,"

Tony Hoagland writes in his poem, "Bible Study." "What kind of idiot would think he even had a destiny?"

As of yet, this is just a vague idea in my mind, a feeling, a sensation, as troubling as it is attractive: *maybe none of this is my fault.* Not even getting older. This is not as obvious as one might think: my father blamed himself for his aging, and could never forgive himself, either. But one's life shapes itself, regardless of one's efforts to curve it one way or another. I'm not saying to give up, stop trying, abandon all dreams, ye who enter here, merely that the best dreams may be the ones we least suspect. As I say, this is still an apprehension at this point, but it would be gratifying (that's the word) to think the shape of my life might emerge out of the future mist, and that it might still be a surprise. While I am sometimes not sure I like what I see, there are other times when the shape of me seems more forgivable than I thought possible. Did some futile pursuit keep me thinking? Isn't that more important than commercial success? (What did Cheever say? Every writer's life is an education in love and economics.) Take it as it is, and make that mean something. I mean, yes, sure, I would like to be younger next year, and faster, and stronger, aging backwards, or aging successfully, or aging beautifully, and a wealthy barber, as the books tell me I should be. But the fact is that, try as I might, time is running out faster than I can know.

The name of the marijuana store is Soma, the word used by so many writers (Huxley, Burroughs, dozens of others) to connote a drug that solves the pain of life and makes everything bearable. It's the high-end joint (sorry) of the three emporia serving Crested Butte, a town of 6,600 people, which suggests to me that at least one will be going out of business soon. It was six when we arrived, and they were open to nine, this being the eve of Christmas Eve, for those last-minute gift-buying opportunities. You had to show government ID—a driver's licence—to get into the pot vault, otherwise you could watch skiing videos on the comfortable couches in the waiting room. Johanna and Hayley stayed there. Inside, a young woman—Tara? Christine? Kelly! that was her name, good for me, I retrieved that from the deep bin—gave us the tour: a wall of extracts, mints, chocolates, gummies, drinks (teas and energy fizzes, mostly), a display case of rolled joints, and then another wall of buds in jars, the besmoke section of the store, divided between *indica* (downer, thinker pot) and *sativa* (uplifting, energizing pot). Kelly spent a lot of time explaining how the dosage works, because my dear brother, who is five foot eleven and weighs 210 pounds and is as strong as an ox, is obsessed with overdosing. Yes. He was taking everything in, very, very precisely, as if he was being handed the secret numbers controlling the fate of the universe and was the only person who could save it. Captain Tim, the high flyer! One aluminum bottle of carbonated energy drink infused with *sativa* pot is 8.5 ounces, and of that, an ounce is a dose; Kelly suggests starting with half an ounce. I thought maybe two ounces would be a good start. After twenty minutes in the pot shop, we spend thirty bucks on a bottle of carbonated *sativa*. "Enjoy safely!" the woman at the door tells us as we leave.

The one remaining problem, for me, is Hayley: she knows I have smoked pot, but I have never indulged in it in front of her. So I ask her. "I want to keep Tim company on this journey, because he is nervous," I say. "Should I do it? I don't want to disappoint you."

"Of course you should do it," she says, laughing.

But all a half ounce of *sativa* pop produces, after half an hour, is a mild sense of amusement and a grating self-consciousness, a low-grade anxiety: is this the way I should be behaving on the night before the night before Christmas? I suspect that question does not have an answer.

DECEMBER 24

More skiing. Tim is *really* in bed now. Apparently half an ounce of *sativa* pop *was* too much.

Back in Toronto. Last night was New Year's Eve at Ian and Sue's; it's their turn, among the five couples who have rotated the hosting on New Year's Eve for the past . . . fifteen years? A lovely evening, which ended by 2 AM. No more all-night carousing.

I begin my usual month of no drinking today, and wonder, as usual, if I'll make it to the end. The thing is, I feel less need to drink now. The thrill is still there, the slight loosening of the emotional collar, the relief of garrulousness, the easy, unself-conscious flirting. But losing the early morning of the next day now feels like too high a price to pay.

At home afterward, I said to Johanna, "That was a very good party, given that we are now older people."

"Don't include me as one of your older people," Johanna said. After all, she's fifty-two.

JANUARY 5

I never used to be a creature of habit. But every night now, my habit is the same: brush my teeth (sometimes with flossing); add the eye drops, to stave off glaucoma; rub in some lotion to keep rosacea away. Undress, clothes away, into the T-shirt. Find the dog, make sure she is in the room, possibly on the bed; into the bed (usually before Johanna, by a few minutes anyway); read for fifteen minutes (from the stack of books beside my bed, at least five books at a time in various stages of undress); an adjustment of the pillows, reducing them to one; kiss my wife good night (most nights); a murmured joke or two, something to make her laugh; fall asleep. Johanna says I always go suddenly. She says she envies me that.

JANUARY 8

A letter from one of my oldest (we met when we were sixteen) and closest friends, describing his struggles to face each day. He's sixty-one: successful, self-sufficient, still dating, well-read, a nascent writing career in the works. And yet there are mornings he wakes up fighting the desire to go back to sleep, permanently. It's the mornings that are hardest for me too: waking up and feeling the dread there, waiting like a pet to be watered. Get up and fail, get up and fail. Get up, and try to make up for what you never managed before now. Try to make up the lost time. This is what the self-help books never talk about. (Tim was on the phone yesterday, telling me about some new book he's reading, about value investing. How does he do that? Lurching from one batch of advice to the next, like little psychological inns along the road?) Get up, throw yourself onto the pyre of the sameness of days, hoping, maintaining one's thin faith, that this one might be different. Will this be the day that you manage to do what you have never been able to do, which is take this life as it is and make what you can of it? Probably not. Better happen soon.

I throw myself out of bed, literally, hoping the catapult will get me as far as the bathroom. Hoping that some kind of inertial force, once moving, will keep me moving. Distractions lurk at every corner. Don't get waylaid by email, never mind the paper, forget about Solitaire (or even worse, Spider Solitaire). Downstairs, kettle (don't forget to turn it on after filling, the tasks never end), grind the coffee, all these things in familiar places, in the brain and in the kitchen. Coffee into the coffee pot. Upstairs again to the shower? Hope that defecation doesn't throw off the schedule. Dress, downstairs, paper, breakfast, read the paper (if you're lucky, because the time is streaming past now). Clothes. Wallet. Keys. Phone. Phone? Keys? Wallet? Bookbag? Yes. Out the door. Forgot the car keys. Back in. Forgot the coffee travel cup. And so on. Twice a year I forget my wallet. I am afraid I had one too many concussions as a kid, falling off the table, getting knocked out dancing (I was four, and it happened during the twirling part of the Mexican Hat Dance, some French-Canadian girl flung me to the floor), playing soccer.

JANUARY 10

A strange dream last night: I was in a huge, modern, circular library, talking to two librarians—one a redhead, the other a brunette, one working away, the other slouching and chatting. The chatty, slatternly one mentioned a librarian who was also a writer, at Robarts Library in Toronto, and I said, oh, yes, I know him/her . . . I was pretending, I wasn't sure whom she was talking about, obviously someone a real student of libraries would know. But I tried to pass myself off as knowledgeable, and breezed on. Then the chatty librarian held a file folder up and behind it made a face at the other librarian, a face I wasn't supposed to see, and I realized that she realized that I was talking out of my ass. I tried to backtrack and repair the damage, saying, "Wait, do you mean so-and-so? Maybe I'm thinking of someone different." But it was done. Shortly after this, I took my leave of the librarians—the industrious one shook my hand, the tarty one pointedly did not—and set off to find a place where I could leave . . . a file? Some papers? I thought about leaving them on a desk with a note saying, "These are from Ian Brown for X.," but realized that would not suffice. So I decided to take the notes with me, wherever I went. That was a better solution, I realized, because then the notes would always be with me.

I set out through the vast corridors and rooms of the library; I kept noticing the corner where the floor met the wall, and how the library was designed on the same principle as a lot of buildings, a kind of interlocking hexagonal shape. I passed through the court of a large mall. I was looking for my sisters, who were still with my parents. I was worried that my mother would not be able to walk very far. I exited the mall, and found myself in a kind of suburban landscape, with a wide arterial multi-lane, business- and outlet-lined road between me and my sisters and my parents, who were not quite in sight but who I knew were walking toward a thick green park full of paths. The first job was to get across the road, which the girls had managed to do with my parents. I finally saw them slip between two buildings to get to the park. I followed, encountering three or four people a few minutes later. Had they seen my family? They had. They pointed off toward a green ravine. They had come this way. I was on track to reach them. That was all the comfort I could find.

JANUARY 15

The story about domestic abuse is out. It's so long I can't imagine anyone will want to read it. But it is comprehensive, and it is fair, and it is factual, and it takes the feelings and position of women (the victims) into account even as it describes the motives of batterers, and it doesn't pander, at least not a lot. I did what I set out to do, which was to find out why men hit women. Mostly, however, I am orgasmically relieved that it's finished. I can move on to something else. My editor tried to get me to take on assisted suicide next. "What are you trying to do," I said, "kill me? Or have me kill myself?" She gracefully let me off the hook.

I read three Larkin poems last night, from *Complete Poems*, edited by Archie Burnett, and they absolutely floored me. I'm still not sure, years after I first read it, that I understand "High Windows": The poet sees a couple of kids, thinks how lucky they are to live in an age when morals and manners have fallen by the wayside, "bonds and gestures pushed to one side/Like an outdated combine harvester,/ And everyone young going down the long slide." Then he wonders if someone thought such a thing about him, how he'd be free of God and the conscience of the priest, how he'd go down the long slide "like free bloody birds." And then immediately, instead of words, "comes the thought of high windows" (in a church? in an institution? in a library, where Larkin worked?). "The sun-comprehending glass,/ And beyond it, the deep blue air, that shows/Nothing, and is nowhere, and is endless." Is that about the oblivion of death, and the pointlessness of worrying about what others think? Or is it about lives untethered from any greater sense of purpose than satisfaction? I couldn't decide.

Another poem, "Friday Night in the Royal Station Hotel," was about a travelers' hotel attached to a railway station. "Through open doors, the dining-room declares/A larger loneliness of knives and glass/And silence laid like carpet." And later, "The headed paper, made for writing home/(If home existed) letters of exile: *Now/Night comes* on. *Waves fold behind villages.*" It's about the grace loneliness conveys, and how you can find it anywhere. I was glad I'd read it. Later, it reminded me of my father.

I was about to go to bed when I made the mistake of reading the third poem, "The Old Fools," which turns out to be about aging people. It was all I could do to read it without moaning, and when I read it out loud to Johanna, she actually cried out, again and again.

> What do they think has happened, the old fools,
> To make them like this? Do they somehow suppose
> It's more grown-up when your mouth hangs open and drools,
> And you keep on pissing yourself, and can't remember
> Who called this morning? Or that, if they only chose,
> They could alter things back to when they danced all night,
> Or went to their wedding, or sloped arms some September?
> Or do they fancy there's really been no change,
> And they've always behaved as if they were crippled or tight,
> Or sat through days of thin continuous dreaming
> Watching light move? If they don't (and they can't), it's strange:
> Why aren't they screaming?

That was the first stanza. Larkin was in his fifties when he wrote it, an age when you can still ignore the oncoming breakup of your mind and your body, before you begin to run into daily intimations of your own mortality.

In the next stanza he does a lot of metaphysical playing about, as he turns life, like some memento mori, over in his mind:

At death, you break up: the bits that were you
Start speeding away from each other for ever
With no one to see. It's only oblivion, true:
We had it before, but then it was going to end,
And was all the time merging with a unique endeavour
To bring to bloom the million-petalled flower
Of being here.

A now-famous phrase. But then he gets serious, and
starts to mark out the signs of decay:

Next time you can't pretend
There'll be anything else. And these are the first signs:
Not knowing how, not hearing who, the power
Of choosing gone. Their looks show that they're for it:
Ash hair, toad hands, prune face dried into lines –
How can they ignore it?

Those are the lines that get me, of course: not knowing who some singer or actress is, not being able to hear,
circumstances taking over my life. The money worries, the
small decisions, the small forbearances and denials—so far,
anyway.

Perhaps being old is having lighted rooms
Inside your head, and people in them, acting.
People you know, yet can't quite name; each looms
Like a deep loss restored, from known doors turning,
Setting down a lamp, smiling from a stair, extracting
A known book from the shelves; or sometimes only

The rooms themselves, chairs and a fire burning,
The blown bush at the window, or the sun's
Faint friendliness on the wall some lonely
Rain-ceased midsummer evening. That is where they live:
Not here and now, but where all happened once.
This is why they give
An air of baffled absence, trying to be there
Yet being here. For the rooms grow farther, leaving
Incompetent cold, the constant wear and tear
Of taken breath, and them crouching below
Extinction's alp, the old fools, never perceiving
How near it is. This must be what keeps them quiet:
The peak that stays in view wherever we go
For them is rising ground. Can they never tell
What is dragging them back, and how it will end? Not at night?
Not when the strangers come? Never, throughout
The whole hideous inverted childhood? Well,
We shall find out.

Well, yes, we shall find out. It's a group exercise. The
prospect already gives me pause: that funny look my father
leveled at me as he said, "Don't get old, Will." But really
saying, in his kind way: you will get old, you'll see, I can't
help this, and neither can you. I wonder if it gave him
any satisfaction to know that he wasn't alone, that I was
headed there too, that I would eventually understand?

A year ago, I wrote that Facebook post about turning sixty, and what a massive turn it seemed. Today I am sixty-one, and I have to admit I almost forgot to anticipate the onset of the dread of being a year older. I knew it was my birthday, but I didn't really register what another birthday meant, so I can honestly say that I do not feel any older: being sixty-one feels no different than being sixty. (Which in general feels like the car is in excellent shape, and running beautifully, considering that it's a 1954 Plymouth Belvedere.)

Maybe the damage from the obliterating transition to sixty was so extensive, so widespread, that it flattened a couple of birthdays on either side, and managed to take sixty-one with it. But I have the feeling I will barely notice my age until I come braking fast on sixty-five, the next official cliffside drop-off point. In any event, Christie Brinkley and I are still exactly the same age.

I'm not saying turning sixty-one was without incident. No. My daughter Hayley called, first thing, and asked me what it was like to be so old. She was joking, and I laughed, and that was (I say this in full sincerity, which I am allowed to indulge in at my age) a great present. My brother called to commiserate, and that made me feel better. Then Johanna walked up to the kitchen window and said, "The bad guys have been around." I couldn't hear her, of course, since I had not yet slipped in my hearing aid, so I said, "Who has been around?"

"The bad guys."

"The backyard guys?" I thought she meant the fellows who have been replacing the soffits on the third-floor dormer, which were chewed away by the atomic squirrels we have in our neighborhood. (They knock the green compost bin over every night, but they no longer care for its ordinary vegetal fare: they prefer to chew directly on the plastic. I guess it has more fluorocarbons.) "I thought the backyard guys finished long ago," I added, helpfully.

"Who?"

"The dormer guys. Didn't you just say they'd been around?"

"The bad guys. Ginny and I call the raccoons the bad guys."

That really surprised me, because Ginny is our dog, and my wife's still in her early fifties. Ginny's a very sweet dog, but as far as I am aware, she does not converse in English. "Ah," I said. "Was that Ginny's term, or yours?"

"Well," Johanna said, "it was Ginny's name for them, originally, but I agree."

I guess this is the way it is later on in life, when the kids are out of the house and the mind is free, more or less, to roam where it may, hilariously or otherwise. When I work at home, I talk to the dog as well.

Then we had a discussion about money, and how nice it would be to have some more, and then we discussed what I would like for my birthday dinner. Shrimp and eggplant parmigiana, from that morning's *New York Times* dining section, as it turns out. Then I started typing again, and my wife came out into the kitchen and said, "You're not writing that down about the bad guys, are you?"

"Of course not," I said.

By that hour of the day—9 AM—I had been up for a while, given that at sixty-one I no longer sleep beyond 6 AM, latest. I made the mistake, however, of beginning the day on the couch in the living room, waiting for the kettle to boil while looking at Instagram pictures from friends. Error. Naturally, I was a little taken aback by how much human life had transpired without me. Not mentioning any names or anything. I'm not complaining, everyone has his or her own life, and Ian Brown cannot be included in *every* scene. And of course I experience the usual and much-discussed Instagram location envy, my friends jetting to Berlin and Arizona, to Chile or China.

But Instagram always makes me feel worse in a deeper way as well. What discourages me about Instagram, *every single time*, is that it is by default a record of what I do not have. It may be a great way of sharing—maybe that is the way we now do things in this wondrous connective collectivity that is life lived online, bringing us all together in the hive—but it is no way to start the day. You should never start the day staring at what you do not have—and that pretty much excludes everything the news and social media have to offer. They are always about what you have not noticed, what you did not see, what you do not yet know. Starting the day with Instagram is like starting the day by signing a contract recognizing that life is a bottomless hole of desire, and that however you strive to fill it, you never, ever will, my friend. It should be called Instaregret.

So I have come to believe, in my adolescent agedness, that the best way to start the day is with something you do have, whatever it may be. Thus, after my shower—after the ritual of rinsing myself clean of what has accrued and stuck to me—I walk around in front of my bookshelves (as I air-dry with a towel around my waist, because toweling off has always seemed both inefficient and, more importantly, a waste of time, as you are going to be dry in a few minutes anyway), trying to find something good to read for a minute or two. To launch the day, and everything that might then ensue from such an act of faith. Because as a friend of mine once said, in an entirely different context, quoting the slogan of the New York State Lottery, you never know.

The books in our house desperately need reorganizing and re-alphabetizing, so I don't know what I'll encounter. I have no preconceptions, and pull a book at random:

Shakespeare (though that's rare), the poems of Tony Hoagland, something out of Woolf's *Common Reader*, a couple of paragraphs of Thomas Bernhard or A.J. Liebling (I'm fond of the opening to *The Earl of Louisiana*, where he compares Southern politicians to fresh-picked corn that gets less palatable the farther it travels from its field) or Hooker or Roth or maybe a poem by Vasko Popa (say, the one where he compares his lover's breasts to aspens) or some drop-dead verse by Szymborska. Milton, even.

Of course, I don't always keep to the regimen: there are days when the paper falls in the way first, or when I get seduced by a message on my phone in the course of trying to find out what time it is/how late I am. But what I read first makes an enormous difference to the rest of my day. It makes such a palpable difference, in fact, that I began, quite a long time ago now, to write some of these mini-readings down, in service of what I am telling myself will one day be an art project. I write the best lines of the day's reading (and it does have the feel of the lesson in a daily Mass) on a shirt collar cardboard, the little 1½-by-8-inch stiffening strips that line the collar of your shirts if you have them laundered (which I do, at an expense I can't really afford, because I don't have time to launder and iron them myself). Sometimes I even type what I've read onto the cardboards, on an old upright Remington. I intend one day (sooner rather than later would be best at my age!) to varnish them and assemble them into rectangles, over which I will then paint acrylic, or thin watercolor, portraits of people I care for or miss or rely on for mental succor. I suppose it is a way of amassing a record of the contents of an ordinary mind. As usual with projects of mine, this one is in a state of suspended animation, waiting for the next step—in this case, figuring out how to paint on the cardboards so that the sentences of the passages I woke to will still be legible through the paint. But that's just a detail, a practicality.

A few examples.

A column of smoke rose thin and straight from the cabin chimney. The smoke was blue where it left the red of the clay. It trailed into the blue of the April sky and was no longer blue but gray. The boy Jody watched it, speculating. The fire on the kitchen hearth was dying down. His mother was hanging up pots and pans after the noon dinner. The day was Friday. She would sweep the floor with a broom of ti-ti and after that, if he were lucky, she would scrub it with the corn shucks scrub. If she scrubbed the floor she would not miss him until he reached the Glen. He stood a minute, balancing the hoe on his shoulder.

That's the opening of *The Yearling*, by Marjorie Kinnan Rawlings, which I apparently opened up and reread a few pages of in February 2012. As I've mentioned, I was in the fifth grade in Montreal in 1965 the first time I read it, in Miss Wilkie's class. I had pneumonia that year, and read *The Yearling*, which was a big book, in two non-stop days while I was quarantined at home, sitting in an orange Naugahyde armchair in our back sunroom, while my mother worked in the kitchen. I remember thinking: "This pneumonia thing is the greatest, I can just sit here and read without having to do chores." That never happened in that house. I like that memory, and I like the specificity of the book's opening, how efficient it is (you learn that Jody doesn't go to school, for instance), and I like how it sets up Jody's escape plan (and the implicit hiding he will get when he returns home, having shirked his hoeing).

On November 16, 2014, in *The New York Times* (I succumbed to the newspaper that day, but at least it was a foreign newspaper, and therefore of less pressing relevance to my daily life), I read:

> *Matt Haag, a professional video game player, makes close to a million dollars a year sitting in a soft chair smashing buttons. It is a fantastically sweet gig, and he will do almost anything to keep it.*

That's a snappy shred of feature writing, and a description of an entirely new kind of job.

Or this, from several years earlier and page 189 of David Gilmour's *The Perfect Order of Things*, which I found to be an excellent book:

> *It was a brief moment of prosperity. I was forty-three, I was the host of a harmless little television show on the arts; guests came and went, actors and writers and musicians flogging their novels, movies, CDs and what have you. It was like the*

provincial branch of an advertising agency that disguised boosterism as "arts journalism." But it paid well and it satisfied the cravings of my almost insatiable vanity.

Or there is this, from Martin Amis's *The Pregnant Widow*, which a lot of people claimed not to like, but which is underrated as satire:

The exercise bar was a fixture that Keith had barely noticed until now. He'd assumed it was some kind of towel rack.

That's from page 83.

I realize that a project this weird makes me sound like a lot of people as they soft-shoe into their sixties, the decade when a startling number of us start wearing caftans or symbols of the Shambhala and talking about mindfulness and being free from the obligations of middle-aged life. When some of us start saying, "Best decade ever!"—at which point I quietly wonder if they've fallen off their meds. But I am no different. A year ago, on the day I turned sixty, I started this diary of my sixty-first year, a chronicle of the passing of time and its effects. This is the last entry of that year. I have no idea if any of it amounts to anything—I find it harder than ever to make that judgment—but I keep writing down the details that go whizzing by. Just as I don't know what the point is of recording five minutes of morning reading, or why a record of those perusals matters, especially when they are written on shirt cardboards. I have no doubt that they don't—matter, I mean.

But the world would be a desolate place if we insisted that everyone pursue only those routes that are collectively agreed to be worthwhile and useful. We would not have, say, Hockney's beautiful perspective studies or his paintings of swimming pools—strange things, and perfected in later life—or Matisse's cut-outs (ditto), or any number of poems. Nicholson Baker wouldn't have written most of his novels, and a guy I used to know whose name was Bob Blue wouldn't have painted a bunch of mothers and children playing at low tide by the seaside, on the delicate verge between danger and freedom—to name just a few items that have kept me company in the past year.

So I think I will keep writing down the words I read first thing in the morning, on my shirt collar cardboards, and stuffing them in the left-hand top drawer of my small bureau, the one laden with all my framed photographs, if only to honor the example of other people who have done such things, and the genius of their single-minded conviction that what was passing through the chambers of their being and somehow got caught there was worth recording. For posterity, for the mere possibility of its future.

I believe in that place now, and in that strange process. I'm not sure I did a year ago. But I was younger then, and only just setting out on the transition to getting older—to becoming the Other inside me who has been getting older all along. He turns out not to be so frightening if I can sit still long enough to simply observe him, without panicking. I figure, what with so many of us so often terrified of what is coming down the road, and averting our gazes to the nearest distraction, someone ought to keep his eyes open. Otherwise, you could miss a lot along the way.

ACKNOWLEDGMENTS

This diary is not simply the raw material and scrambled notes I made each day: I collected and edited and rewrote entries as I went, and then tidied them up again when the year of living observationally was over. I have obscured some names and details to protect identities. In some instances the chronology of discovery I've depicted was not quite chronological; for instance, for reasons of pacing, some research on what happens to the human body and brain after sixty is spread over several weeks of entries, rather than when it was actually ingested. Some of the material in my notebooks and diary later became stories, in not so different form, in the *Globe and Mail*, the newspaper where I work as a roving reporter; I am grateful to the *Globe* for the permission to use that material again here. Those journeys and events, however, were events in my life and details in the diaries before I decided to make them into stories in the *Globe*. Whatever else this book is and isn't, it is a true account of what passed through my consciousness and life in the course of the year I embarked on my seventh decade.

I was helped by any number of clever people, though I can only thank a few here. Matthew Lore, Dan O'Connor, and Jeanne Tao at The Experiment turned their exacting eyes on the US edition, to instant effect: I am grateful for their efforts and especially their faith that this book was worth publishing. My editor at Random House Canada, Anne Collins, wielded her usual genius in turning this manuscript into a book in the first place, all the while reassuring me (and I needed a lot of reassuring) that it was worth writing. Gabe Gonda and Hamutal Dotan, respectively my boss and my editor at the *Globe and Mail*, cleared a month to let me work on this book, for the promise of an article later. My brother, Tim Brown, and his husband, Frank Rioux, lent me many stories, not to mention their gracious company and beautiful places to write in New York and on the Atlantic Ocean. Bruce Barnes was a good friend along the way, as was my old pal Philip Keddy. Cathrin Bradbury, my friend and former editor, also read the manuscript, gave it the benefit of her assured editorial judgment, and reminded me of what I had forgotten.

Finally, I am immensely grateful to my wife, Johanna Schneller, who offered gracious counsel and encouragement, always. Most of all she made me laugh, as she always does, as did my children, Hayley and Walker, as I stumbled along, figuring out what it felt like to be getting older than I wanted to be. I must offer special thanks to Hayley, who (like her mother) shows up a lot in the diary—a thankless role—and who was thoughtful and principled company throughout the project. I hope for the love of my family and friends for as long as my life might continue: that way, not much can go wrong.

PERMISSIONS ACKNOWLEDGMENTS

Gwendolyn MacEwen's poem "Late Song" is taken from *The Selected Gwendolyn MacEwen*, published by Exile Editions, Toronto, 2007. Copyright © to The Estate of Gwendolyn MacEwen. Permission to use Gwendolyn MacEwen's poetry was provided by her family.

"Outdoor Shower" from *Blood, Tin, Straw: Poems* by Sharon Olds, copyright 1999 by Sharon Olds. Used by permission of Alfred A. Knopf, an imprint of the Knopf Doubleday Publishing Group, a division of Penguin Random House LLC. All rights reserved. Any third party use of this material, outside of this publication, is prohibited. Interested parties must apply directly to Penguin Random House LLC for permission.

"The Old Fools"; Excerpts from "Aubade," "Friday Night in the Royal Station Hotel," "High Windows," and "This Be The Verse" from *The Complete Poems of Philip Larkin* by Philip Larkin, edited by Archie Burnett. Copyright © 2012 by The Estate of Philip Larkin. Reprinted by permission of Farrar, Straus and Giroux, LLC.

ABOUT THE AUTHOR

IAN BROWN is an award-winning author and feature writer for the *Globe and Mail*. His most recent book, *The Boy in the Moon: A Father's Search for His Disabled Son*, was a #1 national bestseller in Canada and named one of *The New York Times*'s ten best books of the year and a *Globe and Mail* Best Book. It won all three of Canada's most prestigious non-fiction literary awards: the Charles Taylor Prize for Literary Non-Fiction, the Trillium Book Award, and the BC National Award for Canadian Non-Fiction. His previous books include *Freewheeling*, which won the National Business Book Award, and *Man Overboard*, an examination of modern masculinity. He lives in Toronto.